Bill Barnes
10/9/67

Minister/Mayor

Minister/Mayor

William H. Hudnut III
with Judy Keene

The Westminster Press
Philadelphia

Book design by Gene Harris

First edition

Published by The Westminster Press®
Philadelphia, Pennsylvania

PRINTED IN THE UNITED STATES OF AMERICA

9 8 7 6 5 4 3 2 1

Dedicated with love and appreciation
to my father, William H. Hudnut, Jr.
May 29, 1905—May 31, 1985
and my mother, Elizabeth Kilborne Hudnut

Library of Congress Cataloging-in-Publication Data

Hudnut, William H., 1932–
　Minister/mayor.

　Includes index.
　1. Hudnut, William H., 1932–　　. 2. Mayors—
Indiana—Indianapolis—Biography.　3. Indianapolis
(Ind.)—Biography.　4. Presbyterian Church (U.S.A.)—
Clergy—Biography.　5. Presbyterian Church—United
States—Clergy—Biography.　I. Keene, Judy, 1943–
II. Title.
F534.I353H834 1987　　　977.2'52 [B]　　　86-32512
ISBN 0-664-21321-9

Contents

A section of photographs follows page 97.

Foreword

The best lack all conviction, while the worst
Are full of passionate intensity.

—William Butler Yeats, 1921

When I first met Bill Hudnut at college in the 1950s, I scarcely dreamed he'd become a kind of living antithesis of the Yeatsian portraiture. Yet in this book he proves just that. He demonstrates not just the verve and wit of the accomplished politician which he has become, but also a sensitivity and a humility somewhat rare among those who share his second calling. And in this book he brings us a caring but also penetrating treatment of that critical and controversial area of American life: the interplay of church and state.

The message could scarcely be more relevant in a season when a strident religious Right, chock-full of passionate intensity, seeks to impose and enforce its worldview on us all. If we needed a thoughtful alternative to intolerance in clerical garb, Bill Hudnut is clearly our man. He stakes out a biblical faith of Lincolnian simplicity and directness. Then he applies his credo to his own political experience, city and national. When this remarkable intellectual, personal, and religious odyssey is complete, it is not just both the Bible and the First Amendment that emerge unscathed and magnified. So does this minister/mayor, thoroughly human, level-headed, and, as his friends will attest, a man at whom you can toss any idea and expect a caring and thoughtful response.

Let it be said: Hudnut is a bit carried away by this Colts football fanaticism. One wonders if the Deity in fact took note of Indianapolis conspiring to snatch away Baltimore's team. Maybe the Colts would have left Baltimore anyway. A skeptic might still talk of robbing Peter to pay Paul.

But if one is mayor of an upwardly mobile city, a few such excesses are tolerable. For beneath Hudnut the politician and Indianapolis booster, there is this core of a deeply sensitive man. At least he *thought* of Baltimore's feelings, tried vainly to make peace with the self-possessed Baltimore mayor (and later Maryland governor), William Donald Schaefer. To be the "sorest loser" in Hudnut's book is a pretty heavy rap.

Of the sterling features of this book, several leap to attention.

First, Bill Hudnut is an extraordinarily fortunate man. Disappointments he has had (and candidly recounts). But how many Americans have as rich a family experience to draw on as this son and grandson of Presbyterian ministers? The majesty of the Hudnuts' faith, the richness of the family experience, fostered by the matriarchal as well as the paternal line, shine through in these pages. Who with such a tradition behind him could bear to have the God of the Old and New Testaments trivialized?

Oftentimes it seems as if these United States are drawing on the accumulated strength of the more faithful, religiously inclined generations that went before. Perhaps the Religious Right has at least a sliver of justification in attacking secular humanism, not because there is a smidgen of justification in calling it evil, but because humanism without a refreshment of biblical faith may be a wasting asset.

So it is heartening to read Bill Hudnut's testimony to the bedrock of biblical faith. I delighted in reading how he aspires to translate that faith into risk-taking, joyousness, openness, modesty, courage. Not to mention resolve, vision, partnership and dialogue, an understanding of the interrelatedness of all things human. And above all, social justice. There is a Hubert Humphrey quotation about caring for those in "the dawn, the shadows and the twilight of life." Then this Republican politician reminds us: "The Bible is a story about oppressed people going free. . . . If my decisions can free people from poor housing or hunger or racial prejudice or sexism or illiteracy or any other kind of chains, my decisions are proceeding in the right direction."

If that is so, is it then specious to think, as Bill Hudnut would have us, of a stadium and downtown revitalization as positive goods because they create entry-level jobs for the least fortunate? Or to doubt long that he was about the Lord's work when he told the Reagan administration it was wrong—"wrong legally, morally, and politically"—when it tried to overturn the affirmative-action orders that had opened the doors of government employment to long-oppressed minorities in Indianapolis and other cities across America?

The mix of humor and level-headedness and vision embodied in Hudnut's overwhelming political success as minister/mayor are hard to miss as he recounts the stories of his Indianapolis mayoralty, from aesthetic and economic breakthroughs to dealing with irate citizens whose trash pickup has been neglected. Indianapolis is indeed now a model of public-private partnerships, of remaking a gloomy downtown into a highly attractive one, of thoughtful economic planning and viable governance. But we are spared here a rah-rah book. Indeed, we're let in on Hudnut's approach to decision-making and the pros and cons of some of his more difficult calls, from an anti-pornography ordinance eventually struck down by the courts to a neighborhood's fight against a "family home" for abused and abandoned children. Anyone who has watched good politicians practicing their craft will understand his rendering of the essential ambiguities—"grays," as he calls them—in decision-making.

Here, palpably, is a man who believes intensely in the glory of cities as the places where the best and the worst of the human condition are etched out, where the redemptive processes of life must be given rein. With such distinguished mayoral contemporaries as George Latimer of St. Paul, George Voinovich of Cleveland, and Henry Cisneros of San Antonio, Hudnut rose almost naturally to the presidency of the National League of Cities, where I watched him perform the balancing act of standing up for the urban cause without overtly attacking the Reagan White House.

But lucky for us, Bill Hudnut in these pages talks directly about the phenomenon of losing, of defeat in public life, as well as the triumphs. How seldom politicians ever talk about this darker side of their calling. Or when they do, how often they pretend the pain, especially the blow of electoral rejection, is not real. Bill spares us such nonsense. He recalls the big defeat, when he lost his seat in Congress, but more particularly he deals with the everyday defeats each of us inevitably experiences. I find it incredibly refreshing for a politician to note that "suffering can gentle us, and losing can release love within us." Or to recall that when ancient Israel's "circumstances were the darkest, Hebrew faith glowed most incandescently."

Which brings us to Bill Hudnut's ultimate hero, that homely, unpretentious, biblically driven politician, Abraham Lincoln. For while our minister/mayor strives mightily in this book to formulate a theory of appropriate division between church and state, while he labors to navigate between the Scylla of overbearing religious absolutism and the Charybdis of coldly removed separatism, while he carefully shows how religion can infuse political will and action without becoming its own tyranny, one paragraph of his narrative almost says it all. It is to be found in chapter 3 when we are given a glimpse into the sermon which as a freshman congressman he delivered, of all places, within the White House during the Nixon Presidency. "The Religion of Abraham Lincoln" was the chosen topic. The timing was in the midst of the Watergate crisis, the political fallout of which would cost Hudnut his seat in the U.S. House (a providential defeat, in retrospect). Mr. Nixon himself listened—apparently absentmindedly. But hear the words:

> There is a great difference between worshiping God and domesticating him, between looking upon him as the lord of all nations and regarding him as the ally of one; . . . between affirming "My country for God" and boasting "God for my country"; . . . between making ours "a nation under God" and making a god of our nation; . . . between humbly praying, as Lincoln did, that we might be on God's side and self-righteously asserting that he is on ours.

The vast majority of Americans, I firmly believe, would resonate to that message. It expresses what most feel, yet have never adequately articulated. There is grave danger that we may have thrust upon us in America the notion of a nationalized, politicized Deity, exclusionary rather than inclusive, militarized rather than peace-giving, the antithesis of the caring Almighty whom Lincoln knew.

I can hear my friend Bill Hudnut laughing at the presumptuousness of the effort, not because it may be taken lightly, but because one ought to take joy in the good battle to defeat any destructive, divisive force within our society, political-religious pretense included if not foremost. This little book might even, St. George style, be the sword with which to slay that particular dragon.

Neal R. Peirce
Syndicated Columnist
Washington Post Writers Group

Preface

In early June of 1985, the General Assembly of the Presbyterian Church (U.S.A.) met in Indianapolis. I was invited to speak at a morning prayer breakfast and chose as my topic "Biblical Touchstones for Public Service." It was a scant four days after my father, a Presbyterian minister, had died at the age of eighty, and in the course of my remarks I naturally made several references to him, because he and my mother were very much on my mind.

After breakfast, Keith Crim, Editorial Director of The Westminster Press, asked for an appointment to visit with me in my office. I told him I'd be glad to see him, and when he came in, he asked me if I'd ever thought about writing a book on the general subject of my two careers, one in the church as a pastor, and one in political life, first as a congressman, and since 1975, as a mayor. I hadn't, and told him I didn't think I had the time or the talent. But he persisted, and with the friendly prodding of two members of my staff, Kae Browning and Lesa Dietrick, I finally agreed to give it a try. Keith specifically asked me if I would incorporate some family references as well as some ideas from Lincoln that he had heard me mention in that speech; hence the chapter on my family, and the frequent mentions of both my dad and the sixteenth President.

I began by writing notes and dictating thoughts in my spare time—weekends, nights, early mornings, during airplane trips, vacations, and so on. I could not take away time from my regular work to write this book. Realizing it was too big a task to undertake alone on this basis, I asked Judy Keene to help me bring my material into final form. Judy is a freelance writer in Indianapolis who has been a joy to work with on this project. I had come to know her in connection with an article she once wrote about me for the *Princeton Alumni Weekly,* and I thought she would be able to help me. I was right! Her assistance has been invaluable. I must take sole responsibility for the contents and interpretations contained herein, but I could not have prepared it without Judy's fine professional hand in the editing process.

It is easier to say what this book is *not* than what it is. It is not the memoirs of a big-city mayor. It is not an account of the emergence of Indianapolis into major-league status. It is not a book about how to run a city or how to handle the job of mayor, which is probably the toughest job in politics today, except the President's. It is not an analysis of a modern city's problems or an answer book about how to solve them.

Nor is this a book of devotions or a collection of meditations by someone in public office. It is not a study of the church's mission in today's world. It is not a description of "ministry" in that world.

This book is not an essay on the relationship of religion to politics, nor is it a commentary on the evolution of religion's role in political campaigning from the days when the liberals dominated the dialogue to the dominance of the conservative evangelicals today.

Rather, this book portrays my journey from minister to mayor, describing how I made the transition and the way in which my theological training and family background influenced my thought and activity as a public servant. My feeling is that religion should be like leaven in the bread rather than frosting on the cake; it's there, it has an effect, it's important, but it is unobtrusive, quiet, not something to be displayed. Religion develops "habits of the heart" (de Tocqueville's choice phrase) that in turn form our character and inform our decisions and actions; in its relationship to political activity, I understand religion to be primarily internal, not external, "of the heart," not "on the sleeve." So I would have to agree with Karl Barth, the famous Swiss theologian, who is reported to have said, "A Christian cobbler does not make Christian shoes; he makes good shoes." I want to be elected because I am good, better qualified than my opponent, not because I am a Christian.

My aim in this book is to set in a biblical context certain subjects with which I have dealt during my public life. If the reader gleans any insights about how the Bible understands the city and the task of building a better one, how it supplies helpful resources for public service, how decisions are made, how religion relates to political campaigning, how losing should be faced, and how and what we learn from tough controversies in which we are involved, then my task will have been worth the effort.

I make no pretense at objectivity; I want it to be clear at the outset that I am writing from a certain vantage point. History is really historiography—everything is seen from a subjecti e point of view. My frame of reference is that of an ordained Presbyterian minister involved in politics. I believe that Jesus Christ is my Lord and Savior and that the Bible is the Word of God written. But having confessed that, I want to go on to say that I hope my approach is inclusive, not exclusive; irenic, not polemical. I respect the right of others to believe differently, and I only hope that those who read these pages, regardless of religious or political persuasion, will forgive me if my understanding is different from theirs. I hope the book's appeal is broad, rather than narrow or sectarian, and hope it will have relevance not only to those who have a specific focus of interest, like the transfer of the Colts NFL franchise to Indianapolis or my stand against the U.S. Justice Department on affirmative action, but also to all men and women who seek to live out their lives creatively, responsibly, and biblically, keeping their feet firmly planted in the earthly city but fixing their heart and eye on the "city which has foundations, whose builder and maker is God."

In addition to the persons already mentioned, I want to express my appreciation to my sister Holly and my son Bill, who have helped Judy and me in assembling the final draft, and to Kae Browning, who assembled the photographs. I also want to thank Neal Peirce, a classmate of mine at Princeton and a very keen observer of the urban scene, for writing the foreword. And thanks are due to Beth Logan, who spent many of her evenings and weekends cheerfully and efficiently typing the manuscript. I feel very indebted to the congregation of Second Presbyterian Church, the Marion County Republican organization, the Mayor's Staff and Cabinet, all of whom have contributed indirectly to making it possible for me to be involved in these two careers and to write this book. And finally, I would like to thank the members of my family, and particularly my wife, Susie, for their patient understanding and loving support when I took time away from them to pursue this project.

Indianapolis, Indiana   W.H.H. III
September 1986

1

"The Guy Who Stole the Colts"

Dave Frick and I shivered as we paced back and forth on the tarmac in front of the executive terminal at Indianapolis International Airport. April 2, 1984, was a typical early spring day in Indiana, complete with blustery winds that whistled a bone-piercing chill through our clothing. We drank coffee in an effort to stay warm and scanned the horizon, watching for a multi-engine Lockheed Jet Star 8 to poke its nose through the clouds.

Dave was a close personal friend, a former Deputy Mayor, an attorney, a political ally, and a young man with one of the finest minds and largest hearts in Indianapolis. He had acted as my chief negotiator during the past eight weeks, and his skill was largely responsible for the visit we were now awaiting. We were both dog-tired but at the same time elated. This was a day we had been working toward, not only for eight weeks but for many years. It was a dream come true for our city, and an event that would soon prompt *Time* magazine to declare, "India-no-place is no more."

Finally the plane appeared, and we watched as it landed on the long runway and taxied toward us. We tossed our coffee cups in the wastebasket and walked out to greet the man of the hour. As he stepped down on to Indianapolis ground, we shook hands in welcome. He smiled broadly, brushed his hands through his thick white hair, and answered in the kind of taut, nervous way he expressed himself. "Hiya, Bill. Hiya, Dave."

We hustled our guest out of the weather and into a waiting car, then headed downtown. On the way in, Dave and I talked about the reception that was waiting in our new domed stadium. It was a workday, so we were uncertain whether we would have much of an audience, but we were sure the press would be in attendance, for we were bringing with us a really dynamic and controversial person.

The car pulled up to the back door of the stadium. We climbed out and went into a holding room where we met others in the party. Then, on cue, we all walked through the revolving doors, down a long chute, and out onto the floor. Our destination was a platform that had been erected in the middle of the field of green turf, facing the north stands in this 61,000-seat domed stadium. We took a deep breath and pushed our way through the swinging doors.

The scene before us was incredible. It was beyond all our expectations. Twenty thousand people jumped to their feet and began to cheer the moment they spotted us. The atmosphere was electric with excitement, and as we climbed the steps to the platform, the crowd went wild. This was the most emotional moment I had experienced during my nine years as Mayor of Indianapolis. I had a lump in my throat as I grabbed Colts owner Bob Irsay's hand and lifted it aloft prizefighter-style—signaling a champion, celebrating a victory.

Later, we would learn that these great fans had jammed city streets for hours waiting to be a part of this momentous occasion, and thousands more had been caught in traffic. And later we would look back to reflect on the importance of this day—not just for the welcome to the Colts that had taken place, but for the galvanizing effect it had on the optimistic spirit already alive in our city.

Indianapolis had become one of a growing number of "entrepreneurial" cities, communities that aggressively seek positive alternatives to the challenges they face, then take the steps necessary to implement the best solutions. An entrepreneurial city encourages vital partnerships between the public and private sectors and supports leadership that will take risks. Gone are the days when politicians can afford to ignore the help available from non-government circles simply because they are unwilling to share the spotlight. An electorate that supports only those candidates who lie low and play it safe is an electorate that will be poorly served.

Indianapolis has certainly not been insulated from the problems that face all major American cities, but during the early 1980s, the determination to deal with these issues had earned us the title "Star of the Snow Belt" from the *Wall Street Journal,* and the *Chicago Tribune* had described the city as a "bullet train" of progress in the Midwest. Tax structures designed to encourage development had resulted in hundreds of millions of dollars being pumped into the construction of new buildings and the rehabilitation of existing structures in the heart of the city, and the pride that our citizens took in the city's progress resulted in two All-American City awards and a Keep America Beautiful award for being the cleanest city with a population above 500,000. A strong spirit of voluntarism, which is evidenced every May during the month-long Indianapolis 500 Festival, was a key in the unprecedented success of the National Sports Festival we hosted in 1982. We believed an important element in the continuation of the momentum generated by earlier successes would be the construction of a first-class domed stadium in the heart of the city.

We called it the Hoosier Dome. The name was chosen from 50,000 entries in a contest held shortly after we had broken ground for construction.

"Hoosier" means somebody from Indiana, and although the word was well established by the 1830s, no one is quite certain about its origin. There has been speculation that it was derived from the pioneer's habit of calling "Who's yere?" when a stranger approached his cabin. It could have originated when a contractor on the Louisville and Portland Canal, Samuel Hoosier, hired Indiana laborers who became "Hoosier's men." The most colorful explanation came from Indiana poet James Whitcomb Riley, who claimed the word grew out of the pugnacious habits of the state's early settlers. "They were very vicious fighters, and not only gouged and scratched, but frequently bit off noses and ears," he explained. "This was so ordinary an affair that a settler coming into a bar on a morning after a fight, and seeing an ear on the floor, would merely push it aside with his foot and carelessly ask, 'Who's ear?' "

At any rate, many people did not—and do not—like the word, for they believe it to be a pejorative term, a derogatory name implying country bumpkin or frontier hick. Consequently, when we finally announced the name "Hoosier Dome," some people in the press complained, asking how we could possibly have chosen such a dumb name for such a beautiful building.

But I liked it. To me it was an inclusive and generic name for Indiana. We rejected suggestions like "The Indy Dome" or "The Circle City Dome," because this facility was for the entire state, not just for Indianapolis. We hoped everyone in Indiana would feel included in the excitement surrounding its construction, and we wanted everyone to know they would benefit from it, whether they lived up by Lake Michigan or down by the Ohio River or in any of the other ninety-one counties in "Hoosierland."

On the day Bob Irsay was welcomed into our city, the Hoosier Dome was not quite completed, and the shiny newness and smell of paint and sawdust undoubtedly added to the excitement of the fans, who were seeing the inside of this great stadium for the first time. The first official function would be the annual Mayor's Breakfast to kick off the month-of-May festivities leading up to the 500 Mile Race, and at that time I had the honor of clipping a huge ribbon and declaring the Hoosier Dome, "this all-American facility in this all-American city," open and ready for business.

Dreams of a domed stadium had begun to take shape in Indianapolis in the late 1970s. All through that decade, people had hoped we might position ourselves for a National Football League expansion franchise, and one of our most prominent civic leaders, Bob Welch, had been working toward this goal for the better part of ten years. We had been through a couple of false starts, then were disappointed again when we learned it would be inappropriate to include a new stadium in the White River State Park, a large urban park being planned for the city. That decision, however, turned out to be for the best, because it forced us to search for an alternative. A small group of people who met periodically during that time to discuss the city's future came up with a solution—the suggestion that we could build a domed stadium adjacent to and connected to the Indiana Convention Center in downtown Indianapolis.

In early 1980, soon after I had been elected to a second four-year term as Mayor, the time seemed right to pursue this idea. Dave Frick and I first talked with the executive committee of the Chamber of Commerce and found them eager to help. They authorized a committee to study the desirability of attaching a domed stadium to the Convention Center and, assuming this was considered a feasible idea, to offer suggestions on how such a facility might be financed. As part of this six-month assignment, the committee paid a call on NFL officials in New York to make sure that whatever we undertook would be in keeping with their specifications. (It wouldn't make much sense to build a 60,000-seat facility if the NFL required 80,000 seats!)

The committee's report endorsed the concept we had offered, and right from the beginning the project was advertised as a multipurpose facility and expansion of our Convention Center. We would double the amount of floor space available for exhibits and meetings, and we would build a number of new meeting rooms. The new facility would be yoked to the existing building, rising on top of a street that would be vacated, a few warehouses that would be acquired and demolished, and a lot of vacant ground. It would *not* be a free-standing stadium designed solely for professional football.

It was one thing to have the concept of a domed stadium in downtown Indianapolis, but it was another thing to pay for it. We would have to be careful to finance the $60 million project (which eventually climbed to $80 million as the scope of construction was broadened to include more convention space) in a way that would be agreeable to the citizens of Indianapolis and Marion County. We did not want to raise the property tax by floating a general-obligation bond issue, and we were also very leery of federal dollars because of all the incredible strings attached and the red tape and long time frame that money from Washington carried with it.

(On October 27, 1982, ten days after my fiftieth birthday, I was testifying before a committee at the State House when word came that the President wanted to speak with me. I excused myself and went to the phone to talk with Mr. Reagan. He began by asking me how it felt to be "fifty plus ten." He wanted to wish me a happy birthday and see how things were going. He had been well briefed. He asked about the progress of the Hoosier Dome and how we were faring with our "new building," as he put it. I answered that it was in the ground and going up quite nicely, and asked him, "Mr. President, do you know what the best thing of all about it is?" "No, what?" he asked. "There's no federal money in it," I responded. He laughed.)

The study committee's recommendation was that funding should represent a combination of private and public dollars, some of which would come from the not-for-profit part of the private sector, some from licensing the rights to the stadium's suites to private companies and individuals, and some from the public through a 1 percent tax on sales in Marion County restaurants and taverns. This sales tax would supply the revenue to service the debt on bonds we would float to finance the major portion of the project.

We began by enlisting the help of philanthropies in the city, convincing them that their contributions would assist Indianapolis in some very worthy causes that they could legitimately support—increasing the number of jobs in the community, for instance, and promoting our convention business. Their responses were magnificent votes of confidence in the future of our city. Lilly Endowment approved a $25-million contribution toward the construction of the Hoosier Dome and the Krannert Charitable Trust authorized a grant of $5 million. What splendid expressions of generosity! With a couple of handshakes that followed some serious conversations, we had raised $30 million. Now we could challenge the public sector to match that commitment.

The sales tax proposal could not be presented to the City-County Council without permission from the State Legislature. A bill granting that authority was introduced and received support from Democrats and Republicans, organized labor, and the Chamber of Commerce. It passed both houses during the 1981 session of the General Assembly and was signed into law by Governor Robert D. Orr, a good example of city and state government partnership in action.

As we look back on it now, it seems easy, but at the time we thought it was very difficult. There was opposition from political opponents who hoped to gain some partisan advantage and from the Indiana State Restaurant Association. We had a noisy protest denouncing the tax increase by individuals who carried placards into the City-County Council chambers labeling me as "High Tax Hudnut" at the time of the Council vote, and even after the law was enacted we ran into another roadblock when political partisans filed a lawsuit declaring the tax unconstitutional. The sale of bonds had to be postponed (which cost the taxpayers more money) until the Indiana Supreme Court disposed of the issue by upholding a lower court's dismissal of the lawsuit.

The following April we broke ground, and during the same month $47,250,000 worth of AAA-rated revenue bonds were snapped up by the investment community and individual buyers to finance the public sector's contribution toward the project. In the creative leveraging that had occurred, government had asked the private sector for support, and it responded; then the public sector had responded to the challenge. With the bond money and the $30 million pledged by the philanthropies, all that was left was to raise income from the licensing of the suites (at base costs ranging from $40,000 to $100,000 with annual renewal fees). We thought they would be hard to license because, as one businessman put it, "Who wants to lay out all that money to buy a suite and watch high school football games for the rest of his life?" When the applications went out, however, 68 of 99 suites were committed. (Those remaining went quickly when the Colts news broke.) The stadium was rising out of the ground and everyone was excited about its progress.

The Hoosier Dome had become a symbol for the resourcefulness, creativity, self-reliance, and entrepreneurial spirit of an American city in face of the tough times caused in the early 1980s both by a recession that caused a marked downturn in the production of durable goods and by cuts in federal funding for domestic programs as a result of the initiatives of the new administration (which lacked, as did its predecessors, a coherent, national urban policy and a strong, supportive commitment to the nation's cities). The Hoosier Dome suggested that cities can seize opportunities to reshape the way urban life is structured, to renew themselves as they change, and to promote revitalizing forces in the midst of urban abandonment and disinvestment. If we had listened to those who said the Hoosier Dome could not be built, that it would be a terrible political albatross around my neck (I won the next election by a two-to-one margin), and that it would be a white elephant; if we had listened to all those who wanted to play it safe and not take any chances, it never would have been built. Many American cities are exhibiting this kind of optimistic spirit, convinced that through local initiative they can overcome their problems to enhance their competitive positions and the quality of life their citizens enjoy. Many city governments are no longer relying on federal aid as the dominant resource for addressing urban needs. Entrepreneurial cities have certain characteristics in common, and these emerge in the way the Hoosier Dome was put together in Indianapolis.

An entrepreneurial city is willing to change. It recognizes that "new occasions teach new duties, time makes ancient good uncouth; they must upward still and onward, who would keep abreast of truth," to quote from one of my father's favorite hymns, words written by James Russell Lowell. The Good Book tells us that we must discern the signs of the times and that the children of darkness are often wiser in their generation than the children of light. Translated, I guess that means "the times they are a-changing," and we must change with them. If we remain wedded to old product lines, business opportunities will pass us by. No one stands still in life; we either go forward or backward. So it was with our Convention Center. When it was built in 1971, it was the seventh largest in the United States; by the early 1980s, it ranked forty-second! An entrepreneurial city cannot accept things the way they are but must make them better; this is a theme repeated throughout American history. "The times can be made better if we bestir ourselves," said Ben Franklin. Lincoln said it this way: "The dogmas of the quiet past are inadequate to the stormy present. The occasion is piled high with difficulty, and we must rise with the occasion. As our case is new, so we must think anew and act anew. We must disenthrall ourselves, and then we shall save our country." And our city!

beyond the past

Partnerships are created in an entrepreneurial city. The Hoosier Dome could not have been built if the for-profit and not-for-profit segments of the private sector had not joined forces with government to make it happen. A consensus was established and we moved ahead as a community. This kind of partnership is called the "new civics." In the old civics, government handled government, business handled business, east was east, west was west, and rarely did the twain ever meet. But the new approach brings them together through a form of enlightened self-interest. This goes beyond traditional corporate philanthropy. It means that business views the improvement of social and economic conditions in the community as a goal tied so closely to its bottom-line interests that it requires direct action and effective involvement. It means that many public officials now understand the wisdom of Winston Churchill's remark, "Some people regard private enterprise as a predatory tiger to be shot. Others look on it as a cow they can milk. Not enough see it as a healthy horse, pulling a sturdy wagon." In the entrepreneurial city, public officials know that pulling the cart of economic development in tandem with the private sector makes a great deal of sense for their city's bottom line—and skyline!

An entrepreneurial city is willing to take risks. Its motto is not "come weal, come woe, our status is quo." The Hoosier Dome, as many commented, was a huge risk—"sure built on faith" as one wag put it. The *Sacramento Bee* commented that our "$82 million gamble paid off." The really good local public officials are deal-makers who are not afraid to share power, risks, and rewards with the private sector. Cities are investors who, in return for tangible support of a project, earn a share of the profit (preferably, not loss!) by participating in gross revenues, net cash flows, or rents. No risk, no reward; nothing ventured, nothing gained; no guts, no glory!

An entrepreneurial city treats amenities as economic assets. In Indianapolis, we are trying to leverage amenity infrastructure for economic advantage. Our commitment to sports facilities, for example, is not an end in itself. The Hoosier Dome is a job generator. It creates new business opportunities. As a result of its construction, new convention business is coming to town, new restaurants and hotels are opening up, new national organizations are moving to Indianapolis, and new people are interested in investing in our city.

An entrepreneurial city makes creative use of its resources. Who would have thought that a few relatively decrepit warehouses, some vacant land, and a little-used street had the potential to become an $80-million asset like the Hoosier Dome? Who would have thought that a block from the Hoosier Dome, our Union Station, abandoned when Americans finally said good-bye to passenger trains, a forlorn and derelict building with moss growing up through its floors, water dripping through a leaky roof, and wind whistling through its broken windows, could once again become a vital part of our city? But today, Union Station is a magnificent festival marketplace, filled with new restaurants and boutiques and entertainment places, as well as a 276-room hotel complete with railroad cars for luxury bedrooms, all a result of the joint commitment of public- and private-sector funds and creative vision. Who would have thought that in place of an asphalt parking lot, a new $36-million 343-room hotel in the Embassy Suites chain could rise fifteen stories above nearby Washington Street? Who would have thought that the prestigious Hudson Institute would move away from Croton-on-Hudson to relocate in Indianapolis? The people who thought these and other dreams could become reality, the men and women who believed things could be better, had a very important characteristic in common—creativity.

It might be stretching the case to say that these characteristics of the entrepreneurial city have a biblical basis, but as a minister turned mayor, I cannot help but be struck by the way in which biblical concepts can be interpreted as undergirding them.

For example, when you talk about partnership you're talking about "Come, let us reason together." You're talking about bearing one another's burdens and being your brother's and sister's keeper. You're talking about sitting around the table discussing strategies, maybe as the apostles and disciples did. You're talking about "working together for good." In the story about Peter and his comrades catching all the fish, we read, "They beckoned to their partners in the other boat to come and help them." That's what we need to do in an entrepreneurial city. We help each other, we work together. We're all in different boats, but when there's a challenge to face, we come together in partnership to give each other assistance, knowing that in cooperation there is strength, and that weakness will result if we each continue to go our own way, protect our own turf, look for all the credit ourselves, and do not lend a helping hand.

The Bible is a book about risk-takers. It's a book about entre-preneurs! Abraham left the comfort of the Fertile Crescent to go in search of the Promised Land. Moses led his people away from captivity into the wilderness. Prophets like Isaiah dared to face down the royalty of their day. Jesus Christ "set his face steadfastly toward Jerusalem," knowing that it meant certain death. And just think of all the risks Paul and the other disciples and apostles took, as they sought to be "obedi-ent to the heavenly vision" and endured all sorts of hardships in order to get the word out about "the way, the truth, and the life" as they had been given to understand it.

The Bible expresses deep concerns about social justice and about the importance of providing bread to people who are hungry, which translates into jobs for economically disadvantaged people and doing those kinds of things that can improve the quality of life for those who are oppressed, discriminated against, or out of the mainstream. And I can't help thinking that the entry-level jobs provided by our commit-ment to amenities is a case in point. Every time you add one new hotel room to a community, you create two permanent jobs—one inside the hotel and the other outside. When we were building the Hoosier Dome, we made as strong a commitment as we could (10 percent) to minority and women's enterprises participating in the project, and were pleased that when all was said and done we had exceeded our goals.

There's a story in the New Testament about 5,000 people being fed by the disciples who had "five loaves of bread and two fish," as if to suggest that we must take whatever resources we have and use them to the best advantage possible. When we refurbish historic buildings for cultural activities or build new facilities for sporting events, we are trying to do something good for the city that results in additional economic growth for our people. They are ends in themselves but also means to other ends. We take the assets that we have, build on them, and hope that many, many people will benefit from the effort. We may not live by bread alone, but we cannot live without it either!

From beginning to end, the Bible is a book about people who dreamed big dreams and pursued them, all the way from Jacob in

dreams,
pursued
them

Genesis to the Seer in Revelation. "For lack of vision, the people perish." We shared a dream in Indianapolis that someday we would be in the NFL, someday we would be considered a major-league city, someday we would be a destination city, not a city you flew over to get somewhere else. We were determined to prove that even though we existed geographically in what some people called the "rust belt," our mentality was far different. We were going to be competitive. We were going to make our dreams come true. After it was all over, the *Chicago Tribune* remarked that "the Dome brings Hoosier pride to a head," and the *Washington Post* described Indianapolis as "a city that is awakening and searching for a dream."

The Hoosier Dome would stand on its own, on the basis of the additional convention business it would generate, irrespective of professional sports. There were those who thought it would be empty, a risk that would not pay off until an NFL franchise became a tenant. But that was emphatically not the case, in spite of what they believed. Risk there was, but it was more prudent than the general public understood. Every time one conventioneer spends a day in our city, it means about $100 to our economy. Once the domed stadium became a reality, a half dozen new hotels went up, new restaurants opened at the rate of more than one a month, and $185 million worth of new convention business was booked—all this before the coming of the Colts was announced.

conventions &
city's economy

Indiana University economists subsequently made a study of the total economic impact of conventions on our city, and the figure they came up with (not counting the Colts) is an added $358.3 million per year. That's not a bad return on an $80-million investment!

NFL franchise
30 m. per yr.

An NFL franchise would definitely be an additional asset. We calculated that the direct economic benefit to our city would run in the neighborhood of $30 million a year, and the indirect benefit would be much greater. We hoped to have a team one day, and we assumed all along that it would arrive by the expansion route. For three years, we made presentations to National Football League owners about the Indianapolis project, beginning at their winter meeting in Phoenix in 1982, followed by Palm Springs in '83 and Honolulu in '84. (We thought the NFL would expand rather quickly, not anticipating the problems they had in the early 1980s with the lawsuits resulting from the transfer of the Oakland Raiders to Los Angeles, the players' strike, and the negotiations for a new TV contract.) Although we did not build the facility solely to land a team, we knew landing a team would be impossible if we did not have a stadium in which they could play. And there was obviously some luck involved. The Colts did drop into our laps, but we were ready. We were well positioned. When opportunity knocked, we were prepared to answer, which is really what luck is all

"luck" &
preparation

about. I believe it was Jack Nicklaus who said, "The more I practice, ✳
the luckier I get!"

Word had spread of the Indianapolis stadium, and a comment made
at the Super Bowl in 1984 intrigued Michael Chernoff, Bob Irsay's
right-hand man, his negotiator, a bright attorney with a keen eye for
detail and a persistent knack for hard work, and a very pleasant guy,
who came to Indianapolis unknown to us to look at our uncompleted
stadium in February. About the middle of that month I was told that
an overture had been received from the Baltimore Colts; did I think
we should pursue it? After a few days' thought, I said, "Go for it with
gusto."

When it was all over, there were accusations around the country that
our city had lured the Colts away from Baltimore. A columnist in Fort
Myers called it "a clear case of prostitution," and the *New York Times*
published an article under the title "The Seduction of the Colts." I was
often introduced at speaking engagements as "the guy who stole the
Colts," but as I see it, the truth is that Baltimore lost the Colts, Indianapolis did not steal them.

It was well known in January of 1984 that Bob Irsay was looking at
sites for a potential relocation of his franchise. His relationship with
Baltimore had deteriorated. Attendance was way down, the media in
that city were beating him up mercilessly, and Baltimore's Memorial
Stadium had deteriorated to the point where some people were calling
it "the ashcan." (A famous NFL quarterback once told me that it was
the worst stadium in the league in which to play.) Irsay was looking for
a new home. He went to Phoenix in January, but that blew up for the
stated reason of premature publicity. He may have been looking elsewhere as well. He felt he had the freedom to move if he wanted to,
since Al Davis had moved the Raiders, and a court decision in late
February of 1984 more or less confirmed the free-agency status of
league owners. Pete Rozelle called a special meeting of the NFL owners to discuss the Raiders' decision and the possibility of a Colts move.
The legal situation was such that when the NFL met in Chicago early
in March, permission was neither granted nor denied, so Bob had the
freedom to do what he wanted. (Commissioner Pete Rozelle and his
staff, particularly Don Weiss, were gentlemen through and through,
playing it straight, not taking sides, and treating all issues and sides
and people fairly and squarely throughout this whole transition period.)

Dave Frick, whom I had designated as our chief negotiator, worked
himself to the bone, donating all his time, and wearing his hat of
Treasurer of the Capital Improvement Board rather than that of a
private attorney. He consulted with a small group of individuals I

convened, who became known as the 706 Club because we met in Room 706 of the Columbia Club on Monument Circle on a moment's notice at any time of the day or night. In addition to Dave and me, the group consisted of Tom Moses, Chairman of the Board of the Indianapolis Water Company (who had served as Chairman of the Indiana NFL Committee since 1981); Nick Frenzel, CEO and Chairman of the Board of Merchants National Bank, who stepped up to the challenge and gave us extraordinary assistance; P. E. MacAllister, Chairman of the Capital Improvement Board (who happens to be the most literate layman I have ever met when it comes to a knowledge of biblical and classical history and literature—I once asked him who Joseph's brothers were and he could name them all!); Jim Morris from Lilly Endowment; and Herb Simon, President of Melvin Simon & Associates, through whose organization the original initiative had come to us from Mike Chernoff. We met often to strategize and evaluate the different proposals that were flying back and forth between the two chief negotiators, Frick and Chernoff.

The media soon caught on to what was developing, and the glare of publicity began heating up. I was caught in the middle. Dave kept telling me that if I told too much about the negotiations, I would blow the deal, but I knew the public had a right to know what was going on and the media naturally had a very high level of curiosity. So I tried to do the best I could to sail between the Scylla of covertness and the Charybdis of too much disclosure.

When I attended the black-tie Sullivan Award dinner on February 27 honoring the outstanding amateur athletes of the year, media people swarmed around me to ask what I was doing. Without divulging any details, I tried to explain that as Mayor of Indianapolis my job was to be as aggressive as I could for my city. I asked rhetorically, "What am I supposed to do—sit on the bank and eat bonbons while the river of history flows by?" Every other mayor in the country would be doing what I was doing, if he or she had the chance. My parents, who lived in Phoenix, called regularly to tell me about the press reports and local TV coverage on the activities of their oldest son, and my brother Bob telephoned to express mock concern that I was turning into a horse thief.

The press didn't care what time of the day or night it was if they wanted a story. Kae Browning, my executive assistant, who was doubling as press secretary, said it seemed to her that people deliberately called in the middle of the night hoping that in her somnolent confusion she might make a mistake and tell them more than "We're negotiating. We're working on it. We hope it works out." She talked to the *New York Times*, the *Wall Street Journal,* the *Chicago Tribune,* and many other papers. She was interviewed by both wire services and all the

Baltimore TV stations, radio stations, and newspapers. She did three TV interviews for Baltimore and received several marriage proposals! She said that after it was all over, she was amazed not only at the way people in the media could phrase and rephrase the same old thing, but also at the way she learned to do that too and, as she put it, "sound important in the process."

Kae had many stories to tell about the press. There was the reporter who tried to bribe a baggage attendant so he could ride out to a jet arriving from Baltimore on a luggage cart, and a USAir attendant even thanked her once for all the business their airline was receiving as a result of media people traveling to Indianapolis. As the negotiations dragged on, many reporters were stuck in the city for longer than they had expected. Many had to buy new clothing, and two were even away from home when babies were born to their wives. One reporter for a prestigious eastern paper had dogged Kae for weeks, but when the news finally broke he was in the pool at the Hilton. She bailed him out by providing all the information he needed.

One of the most amusing things I remember happened when I was home with the flu, and nobody in the media would believe I was sick. One of the Baltimore TV reporters came to my door with a huge jar of hot chicken soup. When the doorbell rang and I opened it in my bathrobe, there was the reporter with his soup and a TV camera grinding away behind him. A little later that week, when I went to Washington for a meeting of the National League of Cities, I was astounded at the number of delegates who came up to me and said they had seen me on TV in my pajamas!

As the weeks wore on, it became clear that Bob Irsay was not ready to make up his mind. Finally, during the last week of March, the process began to accelerate. On Tuesday, March 27, Dave and Nick went to Chicago for a final meeting with Irsay and Chernoff. They returned to report that all the details for a lease were completed and we were ready to go. Still, Irsay had not signed.

Then, the next morning a news item appeared in the papers around the country, stating that one house of the Maryland General Assembly had passed a bill giving the City of Baltimore the right to exercise eminent domain over the Colts franchise. The other house would pass it and send it on for the Governor's signature the next day. That was a gun at Irsay's head. At 11:30 A.M. a call came in, letting us know that they had to move quickly to leave Baltimore before the eminent domain action was taken. We put in a call to Johnny B. Smith, our great and good friend and Chairman and CEO of the Mayflower Corporation. He had told me earlier that if we were to land an NFL franchise through the relocation route rather than an expansion of the League, he would be glad to move them to Indianapolis for free, as a donation to the civic effort, and all he would need would be twelve hours' notice.

That is what we gave him on the morning of March 28. By 9:00 P.M. he had fifteen Mayflower vans in Baltimore moving toward the Colts' training center in Owings Mills, Maryland, and by morning the vans had turned around and were heading for Indianapolis. We lost communication with them because of the press of media and other forces, and at one point Johnny B. told Dave and me that he felt like General Eisenhower on D-Day—he knew his troops were out there, he just didn't know where they were!

That morning Jane Pauley asked me on the *Today* show where the trucks were headed, but I could not give her a direct answer. Even while the trucks were on their way, I had to maintain my silence, because I was still being told by Frick that if I made a premature announcement and did not leave it to Chernoff or Irsay to make, the deal would blow up. When Chernoff stepped off Irsay's plane at Indianapolis International Airport that afternoon, however, he announced to the press that the Colts were coming to Indianapolis, and I immediately followed that announcement with a press conference in my office.

The Mayor's Conference Room was packed for the largest news conference I've ever had. Some two dozen reporters, with TV cameras, regular cameras, tape recorders, and pads and pencils, plus all the Mayor's Office staff and City Hall employees who could squeeze in, were jammed together. I made a statement confirming that the Colts were on their way, answered as many questions as I could, and announced that there would be a formal news conference the following Saturday morning with members of the Capital Improvement Board, who were to be convened in a specially called meeting to ratify the agreements Dave Frick, P. E. MacAllister, and I had already signed.

The reality of the Colts' move had sunk in. Reporters from Baltimore who had previously expressed flippant opinions ranging from "Irsay will leave you high and dry" to "You're welcome to him" now realized the magnitude of their city's loss of this historic franchise. I felt bad for Baltimore, glad for Indianapolis.

I said during the news conference that my heart went out to the people of Baltimore. I had many friends there from the old days when I was a member of the Baltimore Presbytery and pastor of the First Presbyterian Church in Annapolis, and I was sorry for the sadness this brought them, to say nothing of the aggravation and anger the loss of the Colts was causing in other quarters. No one believed me. One reporter wrote that when I said this I was grinning "like a Cheshire cat." But I really did mean it. Two years earlier, I had worked very hard to save the Indiana Pacers NBA franchise for Indianapolis. It almost was lost. I knew what an empty feeling it would create in the heart of our community and what an economic blow it would be if our franchise went elsewhere. We saved it, but the experience gave me real insight into how Baltimore must feel.

My sympathy for Baltimore's loss was very real, but it obviously and naturally was outweighed by my excitement about our city's gain. When the long procession of Mayflower vans pulled in, I enjoyed welcoming them and helping them to unload some of the equipment they carried. We had signed a twenty-year contract with two five-year options, and Irsay had given us the right to match any offer to buy the team if he wanted to sell it outside the family. We also assured the Colts that for twelve years they would receive the cash equivalent of some 40,000 seats being filled if the attendance dipped below that number, and we arranged a $12.5-million ten-year loan at 8 percent. We pledged to build a new office and training facility and made arrangements regarding rent, day-of-game expenses, taxes, suite income, and so on. (It is my understanding that Baltimore may have made a more lucrative offer in a last-ditch effort to avoid losing the team, but it was too late.)

So now it was Monday, April 2, and Bob Irsay, Dave Frick, and I were walking across the green carpet on the floor of the Hoosier Dome while 20,000 people in the stands applauded and shouted their welcome to the Indianapolis Colts. The 74th Army Band was playing! The flags were flying! The occasion was as positive and exciting and upbeat as it could possibly have been.

We ascended the steps of the platform and shook hands with the dignitaries assembled there to greet Bob—Tom Moses, Nick Frenzel, P. E. MacAllister, and others. We exchanged some gifts—keys to the city from me to Bob Irsay, his son Jim, and Mike Chernoff, and Colts sweaters and ties for me and Dave and the others. Words of welcome were extended, and the press asked a few more questions before we headed for a giant reception in the 500 Ballroom in the Convention Center.

As we were descending the steps, I saw Dave laughing and pointing to the seats in the stadium. "What *about* them?" I asked. "Dark blue and silver," Dave answered. The Colts colors! Colors selected long before anyone ever dreamed the Colts would come to Indianapolis. "Amazing coincidence," said Frick.

Or was it providence?

2

Do They Mix?

Bill Enright, my current successor as pastor of Second Presbyterian Church in Indianapolis, recently told the congregation, "I listened to the Mayor this week in his State of the City address at the Downtown Rotary Club, and I thought to myself, 'You know, for a preacher, he's not a bad politician.' Then he said something that caught my attention and changed my mind, and I said to myself, 'You know, for a politician, he's not a bad preacher.' "

Preacher-politician, clergyman-congressman, minister-mayor—unusual combinations, to be sure, but ones that I have lived and am living. Moving from the pulpit of a Presbyterian church to the executive offices of America's thirteenth largest city has represented an alliance of two vocations that are much more compatible than many people would believe.

The questions I am asked follow a typical pattern: "How could you leave the ministry?" "How has your experience in the church helped prepare you for government leadership?" "How could a good Christian man like you get involved in a dirty game like politics?" These inquiries were summed up succinctly during a recent conversation with a new acquaintance. After explaining my two careers to him, he asked with a note of skepticism, "Do they mix?"

I was serving as the pastor of the First Presbyterian Church in Annapolis, Maryland, when I received a call from Second Presbyterian Church and the Presbytery of Indianapolis. At thirty years of age, I was relatively young to be asked to serve the large, influential, and affluent congregation that Second represented, but the invitation offered me a significant opportunity, and I accepted it. (Has anyone ever heard of a clergyman making a move without considering it onward and upward toward a bigger challenge?) In the summer of 1963, Mike, Laurie, Timmy, Bill IV, their mother, Anne, and I packed our bags and headed west for Indianapolis and the church first served by Henry Ward Beecher.

The Beecher connection intrigued me, because my grandfather Hudnut had married Harriet Beecher, a distant relative of that notorious, controversial, charismatic preacher. The Beecher name has been passed down through three Hudnut generations, the latest one to be given it being my youngest son, Theodore Beecher Hudnut, who was born in 1964. Our family has always been proud of this connection with one of America's most illustrious families in the nineteenth century. Lyman Beecher, Henry's father, has been described as "the father of more brains than any man in America," with at least six of his thirteen children achieving considerable distinction! It seemed more than a coincidence when I was tapped to fill the pulpit first occupied by the famous Henry Ward Beecher in 1838.

At Second Presbyterian, my first task was to spread a lot of love around and heal as many wounds as possible. The church had been seriously divided in the early 1960s. The Presbytery had suspended the Session, the minister had left, an interim minister was holding the fort, and permission had finally been given to form a pulpit committee to look for a new permanent senior minister. My father mentioned my name to Walter Leander, a member of this committee who had been a member of Dad's church in Rochester, New York. Walt passed my name on to the committee, and visits were exchanged—some surreptitious, some not so. I preached in a neutral pulpit in Chicago, then the committee brought us down to look at Indianapolis. I was invited to preach on a Sunday in June 1963, after which I was closeted in an upstairs office while the congregation met and voted. The vote was favorable, and a new chapter of my life began.

There were many wonderful people at Second. The church had a long history of first-rate preaching, and the community leaders who filled its pews endowed this great congregation with tremendous potential. While preaching was my first priority and surest joy, I also enjoyed the pastoral and administrative sides of my job, and I worked hard during those early years to bring people back together. With the help of the good Lord and dedicated members of the congregation, the wounds began to heal, people began working together again, and a sleeping giant awoke.

If my first task was to build the church back up in terms of its internal strength, my second was to move it toward greater involvement in the community. I took a position against the thinking, prevalent at the time, that the church ought to stop meddling and stick to the gospel. (Remember J. Howard Pew's famous *Reader's Digest* article by that title?) I offered the opinion that some Christians can be so heavenly

minded they are no earthly good. I defended the church's right to take
stands on the issues of the day. I preached the importance of volunteering, of being involved, of showing that we cared, of getting under
the load of life and trying to give a lift, of being our brother's and
sister's keeper.

And I tried to practice what I preached. I served on various volunteer boards in Indianapolis, including the Family Service Association,
the YMCA, the Westminster Foundation at Purdue University, and the
Marion County Mental Health Association. With the help of the
Church Federation and Dr. Al Edyvean of the Christian Theological
Seminary, I began a weekly television talk show called *Focus on Faith*,
a program that featured a priest, a rabbi, and a Protestant minister
(me) talking about issues pertaining to biblical interpretation, theology, church history, ecclesiology, and current affairs. (This is perhaps
a somewhat lofty description of what some Indianapolis viewers
dubbed "The Three Stooges.")

And I began to dabble in volunteer political activity. I chaired the
Ministers for Ruckelshaus campaign in Bill's unsuccessful effort to
unseat Senator Birch Bayh in 1968, and I headed the Ministers for
Lugar committee when Dick successfully ran for reelection as Mayor
of Indianapolis in 1971. That year I also served as manager of the
successful campaign of one of our church members for election to the
City-County Council. Three times I tried to garner the endorsement
of the local Republican party for elective office (twice for Indiana's
General Assembly and once for the City-County Council). Each time
I failed, and each time I refused to run against the party's slated
candidate. In the late 1960s, I had been a member of the committee
to work on "Unigov"—the consolidation of city and county government.

Politics was working its way into my blood. I loved the fun, the
camaraderie, the strong feelings of "family," the honest sweat of hard
work in the precinct trenches, the thrill of victory. More than just fun,
however, was the knowledge that I was participating in significant
work. It was meaningful enterprise to become involved where I perceived a lot of action taking place. Politics is a game—the most important game in town. I met new people, made new friends, confronted
tough issues, saw exciting opportunities, and encountered a larger
world.

Perhaps during those initial ventures into the political arena I was
too defensive, but it bothered me when people voiced the opinion that
a minister had no business being involved in politics. As I saw it,
ministers had the same right as other people who cared about their
community to become a part of the political process. I personally do
not feel that it is proper to use the pulpit to endorse political candi-

dates or to espouse partisan political issues, nor have I ever used the political hustings to advance what might be considered to be a partisan religious point of view. But members of the clergy are part of their community. They pay taxes like everyone else, they address themselves to the issues of the day, they work with people in their congregations who are deeply involved in the political process. I could not (and do not) see why their calling as religious professionals should preclude political involvement.

So I presented myself as a clergyman who cared about what was happening in his city and wanted to become involved. Later, when I had won elective office and people asked me why I had "left" the church, I tried to make the distinction between a congregationally based pastorate and a wider understanding of both the ministry and the church. All through the years, first as a congressman and now as Mayor, I have cherished my membership in the Presbytery of Whitewater Valley (formerly Indianapolis) and have done my best to help the church in ways I could. I continue to attend Second with my wife and family whenever possible. Occasionally, I have officiated at funerals, baptisms, and weddings, and much more than occasionally—about three Sundays out of five—I have filled pulpits in many churches throughout Indiana and even beyond the state boundaries. At the end of each year I file a report with the Presbytery's Ministerial Relations Committee listing all the church-related activities in which I have been involved during the previous twelve months, and it is my hope that, in this rather narrow sense of continuing to be involved in things that could be called "ecclesiastical," I have kept up my identification with the institutional church.

In a broader sense, however, I feel that politics is a legitimate form of ministry, in that it constitutes service to people. I hope—without being saccharine about it—that it is reasonable to think of one's constituency as a large congregation which one is called to serve. Once I served a single congregation, then I represented Indiana's Eleventh District, and now I oversee the administration of the City of Indianapolis and Marion County; but if ministry is service, as I believe it is, and if we follow One who came "not to be served, but to serve," then being involved in governmental service can be legitimately construed as a non-parish-based form of ministry.

In my view the distinction between a pastorate and the ministry is a proper one to make, and when people accuse me of "leaving the church" or ask me why I went into politics when it meant quitting the ministry, I try to pursue that distinction with them.

Once I was at the White House back in the days when President Nixon arranged for occasional services of worship to be held there on Sunday mornings. I had been invited to attend as a guest and went with my wife. The officiating clergyman that day was a Roman Catholic priest, and after the service he stood between President and Mrs. Nixon in the receiving line. When it was my turn to be introduced, the President, who knew I was a freshman congressman, nudged the priest in the ribs and pointed at me, saying, "You see this fellow right here? He used to be a minister but now he's a congressman!" I did not intend to give the President a free and unwanted lecture on ordination and the priesthood of all believers, but neither could I let the opportunity pass. "But sir, I still am," I said, and to his puzzled look and arched eyebrows, I responded, "Just because I beat a Democrat doesn't mean I was defrocked!" The President laughed (in those pre-Watergate days, his sense of humor had a little more opportunity to flourish), and then, not to be outdone, he nudged the priest again, pointed to my wife, and said, "See what a beautiful wife a Presbyterian minister can have!"

Another question I am asked frequently is how I could have left a "high calling" in the church for involvement in something as unsavory as politics. Most people have a low regard for politicians and feel they are a self-serving lot. Judging by the perks Congress votes itself, from the postal frank to the gymnasium, from subsidized meals to subsidized haircuts, from junkets overseas to first-class airplane trips home, I do understand the conclusions that people draw; but in reality they are way off the mark if they think that most people in politics are venal, out to line their private pockets at public expense.

I remember listening to a call-in radio program while driving to the airport after delivering a speech in Indianapolis. It happened to be the morning after the news had broken that Vice-President Spiro Agnew had been caught with his hand in the cookie jar, and the question of the day was, "What do you think about what Vice-President Agnew has done?" Practically everyone who phoned had the same answer: "He's no different from everyone else in Washington—he just got caught."

Well, I don't think that's true. There are many fine, decent, dedicated public servants in politics; many honorable men and women who are practicing the fine art of politics as honestly and effectively as they can, on both sides of the political aisle, at all levels of government. I know politics has its share of disreputable characters, but I'm not sure that just because politicians receive an enormous amount of publicity when they get into trouble, they are a worse lot than others. Every profession has its bad apples—business, labor, education, reporting— yes, even the ministry! Wasn't it Augustine who, speaking of the church, remarked that there were a lot of wolves on the inside and a lot of sheep on the outside? And Robert McAfee Brown framed the same comment in a different way when he expressed the opinion that the church is much like Noah's ark—the only reason we can stand the

bad apples in church too

stench inside is because of the storm outside! If someone thinks everyone in politics is grubby and everyone in the church is holy, that person has probably never been very closely involved in either.

During my first week in Congress back in 1973, an old-timer came up and introduced himself.

"Hello, young man, who are you?"

"I'm Bill Hudnut. Glad to meet you."

"Where're you from?"

"Indianapolis."

"Where's that?" Some congressmen have a rather limited view of the world.

After I had given him a brief lesson in geography, the questioning continued.

"Tell me, what'd you do back in real life?"

"Well, sir, back in real life I was a preacher."

We had been having this friendly chat in the well of the House before a roll-call vote was finished, but my last answer had clearly changed the tone of our conversation.

The congressman scowled and clapped his hand to his forehead unbelievingly.

"My goodness"—that's not really what he said but that is the way I will translate it—"you guys are taking over this place."

I did a little mental arithmetic, thinking of myself and Andy Young and Father Robert Drinan (I was very disappointed when the Pope forbade him to continue his involvement in politics) and a couple of others.

"Yes, sir, that's right. There are five of us clergymen and two hundred and eighty-nine of you attorneys in the United States Congress. We sure are taking over!"

Perhaps it is easier for a minister to be accepted in politics today than it was for me fifteen years ago, but certainly it is still very difficult for a clergyman to branch out and run for elected office. It cannot be done without the approval of the congregation you serve and the church authorities to whom you are responsible, unless you simply don't care and want to cut yourself off. In my instance, nearly nine years of service at Second Presbyterian had established my standing to a point where I was able to use my relationship with the congregation as a springboard into public life without severing those ties. My entry into politics after a decade and a half as a Presbyterian minister was at once an end and a new beginning—something different, radically so, but also more of the same (serving people). This transition from a clerical to a political life would have been impossible without the support of the congregation I served, and I will always be grateful for that.

Some of the support came from individuals in my congregation who had encouraged me over the years to pursue my interest in government service. There was Gene Beesley, an elder in our church who served as chairman of the board of Eli Lilly and Company. Gene had taken me as his guest to Richard Nixon's first inaugural in January 1969, an event that proved to be quite exhilarating. As I sat on the hard bench looking up at the dignitaries assembled on the east front of the Capitol, I wondered if I would ever be among them—just as in the old Annapolis days, when I had taken the kids to stand in the balconies of the House and Senate, I had wondered the same thing. On the night of the inaugural ball, Gene and I and one of his Lilly compatriots, Henry DeBoest, sat up in our tuxedos until three in the morning talking about politics, about government service, and about Bill Hudnut getting involved in this strange new exciting world.

Dick DeMars, president of Geupel-DeMars Construction Company and, like Gene, a leader in both the community and the church, added his words of encouragement. I remember an evening in his home when we discussed my idea of taking the plunge into politics. At first he did not cotton to it, but as our conversation concluded he gave me a pat on the back. "Bill, if it's what you want to do, I'm all for you," he said. What a great kind of friend to have!

Even Gordon St. Angelo, the State Chairman of the Democratic Party, spent hours giving me the benefit of his insight into political life. Here was a masterful practitioner of the game, a true professional in every sense of the word. Gordy's business was to elect Democrats, but he was broad-minded enough, fair enough, and generous enough not to discourage his minister from getting into politics just because he was a Republican.

Gene's and Dick's and Gordy's attitudes were typical of the people at Second Church. After nine years, we were good friends. It was not that I wanted to leave them, or that they wanted me to leave, but if this was the direction I chose to pursue, they were ready to support me. I was convinced that political office was right for Bill Hudnut. Now all I had to do was convince the Republican Party and the electorate of central Indiana that Bill Hudnut was right for political office!

L. Keith Bulen, Chairman of the Marion County Republican Party, had to be convinced. Keith was a pro and knew more about polls, campaigns, public relations, and fund-raising than 95 percent of all politicians. He had the ability to elicit people's best, he could light a torch in your mind's eye, he could instill pride and kindle your desire to win. He knew how to attract good people to politics, foremost among them Bill Ruckelshaus and Dick Lugar, and he wanted a Republican congressman very badly. He finally decided it was timely for me to put my hat into the ring, and it is to him that I owe my political start.

During the winter of 1971–72, I spent a great deal of time going one-on-one. Base-touching is exceedingly important in politics, as it is in the church. I talked with members of the Marion County Republican Party hierarchy, with literally hundreds of precinct committeemen, with volunteers who wanted to help if we got geared up, and above all with the members of the screening committee, who would decide whom the party would support for the congressional nomination. I also talked with the people in my church—the officers and the members of the congregation. I consulted with the Presbytery and the members of its Ministerial Relations Committee.

And then, in February 1972, I went to the two big group meetings that could determine my future.

The first was the meeting of the Republican screening committee. Since 1964 several people had attempted to unseat the incumbent congressman, U.S. Representative Andrew Jacobs, Jr., but none had been successful. Andy was going to run for another term, and several individuals vied for the support of the Republican Party in opposing him. One by one we appeared before the committee. Of the primary contenders, I was the least well known and could claim little political experience, but I told the committee that I thought I had the ability to work hard, to articulate the issues, and to beat Andy in the fall. I said I knew I could not do it alone, but I thought I could do it with their help. When the day was over, the committee had given me the nod, but one of the other candidates had vowed to run anyway, which meant that we were in for a tough fight.

The second important meeting that month was the specially called gathering of the Second Presbyterian congregation. It had already been announced in the papers that "The Reverend Dr. William H. Hudnut III" had been selected by the Republican Party as its endorsed congressional candidate for the Eleventh District, but before I could really run, it would be necessary to take a leave of absence from Second Presbyterian Church. On February 29, the congregation met for the purpose of voting yea or nay on my request to be granted a sabbatical leave—not to study or go abroad, as was usually the case, but to run for Congress! Without approval, I would have two choices: I could abandon my political career before it started and stay on in the congregationally based ministry, or I could resign and run for Congress on my own, without any visible means of financial support for me or my family of seven. Most of the officers of the church were favorably disposed toward granting me the leave and recommended this to the congregation. But the key was whether Gordon St. Angelo would oppose the motion. He stood to speak. Everyone had been waiting for this moment. They knew, as I did, that he could oppose my request, saying that it was inappropriate, that church money should not go to fund a political candidate, that the church should not be involved in partisan politics, and all the rest of it. My request could be denied and the congregation could be seriously divided.

It would have been easy for Gordon to create a lot of static, but, Christian gentleman and friend that he is, he did otherwise. He told the congregation that although he might disagree with my politics, and while he undoubtedly would never vote for me(!), he still believed Bill Hudnut had a right to do this if he really felt that it represented God's will for his life. Gordon said that clergymen were not second-class citizens and that I should be allowed to practice what I preached, which was involvement in the life of our community. He evoked images of great Presbyterian leaders in the past who had taken the plunge into politics—John Calvin in Geneva, John Knox in Edinburgh, John Witherspoon in Princeton. He added that the congregation should be supportive as Christians, regardless of their political views, and he expressed approval of my request. When the vote was taken, it was unanimous in my favor! The congregation would release me and I would jump into a political campaign, with the understanding that if I won I would resign my pastorate, but if I lost I would return to the church after the November election (or earlier if I did not survive the May primary) and continue to be Second Presbyterian's pastor.

With this moment, my life was irrevocably changed. I was leaving the relatively quiet setting of a ministry, where I had tended to pastoral duties, and entering that of a hotly contested political campaign. To climb down out of the pulpit and into the rough-and-tumble of politics where everyone was not your friend was quite a transition. I went to hundreds of coffees, political rallies, meetings of every description, factory gates, bowling alleys, and all the rest. Billboards went up with my name on them. I had debates on TV. I spent a great deal of time cultivating the approximately 400 precinct committeemen and women who would be responsible for carrying the message of my endorsement by the party to the voters in the May primary. Some of them supported me; some did not. It was going to be very close.

But none of us realized how close. Some 45,000 people had cast their ballots to determine which of the four candidates would be the Republican nominee: one received 800 votes and another 3,000; the remaining 41,000 were so evenly divided that I had received only 81 votes more than Dan Burton (now a congressman). Don't tell me that a single vote doesn't count! Dan demanded a recount, and after six weeks I was declared the official nominee of the Republican Party by 98 votes.

It's interesting to do a little arithmetic on that figure. If 50 persons had changed their vote, meaning a swing of 100, I would have lost the election instead of won it. Since there were approximately 400 precincts in the district, I won that election by one eighth of a vote per precinct. There are many stories in the folklore of American politics about close elections, but this one is mine alone!

The campaign wore on through the dog days of summer, picking up a more heated pace in the fall. When all was said and done, I defeated Andy Jacobs and went to Congress. I was the beneficiary of a Nixon landslide. In my congressional district, Nixon beat McGovern by about fifteen percentage points, while I beat Jacobs by only two.

I learned right at the beginning of my political life what I think I knew anyway, because it's one of life's most fundamental lessons: there is no such thing as a self-made man or woman. We are all indebted to others for so much that our only possible appropriate attitude is one of humble gratitude. Sometimes in politics, about one minute after the votes are counted on election night, victorious candidates begin to think they did it all by themselves. Getting a big head, they forget the organization that backed them all along the way and turned out the vote for them at the polls.

To be effective, political power has to be organized, for it is the nitty-gritty of campaigns—registration, polling, phone banks, advertising, and getting out the vote—that wins elections. That work is carried on by literally thousands of people who volunteer as workers in the precincts and wards, finance committee members, and many others. All told, the Marion County Republican organization in Indianapolis has some 1,940 officials, now headed by a great nuts-and-bolts technician, John W. Sweezy, a close friend and ally without whose support, following Keith Bulen's, I could not have made my way into politics. Building on Keith's foundations, John has created what is, without a doubt, one of the finest Republican urban political organizations in the country, and I'm proud and grateful to be a member of it.

I was often asked in those early days if being a minister made any difference in the outcome of the election. I think not. Possibly 10 percent of the people were pleased a clergyman was running for public office, 10 percent disapproved, and the other 80 percent evaluated me on my merits, my views on the issues, and my party affiliation.

I spent only two years in Congress, discovering on a certain bleak day in November 1974 that so many people back in Indianapolis missed me that 51 percent of them voted for me to come home—at least that's the way I tell the story now. Actually my defeat had a lot to do with Watergate. Only one Republican congressman running for reelection that year received more votes than in the previous election, and in closely contested races a bunch of us lost. I had taken my position as member of the U.S. House of Representatives seriously and I had worked very hard, but lose I did.

In addition to the grueling pace, my two years in Congress had also been a difficult period for me personally. My wife had left me in

write left... (margin note)

remarried (margin note)

October 1973. It was a sad passage in my life—sad for me, for her, and for our children. I suppose, in retrospect, it worked out for the best, but I did not want it at the time. I could not have made it through those months without the loving-kindness of my next-door neighbors, Dr. and Mrs. J. Neill Garber, who provided me with a place to stay on the weekends when I returned from Washington. Eventually I found my own apartment, and on Easter weekend of 1974 I was introduced to Susie Rice by mutual friends. Susie was single and recently divorced, with three children. We fell in love and were married the following December, after I had lost the election, and we settled down in Indianapolis with no job in sight for either of us. Talk about faith!

My hiatus, however, was not a long one. It would have been difficult for me to return to the church, since Second Presbyterian had already found a successor. Given my professional background, I knew education was probably an avenue for me to explore. Gene Sease, the dynamic president of Indiana Central University (now the University of Indianapolis), offered me a position with an opportunity to teach political science. Simultaneously, I signed on as a management consultant with the Mayflower Corporation, at the request of its CEO, my new next-door neighbor, Johnny B. Smith. Between these two jobs, I made enough to keep body and soul together while Susie studied for her real estate exams, which she passed in early 1975.

I was out of public office, but I had to decide whether I was in or out of politics. If I wanted another run at it, I basically had two choices: I could wait two years and try for another term in the House of Representatives, or I could run for Mayor in 1975, assuming Dick Lugar did not want to run again. Dick had run for the U.S. Senate against Birch Bayh in 1974, and although he had been defeated, his appetite had been whetted for a run against Vance Hartke in 1976. As soon as he announced his intention to do this, I decided to jump into the fray. I held a news conference at Indiana Central and announced my intention to run for Mayor of Indianapolis.

Once again I received the endorsement of the screening committee, which selected me over State Senator John Mutz, who subsequently became Lieutenant Governor of Indiana, and Tom Hasbrook, President of the City-County Council, who continued to serve our community as Deputy Mayor after the election. On election night 1975, I made it past another worthy opponent, Democrat Robert V. Welch, a well-known and well-funded Indianapolis businessman. For the next two months I worked with Mayor Lugar and his people on the transition, and on January 1, 1976, I was sworn in to my first term as Mayor of Indianapolis.

Thus began my residency on the twenty-fifth floor of the City-County Building, in a position I have held through two more elections

and nearly a dozen years. I declined another opportunity to run for
Congress when it was offered in 1982, for by then I had learned that,
for me, serving in that body was much less satisfying than serving as
Mayor of one of America's great cities. It is easy to become lost in
Congress, particularly for a relatively junior Republican. There are
opportunities to serve your constituents, to vote on legislation, and
perhaps to sponsor an occasional bill and make your mark in some
particular area of concern, but I believe I have had a larger and more
rewarding chance for impact in the executive branch of city government than ever would have been the case had I returned to Congress.

People often ask me whether my experience as a pastor has been
helpful (or even relevant) in my work as Mayor. I answer that there is
no question that my ministerial background has been invaluable, even
though it is a given—everyone knows I "used to be" a minister—and
something I never mention or try to trade on. To support this conten-
tion, I often enumerate several similarities between the two, but there
are, of course, differences as well.

My days at Second Presbyterian were full. Like most ministers, I
worked hard at being the best pastor I could be and I stayed busy with
the needs and concerns of my congregation. I learned very quickly,
however, that politics was much more demanding. Eighty- to ninety-
hour workweeks are now the rule, not the exception. One of my major
regrets about being in public life is that now I have much less time to
study, much less time to think. My dad raised me on Harry Emerson
Fosdick's old maxim that for every minute you preached, you should
spend an hour in preparation, and while I did not adhere strictly to
that, I did spend a lot of time in quiet meditation and study, preparing
my thoughts for Sunday morning. Now I must speak off the cuff and
extemporaneously many times a day. In one year I made 600 speeches,
issued 400 proclamations, attended 160 meetings, gave 80 news conferences, received I don't know how many phone calls, and sent out
22,000 letters—activities that certainly eliminated many of my quiet
moments.

In addition, people in politics carry a heavy burden. They must deal
with weighty and complex issues, and some of their decisions can be
extremely difficult to make. The demands not only on their time but
on their resources and patience can be inordinate, and they must
conduct all of their affairs under constant public scrutiny. In the ministry I had a much more private kind of profession—one where I did not
have to operate under sunshine and open-door laws, where I did not
feel compelled to disclose my financial holdings, and where I was not
asked to justify my decisions or react publicly to criticism.

On the other hand, another difference between the ministry and
government service has to do, I suppose, with clout. A member of the

differences

clergy is imbued by his or her vocational choice with a certain spiritual authority, which obviously a person in politics does not possess. But by the same token, as the world understands power, prestige, and influence, a congressman or a mayor has more of it. You're in the newspaper most days, on TV most nights. You're embroiled in things that are controversial. You are doing things that are perceived to be newsworthy. A lot of people defer to you, and you are served by a staff that makes life easier for you. People even return your phone calls!

life of pastor of mayor

A very basic difference, of course, has to do with the subject matter dealt with in religion and politics. I like to say that when I was in the pastorate I was called upon to deal with the ultimate problems of human existence—life and death, sin and grace, marriage and divorce, alienation and reconciliation. But now that I am Mayor, I deal with the penultimate problems of human existence—picking up the trash, plowing the snow, filling the potholes, and putting the stop signs along the roads of life! Obviously, a mayor, who addresses matters of public policy and grapples with such problems as crime, transportation, decaying infrastructure, jobs, health, and education, is dealing with a set of issues and problems different from those facing the pastor, who is working with biblical interpretation, theological insights, and the personal problems of parishioners. Not that pastors do not get involved in addressing themselves to the issues of the day, but that is not their stock-in-trade.

the phone calls

If I were a pastor, I might be expected to answer the phone in the middle of the night because someone's child had been injured in an automobile accident, or my Saturday morning might be interrupted by a couple facing a marriage crisis. As Mayor, I find it rather routine to receive calls at home because people are upset with water backing up into their basement through the sewer system, or neighbors are making too much noise at night, or the proverbial cat is caught in a tree! Once, about one-thirty in the morning, Susie and I had a phone call that rattled us out of our slumber. It turned out to be a woman who was irate because, after an evening out on the town drinking, when she had tried to retrieve her car from a parking lot, she found chains across the exit. She wanted me to come down and help her. Immediately!

Then there was the Saturday morning, after a particularly severe ice storm had paralyzed the city, when a disgruntled citizen came slithering up our driveway. He slammed his car door and stormed up the steps of the house. Susie was out, and I knew I was in for a difficult confrontation. I opened the door, just as he began pounding hard on the knocker, and invited him to come in out of the cold. "What's your problem?" I asked him. "I'll tell you what my problem is," he answered. "My trash hasn't been picked up!"

The fellow did have a real concern, because during that particular winter, Christmas was on a Thursday (and so his trash had not been picked up), New Year's was on a Thursday (and so his trash had not been picked up), and two weeks later, Martin Luther King's birthday was on a Thursday (you get the picture now). The next week the ice storm hit and again the man's trash had not been taken away. I told him I was sorry, and that unfortunately my wife was out with the station wagon or maybe I could help him. He told me not to get fresh with him, and I promised to call the City Sanitation Commissioner to see if we could get a crew to take care of his problem—which we did.

This, however, was not the end of the story. Angered at being bothered on a Saturday morning at home when I was doing other things, I went out and in a fit of petulance removed the numbers from our mailbox. The next evening, Johnny B. Smith arrived at my door as a spokesperson for the neighborhood. Rather sheepishly, he explained that the neighbors wanted me to replace the numbers on my mailbox. I explained to him that on Saturday, while I was at home all peaceful, some nut had come down the street—

He interrupted me before I could finish. "Bill, that's just the point," he said. "If some nut comes down the street looking for the Mayor's house to bomb, we want to make sure he hits the right one!"

Yes, in religion and politics, we are dealing with two altogether different subject matters. More seriously, it is important for clergy in politics to recognize that their views on the issues count for a lot more than their views on God or religion or the Bible. I recollect an evening meeting held early in my political career at the home of Beurt and Cory Jane SerVaas. They were members of Second Church, but, more to the point, Beurt was President of the City-County Council. He invited a number of political and religious leaders in to meet me, and during the course of the discussion, P. E. MacAllister, an elder at Northminster Church and an active Republican, asked me a rather startling question —"What do you think about secondary boycotts?" I don't remember my reply, but I've never forgotten the point P.E. was trying to make: Okay, so you're a preacher, we all know that, but what we don't know is your views on matters of public policy, and that's what we're interested in. You can't coast on your religious coattails here. The subject matter of politics is quite different, and we have an election to win. Where do you stand on the issues?

There are, however, many similarities between the ministry and public service, and in several ways having been a clergyman was a definite aid in becoming a politician.

Most important, in both vocations you spend a great deal of time working with people. It's the people that count. In the church you become deeply involved in people's personal problems. You want to help them. You want to serve them. You want to resolve the issue that is vexing them. And it is the same in politics, at least for me. Basically, politics is a way of serving people, and public servants should be just that—servants.

Alexander Hamilton was once asked what the chief difference was between the new kind of government that he and the Founding Fathers had established on this side of the Atlantic and the government they had left in the Old World. Without hesitation, he responded to his questioner, "Here, sir, the people govern." Abraham Lincoln picked up the same theme in his Gettysburg Address when he defined our system of representative democracy as "government of the people, by the people, and for the people." I keep telling our City department heads that we must be people-sensitive, we must answer people's mail, we must be courteous to them on the telephone, we must not give them the bureaucratic brush-off. When I was elected Mayor, one of the first things I did upon taking office was to establish the Division of Neighborhood Services in place of the old "complaint department." I told our people we never receive a complaint, just opportunities for service, and they do come in!—on an average 90,000 phone calls a year!

The ministry stood me in good stead when I went into government; it not only taught me the value of people, it also helped me to think and speak on my feet. The issues were different, as I've mentioned, but being able to communicate ideas, to articulate your thoughts, and to persuade others is an essential part of both professions. I was visiting with two fellows in my office, when one asked me if being in politics was a lot different from being in the ministry. Before I could answer, the other one replied, "Gracious, no—they're both the same thing. They're both involved in sales." And that's partially true.

It took a lot of learning for me to develop the confidence to address myself to what might be called political issues outside my accustomed field. When you know what you're talking about, you can speak with authority, but that only comes as your knowledge in the field develops. I do feel comfortable offering prayer, of course, but I don't often give prayers in public because I don't want people to be confused about my roles. If I am invited somewhere to preach on Sunday morning, fine; but if I'm somewhere in my capacity as a governmental official, I resist the tendency of some people to call on me to give an invocation just because I am a clergyman by training. Once, though, I acquiesced when a preacher did not show up to give a prayer at a big function in Washington. After the prayer I was quite amused when a "little old lady" came up oohing and aahing and said to me, "Congressman, I loved that prayer you gave. If I didn't know better, I'd think you were a preacher."

Ministers have to work with volunteers and they have to ask for financial support, and experience in these two areas is very helpful in politics as well. Literally thousands of people volunteer their time to the political party of their choice in order to help win elections, and fund-raising is an absolute essential in mounting a successful political campaign. While working with volunteers is essentially a pleasant experience, fund-raising can be difficult. No minister or politician, however, can do without either one.

Still another similarity between the two careers is the way both of them involve hands-on leadership. A good minister becomes involved in all the different facets of a church's life, from bazaars to dinners, from forums to worship services, and from marriage counseling to stewardship campaigns. Likewise, a good politician enters into the life of his or her constituents. I enjoy going around our community attending different events, talking with people about what's on their mind, clipping ribbons, turning spades of earth, and learning about the people I serve. Being a clergyman has given me the joy of involvement in the fortunes and misfortunes of other people, something that carries over very well into my duties as Mayor.

Politics, like religion, can help bring people together—blacks and whites, Republicans and Democrats and Independents, for-profit and not-for-profit, public and private, police and community, labor and management—in pursuit of the ideal that Cicero enunciated when he defined the commonwealth as "a partnership for the common good." People in government, like people in the church, have a good opportunity to overcome the ordinary divisions and tensions that tend to inflame and polarize. Political leaders who act as agents of reconciliation can rally the community spirit and bring healing where there is hurt if they practice the politics of partnership in keeping with the idea of "Come, let us reason together." And that is the way it is at its best in the church also.

In the ministry or in politics, there are many demands on your time. You have to work hard. There is an awful lot of stress. But you wouldn't be in it if you didn't enjoy it. William Wordsworth once remarked, "The religion of gratitude will never mislead us." Nor will the politics of joy! "God daily loadeth us with benefits." In my business, both as a minister and as a mayor, every day is new and exciting; every person I meet represents a new chance to serve. I love what I do, and each day I give thanks for life and the opportunity to live it to the fullest extent possible. It was always that way when I was in the church, and that's the way it is in the Mayor's office.

Do I sound like a preacher? Do I sound like a politician? Am I a minister? Am I a mayor? Am I both? Not long ago I was visiting radio host Gary Todd, a very popular morning man on WIBC in Indianapolis, for our monthly call-in show, *Opportunities for Service.* A listener had brought up a problem that I could not finish dealing with while we were on the air, so I said to him, "Why don't you call the office after the service and we'll talk about this in more detail." I gave him the number and we hung up, but when I looked over at Gary, I found him convulsed by laughter (and on the open airwaves). He pointed out my slip of the tongue, calling a radio talk show a "service" rather than a "program." Still laughing, my friend Gary gave the audience one last line before we broke for a commercial. "You can take the preacher out of the pulpit," he said, "but you can't take the pulpit out of the preacher."

And, Gary, you are so right!

3

Biblical Touchstones
for Public Service

I accepted the invitation to preach at the White House on October 14, 1973, with mixed emotions. On the one hand it was flattering and would be, I thought, an opportunity to speak a true and good word to a relatively prestigious audience; on the other hand, President Nixon's decision to hold services of worship in the White House had brought a storm of criticism centering around the concerns that it was a travesty of real worship and that it was basically a corruption of the freedom of the pulpit. After discussing the situation with my father, himself a Presbyterian minister and one whose opinion I valued highly, I decided to do it. I realized the dangers involved in this enterprise—prostituting the preacher, compromising the integrity of the word of God, and all the rest of it. But I also recalled the biblical precedent of "the church in their house" and concluded that, without scolding the President or abusing the privilege of being there, I would have an opportunity to make some remarks relevant to the debate that was then raging about Watergate.

It was not a comfortable setting in which to preach. Obviously it was not a church. President and Mrs. Nixon, Vice-President-designate Gerald Ford and Mrs. Ford, my family and a few friends, and assorted members of the congressional and diplomatic communities were there, along with representatives of the Executive branch and the press. I chose as my topic, "The Religion of Abraham Lincoln." I thought there might be some relevance in thoughts centered on this theme, and during one of my visits to the White House, I had noticed that the famous portrait of Lincoln by George P. Healy, depicting him seated, resting his chin on his hand, had been moved from the State Dining Room and was now hanging on the wall of the East Room, where the service was to be held. This seemed to me a natural springboard, so I seized it.

Lincoln never made a commitment to institutional Christianity, be-

Lincoln's faith

cause he was scandalized by the divisiveness of frontier denomination-
alism and the petty bickering of Protestant factions about jots and
tittles of the creed. But in a deep and fundamental sense he was "a
biblical Christian." Lincoln's religion has been aptly described by Professor William J. Wolf, in his very enlightening study *The Almost Chosen
People,* as "single-hearted integrity in humbly seeking to understand
God's will in the affairs of men and his own responsibility therein."

Latimer.
"King"/
King

The basic point I tried to make in my sermon was that the implica-
tions of ethical monotheism are still relevant. I used one of my father's
favorite stories about the sixteenth-century English bishop, reformer,
and martyr Hugh Latimer, who was invited to preach before King
Henry VIII. (It set preaching at the White House in the proper perspective!) Latimer kept marveling to himself, "Isn't it wonderful I'm
going to preach before the King of England?" But as he was preening
himself in the mirror of his homiletical ego, he heard a still small voice
saying, "Latimer, Latimer, remember—you're going to preach tomorrow before the King of Kings!" I went on to mention that such an
awareness of the transcendent sovereignty of God, before whose
throne the nations rise and pass away, is necessary if we are going to
avoid moral decay, both personal and national. In support of that
point, I quoted Lincoln:

his sermon

> It is the duty of nations as well as of men, to own their dependence upon
> the overruling power of God, to confess their sins and transgressions in
> humble sorrow, yet with assured hope that genuine repentance will lead
> to mercy and pardon; and to recognize the sublime truth, announced in
> the Holy Scriptures and proven by all history, that those nations only are
> blessed whose God is the Lord.

I suggested that this concept supplies a corrective to the tendency
to idolize the nation by equating God with America, or the American
way of life, or American foreign policy, or our party, or our administration. "There is a great difference between worshiping God and domes-
ticating him," I explained, "between looking upon him as the lord of
all nations and regarding him as the ally of one; . . . between affirming
'My country for God' and boasting 'God for my country'; . . . between
making ours 'a nation under God' and making a god of our nation;
. . . between humbly praying, as Lincoln did, that we might be on God's
side and self-righteously asserting that he is on ours."

After pointing out that affirmation of a higher allegiance is really
what separates totalitarian states from free ones, I said that the American people should understand, as Lincoln did, that biblical religion
implies, from beginning to end, that government is the public's business, that political pragmatism must yield to political morality, that
doing the right as God gives us to see the right should never be

abandoned for the sake of political expediency, and that government should never be fenced off as an amoral field of behavior but rather should be treated, in the words of former Senator Paul Douglas, "as a vital part of ethical life which we should try to conduct on the highest possible level."

[handwritten margin note: "gov't. — highest possible level".]

When it was all over, and the pictures had been taken and the receiving line had dwindled, and my little kids were running all over the White House poking their heads into every nook and cranny of the first and second floors, the press asked me if I had preached about Watergate, to which I responded, "I was talking about the moral foundations of democracy, which are eternally valid, and if the shoe fits, wear it!" (Frankly, the President was quite obviously preoccupied with his troubles, and I'm not sure he heard a word I said.)

The Bible provides us with many touchstones for public service. While it is precarious, in my opinion, to quote scripture in support of a particular partisan political point of view, there are, nonetheless, precepts and concepts in it, eternal truths and resources, that I have found to be very meaningful during my pilgrimage in public life. I would mention six of them.

The first of these touchstones is **gratitude.** The Bible abounds with expressions of gratitude, and I cannot imagine making biblical religion the basis of one's life without concluding that life should be approached with an appreciative attitude. The psalmist said, "Bless the Lord, O my soul, and all that is within me, bless his holy name. Bless the Lord, O my soul, and forget not all his benefits." The psalmist also talked about his cup running over with goodness and mercy, and Paul admonished us to give thanks in all things. When my parents conducted family prayers at the breakfast table, they would invariably "give thanks," and I can still hear Dad reminding us that God "daily loadeth us with benefits" and that we should always pause to be grateful.

It is important to express appreciation to people for their efforts to be helpful, the greetings they extend, and the good times they provide, as well as to recognize the awards they receive and the landmarks they pass. In our office we try to honor kids who have achieved the rank of Eagle Scout, youngsters who excel in various sporting activities, valedictorians, student government leaders, and so on. Periodically we have receptions to honor police and fire department personnel who have acted above and beyond the call of duty, and we have established an awards program to recognize both officers and civilians who have demonstrated bravery or heroism or meritorious service. When people contribute their time and talent to building a better community, it is a valid function of government to express thanks for their efforts.

Most of us who are involved in public life are also grateful for the opportunities our vocation brings; otherwise we would get out of it. I have a friend named George Latimer who is Mayor of St. Paul, Minnesota. George, an energetic, enthusiastic man who throws himself into each day's activities, once remarked to me that he would think something was very wrong if he ever saw a big hole in his schedule. I know many mayors like George—individuals who literally love what they are doing and love to stay busy at it. They welcome each new day with open arms, grateful for the opportunity to serve.

I tell young people who are thinking about a future in government service that it's promising if they can stand the two p's—one is very great (the pressure) and the other not very large at all (the pay). But if they are turned on by wanting to be where the action is, by wanting to have an opportunity to address some of the most serious problems of the day and work toward effective solutions, if they like people and are motivated by the chance to serve, then a career in politics may very well be for them. I remind them that they do not have to run for office to become involved, because there are many civil servants and appointed officials who are deeply involved in the work of government without ever having to go through the ardors of a campaign.

One of the saddest stories in the New Testament has to do with the healing of the ten lepers, not sad because the ten were healed but because only one of them returned to give thanks for the miracle he had experienced. The others went on their way. Only one out of ten people stops along the road of life to say thanks! We say thanks only ten percent of the time! And we should do better. We should pause to be thankful for each new day. "This is the day which the Lord has made; let us rejoice and be glad in it." We should pause to thank God for all life's blessings—for family and work and church and school and friends and neighbors and crises and challenges and mountains and valleys and all the rest of it. As they said in the toast in *Fiddler on the Roof,* "To life!"

In February 1986 my alma mater, Princeton University, presented me with the Woodrow Wilson Award for public service, and in my acceptance speech I expressed gratitude on behalf of America's cities and for those who serve in local government. I told the story about how Lyndon Johnson, at the end of a particularly hard day in the Oval Office, looked around at a sea of glum faces and remarked, "Cheer up, people. Things could be worse. I could be the mayor of a large city!" It's not really that bad, but there is a tendency to look down on city service as the lowest level of government. People sometimes ask me rather patronizingly when I am going to run for *higher* office, as if to imply that work in city government is the equivalent of playing in the minor leagues while waiting for the big break to come along. Most local government officials labor largely unrecognized by the national media, but the many talented and dedicated men and women who serve our cities understand the relevance of the work they do.

The cities are where black and white and red and yellow and brown, rich and poor and in-between, Republicans and Democrats and Independents, blue-collar and white-collar and gray-collar, must live and work together and seek, as much as possible, the good of all. The cities are where tensions can be creative or destructive, where the centrifugal forces tending to polarize America must be harnessed and the centripetal influences innate in human nature released to heal and to bless. The cities are where our inclination to injustice must be curbed and our capacity for justice set free.

The cities are where the ugliness and wretchedness of life crop out, where the homeless sleep on grates at night and the underclass push dope by day. But the cities are also where the beauty of life can be known firsthand, where art and music and culture can flourish, where the ecstasy as well as the agony of the human predicament can be experienced, and where the achievements of the free human spirit can stand triumphant over the wrecks of time.

The cities are where most of the fundamental and intractable problems for the average person have to be solved, problems that have to do with jobs, housing, transportation, education, safety, sewage, leisure time, pollution, and all the rest. The cities are where the shadows and the sunlight of life, the dead-end alleys and the broad thoroughfares, the decay and the renewal, the emptiness and the fullness, the tragedy and the triumph, the bondage and the freedom, the sadness and the joy, the defeat and the victory converge, where all these countervailing forces can come together.

The cities have been called the laboratories in which the experiment of American democracy is being carried out, and there is no guarantee that it will succeed. Cities can stagnate, and when they do, nations decline and civilizations deteriorate. But those of us who work in the cities believe the cacophony of urban life can be transformed into something approaching harmony. Partnerships for the common good can be formed. The quality of people's lives can be improved. That's the challenge of it all, the hope, the glory—and the satisfaction (and the gratitude) when it happens.

Humor is a second touchstone for public service. It is probably more than coincidental that in his biography of the Great Emancipator, Carl Sandburg has a chapter devoted to "Lincoln's Laughter—and His Religion." Connecting laughter and religion suggests the meaningful relationship between humor and faith that any serious reading of the scriptures uncovers.

The Bible does not have much to say about this subject directly, and it obviously is such a serious book that little laughter appears outright. We find the only biblical reference to God's laughter in the Psalms: "He that sitteth in the heavens shall laugh: The Lord shall have them in derision." The standard interpretation of Christ omits any reference to his humor, which is unfortunate as well as erroneous. Jesus indulged in irony quite frequently, and it is not a false portrait to depict him with a smile on his face and joy in his heart. My brother Bob, a Presbyterian minister, has a picture hanging in his study entitled *Laughing Jesus*, by Kozak, in which Jesus' head is thrown back in laughter and his face is wreathed in a smile. Dr. D. Elton Trueblood of Earlham College cites thirty humorous passages in the Synoptic Gospels in his book *The Humor of Christ* and calls it a "misapprehension" to interpret Christianity "as a religion of sorrow and only of sorrow." And Reinhold Niebuhr, the famous theologian who was my mentor in seminary, pointed out in his sermonic essay on "Humor and Faith" that laughter and humor are "vestibules" in the temple of faith, even though in the holy of holies there is only reverence, contrition, and prayer. "Do not look dismal," says our Lord.

I think humor is valuable to a public servant in three ways: it helps you turn nasty situations to good account, it helps you not to cry, and it helps you not to take yourself too seriously.

First of all, laughing with others and at yourself is good therapy, good medicine. Properly timed, it can lighten the load, brighten a dark moment, and relieve tension. It can benefit us psychologically, emotionally, spiritually, and even physically.

One of the people I enjoy working with the most is our Director of Public Works, Barbara Gold. She has an extraordinarily tough and unglamorous job: 2,000 tons of trash to pick up and 900 tons of sludge to handle every day, 1,500 miles of sewers to keep running, air and water pollution to overcome, and serious drainage problems all over the 400 square miles of our county to solve. She must cite environmental violators and despoilers, deal with angry citizens, and manage hundreds upon hundreds of sewer, sanitation, and wastewater treatment plant workers. There are lots of reasons to be depressed in that job. When people's sewers back up into their basements, when sewers break and noxious fumes and untreated wastewater spew out into the streets, when people grow resentful at your commitment to cleaning up the environment, you could pretty easily become a cynic and an absolute bear to work with. But not Barbara! She's living proof of the fact that there's nothing so redemptive as a sense of humor. She has fun at what she does. She pushes away the dark clouds in her Public Works sky with the sunlight of her laughter. Whenever she comes into my office, it's on serious business, but she's a joy to work with because she carries it off with laughter and humor as well as intelligence and an open style of management and determination that are most commendable.

Of course, Ronald Reagan is a past master at relieving tense situations with humor. When he looked up from his hospital bed after being shot in 1981, and said, "All things considered, I'd rather be in Philadelphia," he put the nation at ease, reassured people, and came across as having a lot of guts and being on top of the situation. And when he said with reference to Walter Mondale during their debate on national television in 1984, "I am not going to make age an issue in this campaign; I am not going to exploit for political purposes my opponent's youth and inexperience," he laid to rest one of the opposition's key issues.

Second, the capacity to laugh can save us from becoming bitter. It provides an antidote to cynicism. It helps ward off despair. With all the pressure and problems in public life, you must be able to laugh. It's not at all funny when people make impossible demands on you or when your position makes your family vulnerable to unfavorable publicity. The unjust criticisms that sometimes come your way, the discouragement you feel when hopes and plans don't materialize, and the occasional threats you face are certainly no laughing matter. When someone dumps garbage on your receptionist's desk because the trash has not been picked up, maintaining a sense of humor can give you some poise and perspective. It can help to keep you from being ground down by the burden you carry.

Biblical humor is not a way of denying the tears and heartbreak of life but rather a way of affirming something stronger and more ultimate—and part of that strength comes from humor born of faith in an ultimate meaning beyond the flux of events. It has been remarked that the opposite of joy is not sorrow but unbelief, so it is not surprising that laughter and song should ring through the halls of the temple and the church. People who embrace biblical religion understand, explains Trueblood, that "though there is an ocean of darkness and death, there is also an ocean of light and love which flows over the ocean of darkness."

Lincoln understood this. People close to "Father Abraham" knew that his relish for the comic, his fondness for jokes and stories, his insatiable appetite for the writings of the foremost funnymen of his day —Artemus Ward, Petroleum Vesuvius Nasby, and the rest of them— did not mean that he was a buffoon or that he could never be serious, as some complained. These traits of his, rather, were meant as a cure for drooping spirits, both his own and others'. Lincoln had a lot more to be sad about than happy, and he used laughter as a tonic for his own melancholia. Sandburg relates the story of a rebuke directed at Lincoln

by a congressman who found the President in the White House reading Artemus Ward the day after Fredericksburg—while the ambu-
lances were still hauling thousands of wounded from the frozen mud-
flats of the Rappahannock River and the whole land was bound in
sorrow and shocked in dismay in the presence of the previous day's
fearful reversal. "If I could not get momentary respite from the crush-
ing burden I am constantly carrying," Lincoln said, "my heart would
break!"

Sometimes, then, we laugh so we won't cry. We use a little humor
to get through a difficult or even tragic situation. When I was a teen-
ager and went out to Association Camp, Colorado, for summer vacation, I spent night after night on a cot above which hung a Victorian
quotation from Robert Browning. I've never forgotten it.

> But what if I fail of my purpose here?
> It is but to keep the nerves at strain,
> To dry one's eyes and laugh at a fall,
> And, baffled, get up and begin again.

Third, and perhaps most important, humor can keep us from taking
ourselves too seriously. It enlarges our capacity for self-transcendence.
It helps us to see the "log" in our own eye. There's a real danger in
both religion and politics that we take ourselves too seriously; some
people are so zealous in pursuing a cause that they entirely lose their
sense of humor. They cannot laugh at themselves or with others. They
forget that humor is essential to a healthy faith as well as a healthy
democracy.

I work with twenty-nine members of the City-County Council. We
get along pretty well, and most of our major goals are achieved, usually
with bipartisan support. Sometimes a little kidding helps to keep
things running smoothly. I remember how, when I was president of the
National League of Cities, many of our councillors went to the annual
convention in Atlanta. I introduced them during the course of my
remarks and asked them all to stand up. While they were standing, I
indicated that I had written a letter to the Pope asking him if he would
make them all cardinals—so I would only have to kiss their rings!

And if I am ever tempted to develop delusions of my own self-
importance, I have only to remember the call I received from a woman
in Indianapolis when I was a member of Congress in Washington. She
was really mad. Her trash had not been picked up for some time. She
let me know about it in no uncertain terms. I tried to reason with her
and concluded by suggesting that she call the City Sanitation Commissioner at City Hall in Indianapolis. Quick as a flash she retorted, "Oh
no, Congressman, I don't want to bother anybody that high up in

government!" A comment like that sure helps me keep my job in perspective and not take myself too seriously.

God sits in his heaven and laughs—and we must learn to laugh with him.

A third biblical touchstone is **love,** which in the context of public ③ service can be described both as bearing one another's burdens and as being agents of reconciliation.

Everyone who goes into public life should read the parable of the Good Samaritan, because it's so important that we understand ourselves as servants of others, as burden bearers. "Bear one another's burdens, and so fulfil the law of Christ." "Be your brother's (and *love as* sister's) keeper." "Make love your aim." At the heart of our democ- *service* racy, there is an understanding of government as *service,* as ministry, as making love operational in life. How could anyone read the Bible without becoming consciously committed to trying to live a life of service to others? The Good Samaritan did not stand by on the side of the road. He pitched in and helped.

One of the most important political events of my public career was a blizzard that literally paralyzed our city in late January 1978. (Snow *Snow as* is very political! If you don't believe me, ask former Mayors Mike *political* Bilandic and Jane Byrne of Chicago. If you handle it well, it can make you, but if you mishandle it, it can be your downfall.) I was scheduled to fly to Washington for a mayors' conference and meeting with President Carter, but throughout that Wednesday the weather forecasts turned very gloomy. At the last minute, I canceled the trip, which turned out to be one of the wisest decisions I've ever made.

During the night snow began to fall, and by 4 A.M. I was on the phone to the radio and TV stations declaring a weather emergency. I put on boots, ski pants, and a heavy jacket and knit hat given me by our Racers hockey club, then walked about a mile to a major street where a Department of Transportation truck was waiting. Slowly we made our way downtown, turning back at several points because the roads were impassable. We passed abandoned cars and picked up people walking through the night and gave them rides to nearby shelters. We rescued one woman whose car was in a ditch, her headlights beaming straight up into the falling snow. By 6 A.M. we had arrived at the radio and TV stations to tell the awakening city that the emergency existed and that they should stay off the streets.

I spent all day Thursday and Friday with the Department of Transportation crews, trying to rally the troops and keep morale up as they plowed the tons and tons of snow that had buried the city, and often during these days regular radio and TV programming was interrupted so I could give the community updates on the work that was being done. We were able to reassure the citizens that progress was being made and thereby prevented panic from gripping the city. Finally on Friday night, in a very harrowing ride, a police helicopter took me home. I will always be grateful to "Hutch," who did a magnificent job of piloting that little aircraft and landing in a cul-de-sac amid swirling winds, blowing snows, and swaying treetops.

By Saturday the city was beginning to crawl, and by Sunday people were able to go out and shop. Enough snow had been plowed by Monday that the emergency was lifted and people began inching back to work.

One of the most heartening aspects of that terrible experience was the way in which a larger sense of community immediately surfaced, and people began caring about each other and expressing love in action to their neighbors. Heart-attack victims and mothers about to give birth were airlifted to hospitals, people with four-wheelers set about plowing streets voluntarily, trying to help the DOT, and folks without power had neighbors willing to take them in. Everybody cared about everybody else. Everybody pitched in to try to help.

What could have been a political disaster was turned into a real plus, and to this day people still comment on the blizzard of '78 and how they saw so much of me in my Racer cap while they were cooped up at home. And they still remember how the community reacted in love in the form of service to each other.

Love means not only service but also *reconciliation.* Love overcomes polarization. As my father used to remark, we must learn how to "avoid the acute angle." We must avoid "squaring off" or backing antagonists into corners, for practicing the healing art of bringing people together serves the public better than fighting and confrontation.

Lincoln's example is marvelously instructive in this regard. His qualities of forbearance and patience, compassion and kindliness, his willingness to forgive, and his astounding magnanimity are virtues that have been documented in stories known to every generation of school-children. He had a spirit of love toward everyone that excluded anything mean. His attitude, "with malice toward none, with charity for all," and his emphasis on healing the hurt helped to provide the spiritual adhesive to keep the Union together long after he had been assassinated. To one correspondent he wrote, "I shall do nothing in malice." And from a window in the White House he said to a group who serenaded him upon the occasion of his reelection, "So long as I have been here, I have not willingly planted a thorn in any man's bosom." Without articulating his public service in the theological terms familiar to many of us, Lincoln nonetheless was the preeminent exemplar in politics of an "agent of reconciliation." As he said in his

First Inaugural, "We are not enemies, but friends. We must not be enemies. Though passion may have strained, it must not break, our bonds of affection."

There come to all of us, whether or not we are in public service, many opportunities to overcome the forces that always threaten community (which I like to think means "coming into unity"). Edmund Muskie, the Democratic Vice-Presidential candidate in 1968, asked if we were going to move toward a united country or grow into a divided nation where people fear each other and will not work together. During the same year Richard Nixon seized upon this idea as well, recalling the words on a sign that a young girl carried at a rally in a small Ohio town, BRING US TOGETHER. The theme persisted through the 1970s with both Democrats and Republicans joining in the chorus, until Ronald Reagan promised, in his 1981 Inaugural, "Together, a new beginning."

The issue was—and is—whether a heterogeneous collection of 226,-000,000 people can achieve the goal of *E pluribus unum*. The challenge is the old one laid down in the Preamble to our Constitution, "To form a more perfect union." But it has new dimensions now, as America questions itself and searches for new definitions and new purposes, accepts new groups, new heritages, and new people, and awakens to the realization that the world we live in is much smaller and more endangered than ever before. In his book *America in Search of Itself*, Theodore White suggests that creating a finer and stronger community is the chief challenge facing those who have been elected to govern and to lead as the country moves toward its third centennial and as the twentieth century nears its conclusion.

Cicero once tried to explain to the people of ancient Rome, whose society's texture had changed greatly during the course of the Empire, as America's now has, what a republic was. He failed. Rome declined and fell. Cicero was beheaded. But his hope abides: that the city might become a community where civility reigns and where people live together in peace and harmony. "A commonwealth," he wrote, "is not any collection of human beings . . . but an assembly of people joined in an agreement on justice and partnership for the common good."

A fourth biblical touchstone is conscience, which we might describe as keeping the faith or having the courage of our convictions. We read in the New Testament that Jesus "set his face to go to Jerusalem" and that the apostle Paul was not disobedient to his heavenly vision. The Deuteronomist admonished, "Be strong and of good courage," and Paul picked up that theme when he said to the Corinthians, "Quit you [Behave] like men, be strong."

That was a favorite text of my grandfather's, and he once wrote a

poem around it. I suppose that today the sexist language might be
altered, but be that as it may, Grandpa's words have always meant a
lot to our family. The poem has come down through each generation
and served as a source of inspiration to me many times when my spirit
began to flag. It goes like this:

> Quit you like men, be strong;
>   There's a burden to bear,
>   There's a grief to share,
>   There's a heart that breaks 'neath a load of care—
> But fare ye forth with a song.
>
> Quit you like men, be strong;
>   There's a battle to fight,
>   There's a wrong to right,
>   There's a God who blesses the good with might—
> So fare ye forth with a song.
>
> Quit you like men, be strong;
>   There's a work to do,
>   There's a world to make new,
>   There's a call for men who are brave and true—
> On, on with a song.
>
> Quit you like men, be strong;
>   There's a year of grace,
>   There's a God to face,
>   There's another heat in the great world race—
> Speed, speed with a song.

Conscience, moral courage, doing what we think is right, examining
the issues as objectively and intelligently and honestly as we can, and
then making our decision and sticking by it and letting the chips fall
where they may, is necessary if we are going to structure into the
sinews of the political process a commitment to integrity. It may have
been sour grapes, but Henry Clay was not wide of the mark when he
said he would rather be right than President. Not that we always will
be right, and most certainly we must not always *think* we are right, but
we must always try to *do* right.

Public officials need to be willing, when necessary, to stand up and
be counted, to make the tough call, and to face the consequences when
a decision of conscience is unpopular. This does not mean being a
weathervane or taking a poll to see which side of an issue is the most
popular before making a choice. We should not be thermometers, just
measuring what already exists, but thermostats working within the
framework of good conscience to bring about what should be.

At times during my career in public life I have taken comfort from
Abraham Lincoln's assessment of the criticism that sometimes results

from making decisions based on conscience instead of popular opinion:

> *Lincoln on criticism —* [results for what matter]
>
> If I were to read, much less answer, all the attacks made on me, this shop might as well be closed for any other business. I do the very best I know how, the very best I can, and I mean to keep doing so until the end. If the end brings me out all right, what is said against me won't amount to anything. If the end brings me out wrong, ten angels swearing I was right would make no difference.

Essential to American democracy is a respect for each other's right to be different. If we are asked to do the right and follow the light as we are given to understand it, we must recognize that people will come to different conclusions. They will hold different points of view. The essence of community is not uniformity but being able to achieve an equilibrium among the differences. That's the constant challenge of democracy.

When I was a little boy living in Cincinnati, my father took me to meet Sir Wilfred Grenfell, the famous Episcopalian physician and missionary to Labrador. He was a beautiful man, and though I was only six years old, I can still remember shaking his hand and looking into his kind face. Many years later, my dad told me a story that Dr. Grenfell had told that night. He said he had a Roman Catholic patient in [*ecumenical*] Labrador suffering from frostbite and gangrene, and he had to amputate her leg. He told her that the next time he was down in the States, he would try to find her a prosthesis. One night he was in Boston speaking at a Congregational church when he happened to mention [*story of the prosthesis*] the plight of his patient. Afterward, a woman came up to speak to him. She said her husband, a Presbyterian, had recently passed away and that he had had an artificial limb she would like to donate to the cause. So Dr. Grenfell took it from her, good Methodist that she was, and returned to Labrador. This is the way he summarized it: "When I, an Episcopalian missionary, took that Presbyterian leg given me by a Methodist lady at a Congregational church in Boston and fitted it on my Roman Catholic patient, it enabled her to walk perfectly."

That story suggests what democracy is all about—all of us different, but all of us getting along. And the essence of leadership in a democracy involves the ability to unite disparate strands of interest for a common purpose. The great Presidents are those who can express a sense of national community and national purpose beyond the dissonance of the different sounds in this nation. On a lesser scale, mayors have similar opportunities to do that in the cities where they serve. I like to think of the mayor as an orchestra leader trying to encourage everyone to play the same music even though they are using different instruments. You have to work hard at building consensus and

mayor as orchestra leader (same song, different instruments)

realizing the dream of community, of brotherhood and sisterhood.

You can't talk about the importance of conscience as a biblical touchstone for public service without recognizing that it also involves trying to live out your days with as much integrity as possible. There are, to be sure, public officials who have abused the public trust, and it is important that those of us working in government resist the temptation to exploit our positions by turning them to our own personal advantage. It is also important for the citizenry to see their government at work structuring integrity into the process, with the establishment of viable checks and balances. We have created in Indianapolis, for example, an Internal Audit Division to keep a watchful eye on the accounting and management practices of City departments. (In an operation that has 5,000 people on the payroll and a budget of $360 million, things can get away from you pretty fast if you do not have sharp monitoring capability.) We have also set up a bipartisan Board of Ethics that works to detect potential conflicts of interest and head them off, ruling on matters as diverse as convention trips paid for by contractors dealing with City departments and the use of the City helicopter to save time on short-distance hauls. And we have endeavored to replace political patronage with a merit-based personnel system. The saying that you cannot legislate morality is probably true. But you can build integrity and accountability into the system and make it tougher to do what is wrong. Locks keep honest people out!

Doing what is right, having integrity, and working from the biblical touchstone of conscience are essential to good government. Alexis de Tocqueville visited America in an effort to discover her greatness, then returned to France and wrote a brilliant analysis of American democracy. The following words have been attributed to him:

> I sought for the greatness and genius of America in her commodious harbors and her ample rivers, and it was not there. . . . In the fertile fields and boundless forests, and it was not there. . . . In her public school system and her institutions of learning, and it was not there. . . . In her democratic Congress and matchless Constitution, and it was not there. . . .
>
> Not until I went into the churches of America and heard her pulpits flaming with righteousness did I understand the secret of her genius and power. America is great because America is good, and if America ever ceases to be good, America will cease to be great.

A fifth biblical touchstone for public service is **hope.** Zechariah described the Hebrew people as "prisoners of hope." Jesus told his disciples, "Be of good cheer, I have overcome the world." Whether they were blind or poor or crippled or outcast, he gave them hope that tomorrow could be better.

Harvard philosopher and poet George Santayana divided people into two categories—those whose hearts tilt toward hope and those whose hearts tilt toward despair. Biblically oriented people have hearts tilted toward hope, and they help others look at the future in a more positive way.

Many people feel so overwhelmed that they can no longer cope, and so they drop out. They have had so many false hopes raised, so many promises made but not kept, that their hearts have been taken over by cynicism and apathy. We urgently need leaders who will communicate a believable hope to people. (I believe that is the essence of Ronald Reagan's popularity.) At the local level of government, the grievances against the American city are familiar to all of us—crime, pollution, poverty, unemployment, an eroding tax base, substandard housing— the list goes on and on. The job of the leader is to look at these problems, to wrestle with them, and to communicate a realistic hope that they can be solved. There can be no progress without hope.

When I was in Congress, I never had much opportunity to talk, but I sure had plenty of time for listening, and one day as a debate was going on, my eyes wandered to the ceiling. There, above the Speaker's chair, above the frescoes of Washington and Lafayette, above the American flag and the words IN GOD WE TRUST, above the press gallery, high up where the ceiling and wall come together, the following words from Daniel Webster are engraved: "Let us develop the resources of our land, call forth its powers, build up its institutions, promote all its great interests, and see whether or not we also in our day and generation may not accomplish something worthy to be remembered."

These were the words of a leader who had hope for his young nation and who was able to communicate this hope, not only to his colleagues but to a freshman congressman who would one day be Mayor of Indianapolis. (Webster's words stayed with me a lot longer than the words of the debate!)

Those of us who strive at the local level to "accomplish something worthy to be remembered" apply the same kind of optimism to the problems our cities face. Every time we patch a pothole or unstop a sewer or fix up a street, we do so with the hope that it will make the quality of life better in our city. Every time we try to counteract blight with the forces of revitalization, every time we save and preserve a historic building, every time we put up new housing or conserve existing stock, we do so with the hope that we can provide better places to live for the citizens within our community. Every time we put a deal together to promote a new business enterprise, we do so with the hope that it will create a larger economic pie to be carved up in our community and create new jobs for people. Every time we seek to build bridges between the Police Department and the minority community, we do so with the hope that relationships will improve and peace and tranquillity will someday become a reality. Every time we give a speech about our city, we do so with the hope that people will see us as good ambassadors for our community and want to visit there and invest there. Every time we fight air or water pollution, we do so with the hope that the environment will be a little cleaner than it was before. Every time we insist on equal opportunity for all, we do so with the hope that the evils of racism and sexism will be overcome. In everything we do, we cherish the hope that life will be made better for our constituents as a result of our efforts.

When our progress on these and other issues is slower than we would like it to be, public officials must work to keep hope alive. Once, when I was speaking at the Governor's Prayer Breakfast in Springfield, Illinois, a Roman Catholic State Senator gave the prayer, and I was struck by a phrase in it that, as I learned later, came from the Holocaust Service of Remembrance he had attended the day before. The quotation, once written on a wall in a concentration camp, supplied the theme for the day: "We believe in the sun even when it is not shining, and in love even when we don't feel it, and in God even when he is silent."

A few years ago I went on a Scout hike—or maybe it was Indian Guides—with a bunch of boys and their dads. Indiana weather being very changeable, the beautiful day that dawned soon turned ominously cloudy, and when we were right in the middle of the woods, the heavens let forth tremendous thunderbolts of lightning and a drenching downpour. We sought cover under an overhanging rock, and after about half an hour, everyone began to get a little peevish. One father groaned out loud, "Will it ever stop?" I'll never forget the reply of his nine-year-old son, who patted him on the shoulder and said, "Don't worry, Dad, the blue sky always wins!" Not bad, for a youngster. We could all take a lesson.

Mayors attend many a combined news conference and groundbreaking, but one such occasion stands out in my mind as a good example of biblical hope as it applies to public service.

Along Indiana Avenue, in an abandoned field where weeds surrounded a couple of decaying structures, we had a groundbreaking ceremony. The City was cooperating with the U.S. Department of Housing and Urban Development and St. Paul's Episcopal Church to build 102 units of housing for the elderly, a $4.5-million project to be named Goodwin Plaza in honor of a leading citizen from that area. The speeches had been made, and just as we were putting our shovels into the ground to turn over the earth and start the project on its upward path, neighbors and church leaders and community representatives spontaneously broke into a chorus of the Doxology. Needless to say, the TV cameramen didn't know exactly what to do. The area director of HUD, Martha Lamkin, and I looked at each other and grinned and joined in the singing. It was a first. Never before (and never since!) has the Doxology been sung at a news conference over which I presided. But it was sung that day, and I've never forgotten it. That was a beautiful expression of hope that the glory of the Lord can be revealed in the heart of the city as we work together to make it a better place in which to live and work and raise our families.

Gratitude, humor, love, conscience, hope . . . and, lastly, **grace.** If there's one thing I learned at Union Theological Seminary above all else, it's that God's love follows God's judgment, but you can't have one without the other. (A good Presbyterian sermon usually has three points, but a UTS graduate's has two!) First the confession of sin, then the assurance of pardon. First the hurt, then the healing. People who are well have no need of a physician. The necessary precondition for experiencing God's mercy is the admission that we need it, and pride is the unpardonable sin, because it excludes the pardoner. Before God blesses us, he chastises us. Before his love can flood into our lives, we must open the door of our hearts to him in humble contrition, asking him to enter.

Which is to say that none of us is perfect, and all of us should admit it. The ground before the cross is very level. Nobody can stick a thumb in the pie of life, pull out a plum, and say with Little Jack Horner, "What a good boy am I." With Isaiah, we can only cry out, "Woe is me! . . . for I am a man of unclean lips, and I dwell in the midst of a people of unclean lips."

Sometimes we need to remind ourselves of this. In government, in politics, if you've enjoyed several reelections, if you've been in the limelight of public office for a lengthy period of time, you can develop a real spiritual problem by getting onto an ego trip of outsize proportions. It's called "the big head." You begin to think you can do no wrong—you're invincible. And you assume you're immortal (probably the most disastrous mistake a politician can make). You become less energetic about working for your constituents, and you lose your sense of urgency. You glory in your own publicity. You read your own press releases. You lose your perspective. You become so intense, so concerned with pursuing your own advantage and fulfilling your own ambition that you end up being a rather grim, fierce, and unpleasant person—and somewhat ludicrous in your vanity, living proof of the old adage that when you are elected to a position in government, you either grow or you swell.

But you're not all that you imagine yourself to be! You still have feet of clay. You are still mortal. You can still make mistakes. You are not always right. And you need to retain a little modesty and humility about yourself. You need to be able to say, "I'm sorry." "I'm not as important as I think I am." "I do make mistakes, I have made them and I will again!"

Here, too, Abraham Lincoln's example is illuminating. He held to strong moral positions without becoming moralistic. He proceeded firmly and responsibly to execute historic tasks, but he never became overconfident or conceited or self-righteous. He never identified his point of view with the Divine. Always charitable, always humble, he was nonetheless sensitive to the taint of self-interest in human motives and actions that corrupt the meaning and the activity in which we are involved. Lincoln could make strong moral judgments, but he did so without becoming pompous or censorious. "It may seem strange that any men should dare to ask a just God's assistance in wringing their bread from the sweat of other men's faces, but let us judge not that we be not judged."

President Nixon would never have had to resign in 1974 if he had had the honesty and humility to admit wrongdoing. His tragedy was that he could not say, "I made a mistake." But he did make mistakes. We all do, because we're all human and we all mess up sometimes. When I was in Congress, I voted yea or nay hundreds, if not thousands, of times. Far be it from me to say that I always voted right. As Mayor, I make executive decisions all the time, but they're not always wise. I encounter thousands of people in my daily rounds, but I do not always have the patience and sensitivity I should in dealing with them. I am the CEO of a very large "firm," but if management is the art of getting things done through people, I don't always manage well; I don't always handle the people who report to me properly; I don't always develop the most effective strategies. I receive my share of criticism, and more times than I admit, I deserve it. In short, I have a lot to be humble about and I must not forget it.

At the end of each day, I have to admit my well comes up a little dry. "I am an unworthy servant." "The good that I would, I do not: but the evil which I would not, that I do." I need to be forgiven. I need to know that I am loved in spite of myself. And that's where God's grace comes in. That's the Good News. God still loves me, even when I've blown it! "Lo, I am with you always." I then discover, after I've said "I'm sorry," that love abounds. I discover (it is revealed to me) that God accepts me in spite of my shortcomings—just as Jesus called Zacchaeus down from his treetop perch, going into his house and having a meal with him, despised outcast though he was. I'm assured that "underneath are the everlasting arms." We all need to hear that message— kids need to hear it from their parents, married people from their spouses, employees from their bosses. People in politics need to hear it too, because so often their votes and decisions and actions offend people and they're on the receiving end of a lot of flak.

I am grateful for the way in which God's grace has been mediated to me by others—

By friends who know my faults and foibles and like me anyway.

By political allies who work with me, plan with me, consult with me, argue with me, struggle with me, plod with me, run with me, in an effort to bring good government to the people we serve and leave our city a better place than we found it.

By parents who always hung in there with me, always told me to do my best and leave the rest, always believed in me, always rooted for me, always wanted me to try hard but loved me whether I succeeded or failed, always stayed in touch with me, always supported me, even when—and especially when—my report card had a bad grade on it, or I was cut from the team, or my marriage failed, or I lost an election and found myself out of a job.

By children—Mike, Laura, Tim, Bill IV, and Ted—and stepchildren—Liz, Molly, and Bill—who laugh at me and poke fun at me and keep me from becoming too self-important, who stay in touch even after they move away, who talk to me about the stuff they read about me in the papers or see on TV and always take my side regardless of what the issue is, and who play tennis with me and go fishing with me and send me Father's Day cards that bear cute messages.

And above all *by my wife, Susie,* who does not complain or nag about the incredible amount of time I am away from home, who understands that politics is a jealous mistress requiring sixteen-hour days and ninety-hour weeks, who puts up with the tension and self-preoccupation she sees in me that is job-related and job-created, who handles her public duties as "the first lady of Indianapolis" with a cheerful and willing spirit while working at her profession in real estate, who hurts for me and cries for me and rejoices with me and laughs with me and accompanies me on some of my rounds, who is pleasant and patient with people who call us at home to complain about backed-up sewers and noisy dogs and potholes that aren't filled and garbage that has not been picked up, who wins with me and loses with me and loves me in season and out, and binds all my days, all my comings and goings, all my ups and downs with *chesed,* covenant love, steadfastness, love that never lets me go—and points me to a divine love from the Heavenly Father that I presume to be very similar.

The parable in Matthew 20 about people working in the field for different lengths of time but receiving the same pay has always been puzzling, because you would think that if a person works for one hour, he or she would be paid less than the person who works for ten. But in the parable, everybody was paid what they were promised, and the owner of the vineyard was simply being generous with those who worked a shorter period of time. This suggests that the final determinant of our salvation is God's mercy, not our merit. All are paid equally because of the generosity of the landowner, whether or not they are equally deserving. The parable points us to the trans-moral mercy of God, before which prudential human calculations of virtue and reward dissolve into the ocean of God's grace.

That brings to mind the story about the fellow who was knocking on the Pearly Gates and St. Peter told him it would take one thousand points to get in. Saint Peter asked him, "What have you done to earn your points?" The fellow mentioned perfect attendance at Sunday school for all the years he was growing up, and St. Peter gave him ten points. He mentioned serving on the ruling board of the church for twenty years, and St. Peter gave him twenty points. He mentioned three or four different worthwhile causes in the community that he had supported with his volunteer money and time, and St. Peter gave him twenty-five points. After a while he had managed to accumulate another twenty points, and then, in exasperation, when he couldn't think of anything more to say, he exclaimed, "Good grief! The only way I'm going to get in here is by the grace of God!" To which St. Peter responded, "Nine hundred and twenty-five points! Come on in!"

The Good News is that on the other side of our contrition lies reconciliation with God in a framework of acceptance by divine love in spite of our shortcomings. Nothing can separate us from God's love —not mistakes or failures, not defeats or deficits, not coming in second in an election instead of first, not unfavorable publicity or broken relationships with people, not disappointment or grief or heartache, not the incredible problems that as Mayor I find on my desk every day. No, in all these things we can be "more than conquerors through him who loved us," and at the end of the day we can rest ourselves in the grace of God.

In his book *A Faith to Proclaim,* Dr. James Stewart, one of the twentieth century's great preachers, cites a story of a boy on a battlefield during World War I who gallantly threw away his life for his captain and was being picked up by the stretcher bearers as the smoke from the battle drifted away on the horizon. They saw his lips moving and leaned over to hear him whispering words he had learned long since at his mother's knee, the words of the prayer of a little child:

> The day is done, O God the Son,
> Look down upon thy little one.
> O Light of Light, keep me this night
> And shed around thy presence bright.

> I need not fear if thou art near,
> Thou art my Savior kind and dear.
> So happily and peacefully
> I lay me down to rest in thee.

It's the same with us. At the end of the day, when the sun sets and the busy world is hushed and the fever of life is over and our work is done, nothing remains for us but to throw ourselves on the mercy of Almighty God, confess our sins and shortcomings, ask for forgiveness, and rest ourselves in the comforting assurance that our dear Heavenly Father loves us with an everlasting love that never lets us go.

That is all we know, and all we need to know.

4

"Hands to Work and Hearts to God"

"We rejoice before thee that another has been called into this sacred office of trust and responsibility and privilege. Many are called, but few are choice; and we believe that here is a choice man who has given his life in dedication to thy service."

My ninety-three-year-old grandfather was praying as I knelt before him. My father, my brother Bob, and a host of elders encircled me, their hands resting on my head and shoulders in the traditional "laying on of hands" ceremony that constitutes the heart of the Presbyterian ordination service. My mother and other family members were gathered behind us in the front pew.

We were assembled in the chancel of Third Presbyterian Church in Rochester, New York, where my dad served as senior minister, surrounded by its great choir and organ, its magnificent Willett stained-glass windows, and its wonderful congregation. I had graduated from Union Theological Seminary and was about to leave for Westminster Church, Buffalo, where I had accepted a call as an assistant minister. It was a Sunday evening in September of 1957, the end of childhood, the beginning of manhood, the twilight of dependence, the dawn of independence.

"And so as we put our hands upon him," my grandfather continued in his richly resonant bass voice, "in some way that we cannot understand, but in some way that we believe, may there flow to him a certain grace and inspiration and high purpose, which is in our hearts. . . . Take him now again more deeply, more lovingly into thy care, guiding him in all the ways of life, inspiring him that he may be of great usefulness to the sons of men, to meet a time when the world needs someone in passion, and in conviction and in high purpose, to preach the everlasting gospel of our Lord Jesus Christ, yes, and to live it in glorious unity with him who is the head of the church. . . . And so, in

his grandfather

love, in great love, we do commit this thy servant, our brother, yes and more than a brother, to thy faithful keeping."

My grandfather, William H. Hudnut, Sr., would live another six years before being gathered to his fathers and mothers in "that great Palmer Stadium in the sky," as Princetonians were wont to call it. Princeton, Class of 1886, he would receive an honorary degree on the occasion of his 75th reunion in 1961 and, before he passed away, would be honored as the oldest living alumnus of the university, which was still called the College of New Jersey when he went there.

Grandpa went on to Union Seminary, was ordained a Presbyterian minister, served in Brooklyn and Port Jervis, New York, then went to First Presbyterian Church, Youngstown, Ohio, for a thirty-eight-year pastorate, from 1899 to 1937. He was a strong preacher and cut a classic figure in the pulpit with his Vandyke beard, his cutaway coat, wing collar, and four-in-hand tie. He and my grandmother Hudnut had five children, three girls and two boys, of whom my father, William H. Hudnut, Jr., was the youngest.

On summer evenings we children would sit around Grandfather's knee and listen to his stories, and during the Sunday night hymnsings in front of the fireplace in the family homestead at Windover in upstate New York, we would all sit on the floor while Grandpa offered prayer. His prayers were always long, Cook's tours through family history, and sometimes in our more irreverent moments we would time him. Later, after a couple of us had become preachers, he would warn us always to be conscious of time, and to think about quitting our preaching when we saw people begin to look at their watches. When they took them off and shook them to be sure they were still running, he added, that meant we should stop immediately!

when to quit preaching!

Patriarch that he was, we revered him in his twilight years, and to this day have never forgotten the rough scratch of his beard when we kissed him, his deep voice and his twinkling eyes, and his good sense of humor. We remember his strong sense of family and place as well as his love of the Christian church and his devotion to the cause of Jesus Christ. As some of us followed his footsteps into the ministry, we borrowed a few of his definitions—like that for the upper crust ("a lot of crumbs held together by a little dough") and "blue-dome" Christians (people who believe church attendance is unnecessary and that they can worship just as effectively on the golf course, where the church has stained-grass windows and a blue sky for a roof). We recall some of his actions too, as we heard tell about them—the time he tried to stop a lynch mob in Port Jervis, the missionary trips he took to Africa, and the opposition he mounted to Henry Cabot Lodge and the isolationists who sought to defeat Woodrow Wilson and prevent America's entry into the League of Nations.

We never knew <u>Grandmother Hudnut,</u> but we heard about her gentleness, her sacrificial spirit, her beautiful faith, her loving ways. Hudnut Hall at First Church, Youngstown, was named in honor of the two of them, and, <u>after she died,</u> Grandpa wrote some of the most beautiful words any man could ever speak about the woman he loved, words that have come down in our family across the years and are engraved on my heart forever:

his grandfather's tribute to his wife

> I do not know the standards in conformity with which men and women have been canonized as saints. There were those who because of holiness of life, deeds of mercy, and missionary zeal were so nominated in the apostolic records. There are many saints and saints' days set apart in calendars of devotion. But while Protestantism acclaims no modern saints, there are many amongst us whose lives and services merit such accolades. I may not be qualified to distinguish a saint, but according to the strictest definition I could name a few whom I have seen in action, and whose effigies are as worthy as any to be celebrated in stained glass windows. And amongst these I would canonize <u>my wife, Harriet. I</u> lived with her for 45 years and I can find no fault in her. She walked, without trumpets, in the ways of Jesus. I can pay her no less a tribute.

Both his sons, Herbert and William, went to Princeton University and became Presbyterian ministers. Actually my Uncle Herb had first opted for a career in business, but switched after experiencing an extraordinary and life-changing event during his service in the balloon corps during World War I. His balloon was shot out of the sky, the explosion killing the pilot, but he managed to bail out and landed safely in a tree in the Argonne with sixteen German bullet holes in his parachute. He was pastor of churches in Dallas, Cleveland, and Pittsburgh, and for a quarter century served at Woodward Avenue Presbyterian Church in Detroit. Now, at age <u>ninety-four,</u> he lives in retirement in Glens Falls, New York, where the local Rotary Club recently presented him with a T-shirt identifying him as "the real Herb."

uncle Herb

After graduating from Princeton in 1927, my father went on to Union Theological Seminary, where he met Elizabeth Allen Kilborne, who was earning a master's degree in Educational Psychology at Columbia after having graduated from Vassar College. In 1931 they were the first couple married in New York City's magnificent new Riverside Church, a logical choice for my mother, the daughter of a relatively prominent New York family, and my father, who had worked during his seminary days with Harry Emerson Fosdick, Riverside's pastor.

his father

The Hudnut preachers stood foursquare in the Fosdick tradition of Protestant modernism—a nonliteral interpretation of scripture, topical preaching, a commanding pulpit presence, and a steadfast loyalty to the church. To outsiders they appeared to be the dominant figures in our family circle, but we children could easily see the steady firm hand of our mother's influence on our family's life. The middle child between two Yale(!) brothers, she had given up her missionary career plans when she married Dad and devoted herself henceforth entirely to her family. Kind and thoughtful and self-sacrificing to the core, she always believed in the goodness of the people she loved and, as Dad did, always affirmed their best. She moderated the more authoritarian presence of our father with her gentle loving-kindness, and while she matched the Hudnut men with her own brainpower, she never tried to compete with them. Now that Dad is gone, she lives essentially for her children and grandchildren as well as her friends, and she deserves, every bit as much as Grandmother Hudnut, the accolades Grandpa once penned. For if anyone is a saint, if anyone walks "without trumpets in the ways of Jesus," if anyone is a human incarnation of divine love, it is my mother. When Dad died on May 31, 1985, two days after his eightieth birthday, I spoke of their relationship in the eulogy I delivered at his funeral service:

> We remember the fifty-four years of married life he shared with our mother, the abiding steadfast nature of their love for each other, the serenity that came from being in tune with each other, the peace that "passeth all understanding" that they came to know in their beautiful and tender and gentle relationship with each other as they bore witness to the world's most important truth, that "love can outlast anything. It is in fact the one thing that still stands when all else has fallen."

Our family lived in three different places. My father's first church was in Glendale, Ohio, just outside Cincinnati. He served there from 1932 to 1940, and during those years four of us were born: I came first, followed by Bob, Dave, and Stewart. We really grew up in Springfield, Illinois, where our sister Holly arrived on Pearl Harbor Day. (What a day my father had on December 7, 1941! He had held morning services at First Presbyterian Church, came home, then left me to babysit with my three brothers while he rushed Mother to the hospital. He heard the terrible news about Pearl Harbor, dashed back to church for special prayer services, then back to the hospital to welcome his first and only daughter into the world before finally heading home.)

Our schooling began in a one-room schoolhouse, and whenever any of us are asked to mention the people outside the family circle who had the most influence on our lives, Mrs. Krueger, our teacher, always comes to mind. She oversaw eight grades, each one sitting in a row. She taught us the three R's and added home economics for the girls and carpentry for the boys. She disciplined us, cajoled us, befriended us, and left us with an indelible impression of her devotion, compassion, and integrity.

In Springfield we played rounders and cops and robbers, and when we weren't riding each other around on our bicycle handlebars, our mother was chauffeuring us somewhere or Dad was teaching us to play chess and bridge. We listened to *Captain Midnight* and *The Lone Ranger* and *The Shadow* on radio, played Monopoly, and built models. We traveled to St. Louis to ball games or the zoo, and we watched for letters from our foster brother, Bob Haines. (Bob, who was some fifteen years older than we were, had been informally adopted by my parents and was serving as a major in the medical corps, crossing Europe with General Patton and the Third Army. He would later receive silver and bronze stars for his heroic actions, and his letters sent from overseas were full of lines cut out by censors, which intrigued us.)

By the fifth grade, I had transferred to Butler School, where I played clarinet in the orchestra and acted in school plays. I said the Pledge of Allegiance and Ben Franklin's "Lost time is never found again," and also the Lord's Prayer at the beginning of every school day, never thinking about the hurt or injustice that might have been done to Thelma, the Jewish girl who sat at the desk next to mine. I earned school letters for various extracurricular pursuits, visited New Salem where Lincoln had lived, marched with the Boy Scouts to his tomb on Memorial Day, and loved to sit in the Lincoln pew in the front row of the sanctuary of our church (even though I wasn't allowed to, because it was reserved for Eagle Scouts on special occasions only!). And silently I cried when, in 1946, the family announced we were moving away to Rochester, New York, where Dad had accepted a call to Third Presbyterian Church.

I spent my freshman year of high school in Rochester, learned to drive there, and attended young people's meetings at Dad's church. (I remember that once I was chased all around the block by a member of the church staff who was thoroughly disgusted with this particular P.K. [Preacher's Kid]!) My youngest brother, Tom, was born there, and while my siblings remained at home until it was time for my brothers to follow my lead, I left for boarding school in the tenth grade.

During the summers we went to Windover, deep in the Adirondack Mountains, a family vacation spot with a little lake, a few cottages, and a log cabin built for Dad and Uncle Herb to use every morning as they worked on their sermons and studied. We split wood, dug ice out of the icehouse, swam, and played tennis. In alternate summers we went to Association Camp, Colorado, where Dad was invited to preach, and where the trout fishing and mountain climbing were unsurpassed. At both locations, each of us looked forward to our special day with Dad, a day when we could do anything we wanted—it was ours to plan from beginning to end.

Dad was fond of quoting the famous opening line of Tolstoy's *Anna Karenina*, "Happy families are all alike; every unhappy family is unhappy in its own way," and in retrospect I must conclude that ours was a happy family. What a blessing that was for us kids and what a good start in life it gave us. We were a happy, solid unit, not without our problems and shortcomings, to be certain, but without idealizing or sentimentalizing the past, a good, strong, close family held together by steadfast parental love, hard work, and the competitive camaraderie between us kids.

faith in the family

We began and ended each day with prayer. In the mornings Dad led us in devotions, consisting of a Bible reading or a Bible story from a children's book, perhaps something from a devotional pamphlet or a little book of thoughts like John Baillie's *A Diary of Private Prayer* or George Arthur Frantz's *Book of Mercies*. The latter was one of Dad's favorites, not only for its contents but because George Arthur, a long-time pastor at First Presbyterian Church in Indianapolis, was a dear family friend and fishing companion for many years. The devotions always concluded with Dad leading us in prayers, usually closing with the Lord's Prayer, after which we would devour a three-course breakfast before leaving for school. At the end of the day, Mom usually, but Dad if he was at home, would tuck us into bed, say our prayers with us, and maybe read a Bible story from a big blue book we all, to this day, remember.

Sundays all of us went to church. Always. That was a given. Usually we took notes on the sermon, just in case we were asked what it was about. (Needless to say, we could always count on three points—Dad said a good sermon was portable!) After church, Dad would march straight upstairs to take a shower and go to bed, where Sunday dinner would be served to him on a tray, while we would all go into his bedroom to box and wrestle and play games until it was time for him to sleep. (Unless you've actually done it, you cannot imagine how tiring and draining preaching can be. George Arthur Buttrick used to urge his students to "preach from the heels," to put the whole body into it. My dad did this. He was a vigorous, emotional preacher—not wild-eyed, not hellfire and brimstone, but quite capable of laughing gladly or weeping unashamedly in the pulpit, going slow and low and then rising to heights of power, using his deep sonorous voice to deliver the message, every word of which was prepared meticulously beforehand, carefully crafted, and clearly delivered.)

"preach from the heels." tired after preaching

We had a saying in our family as we were growing up—"I.C. equals I.R.," "Intelligent conversation equals intellectual refreshment." One of my father's outstanding characteristics was his intellectual curiosity, his incredible desire to keep his mind alive and alert with horizons that were always expanding and never contracting. He would have agreed wholeheartedly with Konrad Adenauer, who once commented, "We all are born under the same sky, but we do not all have the same horizons." Dad insisted that we use the talents that were given us instead of burying them, and he had a passion for excellence that made us want to do our best.

For Dad, life was a constant learning experience (he was forever talking about "increasing our fund of general knowledge"), and so, from the earliest days, our family life had an emphasis on honing one's intellect. Homework had to be done, and report cards were taken seriously. In the summertime, in addition to our regular chores, we had to do special homework, little quizzes and tests in arithmetic, English, geography, spelling, and history, prepared by Dad. We were challenged to learn such things as the names of the forty-eight states, the countries and capitals of the world, and Lincoln's Gettysburg Address, and when we successfully met the challenge we were rewarded with a $5 or $10 prize. Around the dinner table, month after month and year after year, we played "games," Dad asking us questions requiring a simple shouted answer, testing us, training us, quickening us. Friends used to dread staying for dinner because they knew they would be subjected to an "infernal quiz" before dessert was over, and they were not ready to compete with the Hudnut kids on an equal footing, since they did not do that sort of thing at their homes!

Later, as we developed, as we came home from school, as we grew up, the conversation turned toward current events and what we were learning in school. And when we were off on our own, the communication continued through letters. Mom wrote us a letter every week. She still does—the family newsletter we call it—keeping us abreast of the news from the rest of the family. Dad wrote us about what we were doing and what he was thinking in relation to our lives. His letters always had clippings in them, good advice, views on current events, cartoons, jokes, articles he thought would interest us. He continued to draw us out about what we were thinking, seeking to train us to articulate, evaluate, and communicate. He worked right to the end of his life, keeping his own mind alive, writing letters, sending his opinions to his congressman, mailing off jokes or stories to the *Reader's Digest.* I will never forget the last question he asked me, just a few days before he died. He was on his sickbed in their home in Phoenix, so weak from leukemia he could hardly hold the newspaper in his hands, but mentally alert and determined enough to ask as he was reading an article about the city budget in Phoenix, "Bill, what's the difference between the Indianapolis budget and the one here in Phoenix?"

Looking back on those formative years, thinking about my family's legacy to us kids, I ask, "What did it all mean? What did we really inherit?" Maybe Bob, Dave, Stew, Hol, and Tom would answer differently, but I believe our family life bequeathed to us a sense of the importance of living life with a certain style and substance, in a certain manner.

Creatively. That was Dad's favorite word. Sometimes he exchanged it with *triumphantly* or *victoriously* or *confidently* or *joyfully,* but it always reduced to the same thing: Make the most of each day, throw yourself into it, embrace it enthusiastically with all your heart and soul and mind and strength, use all your talents, thank God for it. The last time he ever preached was in October 1984. By a nice coincidence he spoke from the pulpit of Second Presbyterian Church, Indianapolis, where he had filled in as an interim minister after I went off to Congress in 1973, and his theme was "Triumphant Christian Living." His text was a favorite passage from the New Testament, from Moffatt's translation of 2 Corinthians 2:14—"Wherever I go, God makes my life a constant pageant of triumph in Christ."

> That's a remarkable thing to be able to say, what Paul said, and as Christians we ought to be able to say it, for the gospel should be leading us into vital, victorious living. Our faith ought to be making all the difference between despair and hope, and our lives ought to be so full of joy, courage and compassion that they could quite genuinely be described as a continuing victory.
>
> Christ gives each of us a self to live with. When we try each day to be guided in all our acts by love, faith, and hope, then we have a self we can use. When we try to be honest and humble, merciful and righteous, understanding and forgiving, loyal enough to suffer for our convictions, and brave enough to follow God's will, then we have a self we can live with. . . . As we live in Christ, as we live for God and other people, our powers are released; as we live in ourselves, they are stultified. There is no disease as deadly as the disease of self-centeredness. . . . The world is full of people whose motto is "I know what I want and I'm going to get it," whereas the world needs people whose motto is "I know what is wanted of me and I am going to give it."
>
> When I was in seminary, I was a student assistant to Dr. Harry Emerson Fosdick. I remember his telling about a mother who discovered her little daughter using a crayon on the bedroom wall. Her mother asked her what she was doing and she replied, "I am drawing a picture of God." Said the mother, "But no one knows what God looks like." To which her daughter replied, "They will when I get through!" Will they? Will they have a clearer picture of God when we get through? Will they have a better idea of what triumphant Christian living is all about? Will they? I hope so.

Those were the last words my father ever spoke from a pulpit— and I can have no doubt that in many people's minds and hearts, a clearer picture of God developed thanks to his life and his witness.

Usefully. My father and grandfather loved to quote the biblical passage "Every one to whom much is given, of him will much be required." Privilege entails responsibility. We are not put here on earth to serve ourselves, but to serve others. When I graduated from college, Dad and I talked about my career choice, and he, hoping I would choose the ministry, said, "Remember, Bill, it's not only the thing you can do best, but also the best thing you can do." And when I talked with him, in 1972, about leaving the pastorate and going into politics, he was supportive, because he saw government service as a broader form of ministry. In one of those little clippings my father sent me, which I have saved, there are two sayings coupled together to drive the point home: The first from that famous author, Anonymous: "There is a four-word formula for success that applies equally well to organizations or individuals—make yourself more useful," and the second, from Grenfell: "Real joy comes not from ease or riches or from the praise of men, but from doing something worthwhile."

"Real joy"

Diligently. That is a bit of a drab word, but it points toward a fundamental truth about life, which is that "nobody ever said it was easy." Perspiration is just as important as inspiration. Hard work, disciplining ourselves, laboring under a yoke, being prepared, having what Dad called "stick-to-it-iveness," are important qualities to cultivate. Chores, homework, piano lessons, memorizing quotations, what did all this mean if not that achievement is the by-product of diligence, that if we do not push ourselves, we will never rise above mediocrity, never amount to very much. Dad talked a lot about living "above the average and ahead of the time."

Publicly. There are other words I could use—civically, responsibly, unselfishly. My parents had a finely tuned sense of civic responsibility. They enjoyed Reinhold Niebuhr's tongue-in-cheek definition of a Christian as "someone who reads his newspapers." My mother participated in community activities that involved her children and her husband, and my dad not only preached on current events, he involved himself actively in trying to build a better community. In Springfield, he helped to found a good government league; in Rochester, he helped rejuvenate the City Club. He loved to drumbeat into us Woodrow Wilson's ideal for Princeton University, which not only he and his brother and father but all five of his sons and a couple of nephews and eventually even some grandchildren attended: "Princeton in the nation's service." He also enjoyed quoting Thomas Carlyle: "Conviction were it never so excellent is worthless till it translates itself into conduct."

Niebuhr: a Xn: "reads the newspapers"

Carlyle! "Conviction into conduct"

Spiritually. How often, growing up, were we reminded by everything in our parents' approach to life that "man does not live by bread alone." They lived out their days "under God," and Christ was their daily companion. The real values we were taught had to do with character, not possessions; with spiritual, not material, things. The point was not so much that we grew up in a home where there was no entertaining with liquor, but rather that we grew up in a home where the emphasis was on living ethically and spiritually.

Hence, there was a strong family commitment to the church, which Mom and Dad saw as the custodian of the values they believed in. We always went to church, even on vacation, even during World War II when gas was scarce and Mom took us to Windover by herself, and we had to walk to the little country church in Johnsburg, three miles down the road! For all its defects and shortcomings, the church has nonetheless been the institution *par excellence* that has been devoted to the care and feeding of humanity's soul, generation after generation. It has had its different roles—pastoral, priestly, prophetic. They are all valid, all worth supporting. Dad liked to say, "The church is not a picture gallery for the exhibition of saints, but a hospital for the healing of sinners." He showed us, by his counseling with people, how the church could help heal wounds and overcome alienation. He showed us, by his preaching, how the church could inspire people to live better lives and focus on the application of the Christian gospel to the times at hand. He showed us, by his generous support of churches and seminaries and his activities on national boards and agencies of the Presbyterian denomination and church-related colleges, that the church should never be abandoned. It was always there; always trying to do good. "Have you ever seen an atheists' home for the aged?" he asked us rhetorically, "or an orphanage run by agnostics?" "Stick by the church," he urged us. "Criticize it where it's wrong, but don't ever forsake it."

> O where are kings and empires now
> Of old that went and came?
> But, Lord, thy church is praying yet,
> A thousand years the same.

Faithfully. My parents always wanted us to live up to our best, to keep faith with the best that was in us. That's how they defined integrity. "Do your best and leave the rest" was our family's watchword. Our parents' letters to us are full of praise and pride and belief in our positive possibilities and our potential for achievement. They wanted us to keep faith with the past, with our heritage, our values, our family traditions, our ideas, our church. "Keep the great securities of your faith intact"—wrote my dad in the front of the pocket New Testament (the Moffatt translation, of course) he gave me when I graduated from school—"by aid of the Holy Spirit that dwells within you."

We were also supposed to keep faith with each other, to stick by each other, to trust each other, to uphold each other and not let each other down; and, indirectly, we came to learn that trust and faith are the glue that holds an open society together. My parents were scandalized by the "breach of faith" that was the Watergate tragedy because they thought it was unconscionable to lie, to cheat, to prevaricate, to dissemble, to stonewall. They believed in the importance of being open and direct and faithful and taught us the difference between a free society based on trust and a police state based on fear. My dad never tired of telling us about his trip to Europe with Sherwood Eddy in 1936, and the brutal way in which his movie camera and film were stripped from him by the police in both Berlin and Moscow; it was quite an object lesson for him, one he never forgot.

Sensitively. In our large family, it was important for us to learn the lesson of respect for each other and each other's individuality. We had to work at getting along, at communicating with each other and understanding each other and sharing with each other. It required real effort to put others ahead of self, to deal with challenges and crises that arose, and to resolve differences of opinion. Mom and Dad genuinely tried to develop that kind of open sensitive style of managing family life. We talked at the table about how each other's day had gone. We divided up household responsibilities and we all pitched in. We never failed to celebrate a birthday, and we opened Christmas presents one by one, each enjoying what someone else received as much as his or her own gift. When problems came up or the folks couldn't "get to the bottom of things," we had family councils (which we kids and Mom always dreaded). We laughed at each other's jokes and foibles. In short, we were raised to be sensitive to and affirmative toward and respectful of and communicative with and responsible for each other. I believe that is the way a healthy family operates.

Appreciatively. We were called to be good stewards of all the blessings we had received, to husband our resources, to protect the environment and to fight those who did not. I'd like to have a dollar for every time Dad pointed out to us a can thrown carelessly along the road or litter along a trail or a birch tree carelessly peeled and told us never to do that. "This is my Father's world," he sang, "and God needs us to help take care of it," he preached. He loved to tell the story about a farmer who had an ugly weed patch one year and when the local pastor visited him the next year, it had been transformed into a beautiful garden. Said the preacher in a rather unctious way to the farmer, "My, what a good job you and the Lord have done with this old weed patch." To which the farmer replied, "Yeah, but you should have seen it when the Lord had it all to himself."

As a family we sang the hymn "For the beauty of the earth," and our parents raised us to appreciate the worlds of nature and culture. They tried their best to open our eyes to the beauty of God's world and see, in beautiful things here on earth, windows opening onto eternal truth. Color-blind though he was, Dad raved about the windows of Chartres and Notre Dame and Ste. Chapelle. He wept over great prose and poetry, from Shakespeare to Keats, from Browning to Sandburg. He devoured biography ("The proper study of mankind is man," he admonished us, quoting from Pope), and he could be brought to tears by the beautiful prayers in the *Book of Common Worship*, the marriage service, and the verses of hymn after hymn.

He often recounted a true tale about a farmer who lived high up on a hill near our place in the Adirondacks. Before going on a hike, we would go up to Harry's to check the view of the far ranges, and depending on how far we could see, we would decide whether to go on our mountain-climbing expedition or stay at home. One day when we went up to Harry's porch and looked out, the view was particularly clear and beautiful, absolutely stupendous as a matter of fact. My dad remarked on it and how fortunate Harry was to live in this spot where he could drink in such a view day after day. To which Harry replied, "Oh, I don't know, you get used to it after a while." That flat and unappreciative response absolutely blew my father's mind! He used the story again and again to emphasize the importance of not taking beauty for granted, and of living life sensitively, gratefully, appreciatively. "Take off thy shoes, for the place whereon thou standest is holy ground."

Courageously. Dad often remarked to us that courage is the most neglected of Christian virtues—not physical courage but moral courage, the ability to hold fast to one's convictions, to stand up to a crowd, to speak a good and true word in the face of criticism, scorn, or ridicule, to laugh at one's fall, to take adversity in stride without letting it drag your spirit down into defeatism and despair, and to carry life off with humor and joy. He agreed with Churchill, "Never, never, never, never give in."

We saw Mom's courage in the way she faced disappointment or physical affliction without a whimper of complaint, and we witnessed Dad's courage often, from the pulpit but also in the way he lived, because he tried to practice what he preached. Our family remembers the tremendous disappointment when twice, in 1957 and 1967, he ran for Moderator of the General Assembly, the highest post in the Presbyterian denomination, and twice he lost. The second time hurt especially, because he had just finished leading the denomination's major capital-fund campaign, which had raised well over $50 million for church mission projects, and because he had given years of service to church boards and agencies and had pastored one of the leading churches in the denomination. But lose he did, and he handled it with grace and style. Asking for recognition from the chair, he congratulated the gentleman who had beaten him and asked that the election be made unanimous. And later, in the family circle or among his colleagues, never was there a word of whining self-pity, never an excuse, never any sour grapes expressed.

He said throughout his life that in his opinion, "the greatest stanza in all of hymnody" was the one from William Cowper:

> Ye fearful saints, fresh courage take;
> The clouds you so much dread
> Are big with mercy, and shall break
> In blessings on your head.

He truly believed that, and that is the way he died. During his two-year fight against leukemia, he never once complained. He would not allow attention to focus on his illness. He joked about "this confounded business" that erupted in sores all over his body and made his nose so red. ("I really shouldn't drink so much," he laughed.) He followed the news and stock market on a daily basis. He stayed in close touch with his family and friends, and when his hand became too unsteady to hold a pen, he dictated his letters to Mom. He tried to keep on preaching, and only with great reluctance did he finally agree to cancel some of his engagements. In November of 1983, when he was quite ill, he and Mom came to Indianapolis (as they had in 1972, 1974, 1975, and 1979) to help me on Election Day. (He loved to go to the phone banks, get a list of people to call in our get-out-to-vote effort, dial them up, and announce himself as "William Hudnut calling for Bill." He got a huge kick out of the disbelief in people's reactions and the opportunity he had to explain to them who he was and to encourage them to vote for "my son Bill.") The day of the election, we went to our friends the Hensleys for dinner, where Dad and Lou talked about fishing and the family watched the returns on TV. Then we all went downtown to stand on the platform while I made my postelection remarks. Dad was so tired by the end of the day he could hardly stand up and had to be taken home early. But he would not have missed it for the world.

He tried to help others live bravely too. One of his letters, to a longtime friend who was going through her own valley of the shadow and had written Dad hoping to console and be consoled, came back to us after he died. He wrote:

> I'm glad you're praying with me. I don't pray that the cup will pass because I know it won't. I just pray very simply that I will have the confidence, the courage and love to live out the rest of my life, however long it may be, triumphantly. I believe this profoundly, that come what may "we are more than conquerors through Him that loves us."

Yes, I do think about those on the other side, and I do hope there will be recognition. As you say, the veil separating the two worlds is fragile. It seems as though a great love must endure, and so we walk by faith, not by sight.

We both accept the inevitability of approaching death with relative calm and confidence. Meanwhile, we are grateful for the measure of health we have.

Let me close with those grand verses from Col. 1—"May He strengthen you in His glorious might with ample power to meet what comes with fortitude, patience and joy." That's great!

Beyond these rather specific components of our parents' legacy to their six children—the importance of living creatively, usefully, diligently, publicly, spiritually, faithfully, sensitively, appreciatively, and courageously—was the general impression of a strong, healthy, caring family unit adhering to traditional family values. Of course, there were problems and tensions and frictions and resentments in our family. We were far from perfect. But when I look back on it all now, my memory is not critical or judgmental, because I know, beyond all shadow of a doubt, that our parents hung in there with us and did the best they could. The door was never slammed shut. They sent us a message of caring concern, of steadfast love that never let us go.

I am grateful for the family I grew up in. Good families, like good marriages, are not made in heaven. They are crafted on earth with lots of hard work and tender loving care. My parents built well. Lots of others have too, and lots of others will. I wish I had built better; I'm sorry my children did not experience as strong a family life in their upbringing as my brothers and sister and I did. But having said that, I must pick up and go on and do the best I can, loving Susie and the kids and never forgetting that they are my first priority, inadequate though I have often been as a father and husband.

I hope it is not nostalgic to feel that family experiences like mine had intrinsic validity and need to be recapitulated again and again if we're going to have a strong and healthy country. I hope it is realistic. Today we hear so much about marital breakdown, spouse and child abuse, single-parent families, role changes, unwed mothers, unwanted pregnancies, crime and delinquency, dropouts, drug problems that disrupt family relationships, and all the rest of it, that we need to be concerned about nurturing the traditional family unit as a genuine growth center where good people, good citizens, can grow up. Not for nothing did Reinhold Niebuhr call the family "the seed pod of the kingdom of God." Building strong family life can help us solve some of the social problems just mentioned. There is no need to be pessimistic, no need to give up. It is a glorious possibility.

Today there are many more single-parent families than in the era after the Depression when I grew up, many more families where the parents both work, many more latchkey children, many more families on welfare, many more divorces and remarriages and stepchildren situations, many more forces to pull the family off center. Some people honestly feel that the American family is at serious risk, and that American children are in jeopardy.

Certainly nostalgia is not the answer, for it would be a mistake to pretend that women are at home the way they used to be, that the father is the breadwinner and the mother is the homemaker in anything like the numbers that characterized my generation. There has been a revolutionary surge of women into the work force. By 1985 nearly 13 million mothers were in our nation's work force, and according to a panel presentation before the American Psychological Association in August 1986, the family with the father as sole breadwinner will account for only 14 percent of American families by 1990. And yet, even if many families today are starting with different foundations, they can still work within the same framework, the same value system, the same commitment to making family life a success. It's a lot tougher now, and more complicated, to build a solid family life, but it's not impossible. Families today can be sources of security and enrichment and joy just like families of yesterday. They can still be strong and successful. They can still inculcate enduring values. A working mother, a single parent, does not have it easy—but that fact in and of itself does not doom the family to failure. The possibility of success is still there.

In extensive studies administered by Dr. Nick Stinnett, Dean of the Graduate School of Education and Psychology of Pepperdine University, six "secrets" of the successful family have been identified and studied, factors that occur over and over in strong family units but are usually missing in dysfunctional ones. The *expression of appreciation* for one another was a key element these families had in common, and the *ability to communicate,* to express feelings and to "listen with the intent to gain understanding," was also deemed very important. Successful families placed a high priority on the *time* they spent together, and consciously "made" time for that purpose. (The person who said that love is spelled t-i-m-e was right on target!) *Religious orientation* was found to provide additional strength and purpose in these families; and *coping ability,* the skills necessary to manage and resolve conflict and to perceive stress and crises as opportunities for growth, was also in evidence. Where Stinnett and his associates found a *strong commitment to the family group,* a dedication to fostering its welfare and happiness, and an active involvement in planning and listening and promoting the well-being of each member, they also found successful parents and thriving children. These are the elements that can make our families strong, even in the face of the changed circumstances in which the

American family finds itself today, and they are ultimately the key to solving many of our society's problems.

My father and mother created a family in which these characteristics prevailed, and I will always be grateful for the upbringing I had. But eventually, it was time to move on. Perhaps because they understood the importance of letting go, perhaps because they thought we would receive a better education, perhaps because they felt it would be good for adolescent boys to be out from under the nose and thumb of their father, my parents decided to send all five of their sons away to school during the high school years. As the oldest, I was the first to go.

I can still remember the pangs of emotion as I unpacked my trunk in September of 1947, far away from home for the first time. I was suddenly overwhelmed with the realization of how much my parents meant to me and how much they had done for me during my first fourteen years. This feeling struck considerable anxiety in my heart, but I realized the truth in the maxim that you can't go home again.

For three years I attended the Darrow School in New Lebanon, New York, a small boarding school in the Berkshire Hills, housed in buildings used years before by the Shaker sect. My parents felt I would have the opportunity to flourish in this rural setting and thought it would be nice for me to attend with my cousin Herb, whose father had been a Princeton classmate of Darrow's headmaster, Lamb Heyniger.

The school's motto was "Hands to work and hearts to God," an old Shaker saying that has stuck with me all my life. Once a week we adjourned classes to do physical labor—tearing down buildings and constructing new ones, clearing brush, cutting wood, among other things, and every day (and twice on Sundays) we went to chapel, where as often as not "the boss" would speak, deploring the "cheap and shoddy" in life and exhorting us to a life of high ideals and high achievement. A giant of a man, 6 feet 8 inches and probably 300 pounds, with a voice of operatic quality, Heyniger was a towering figure in every respect. He took an active interest in the future of every one of us. I still remember the day he put his hand on my shoulder and looked me right in the eye, saying he hoped I would head a college someday.

The regimented approach to life at Darrow provided a framework in which to develop independence, learn self-discipline, and grow in body, mind, and spirit. I played football, basketball, baseball, and soccer and followed Pete Conrad (who later would be the third human to walk on the moon) as captain of the "Red" team, one of two teams that held a yearlong competition in everything from calisthenics to grades.

The abiding value of my educational experience at Darrow was that, with its introduction to Latin, French, physics, math, English, history, and religion, it laid the foundations for my liberal arts education, for which now, in retrospect, I am much more grateful than I was at the

time. Education today tends to be vocation oriented, and the kind of
broad-based introduction to the arts and humanities and sciences that
I received, first at Darrow, then at Princeton, and after that in a more
specialized way at Union Seminary, has always stood me in good stead.
It's not for everyone, but I believe that in our technological age, the
value of a liberal arts education has been considerably underestimated.
Professional education and training are not enough. What is needed
above all else, in the business world as well as the professional world,
is people who can think and communicate clearly, who can reason and
analyze and be constructively critical. An education in the humanities
helps to develop those skills and abilities.

My interpretation of a liberal arts education is one that is devoted
to the cultivation of the intellectual life, giving attention to the ways
of knowing and creating, the structure of science, some knowledge of
contemporary life and how our society came to be where it is. It fosters
an appreciation of literature and art and the great philosophical debates, and it trains us to ask the deep, searching, fundamental questions. It is much more than a bunch of disciplines and academic fields;
a liberal arts education mediates the best that has been said, thought,
written, and otherwise expressed about the human experience, to
paraphrase Matthew Arnold. It trains us to appreciate, to think, to
understand, to synthesize, to hold the events of the moment in proper
perspective, to articulate and communicate and relate, and to exercise
good judgment.

My father used to tell us that the essence of our education would be
what we remembered after we had forgotten what we were taught.
People would never really care whether or not we knew when the
Battle of the Mulvian Bridge occurred, he said, or whether or not we
could conjugate a Latin verb or figure out the hypotenuse of a triangle.
But a lot of people would probably care very much whether or not we
could communicate our ideas and exercise good judgment and common sense and relate to people.

Dad used to kid us and say that we could go to any college we wished,
but he would pay our way if we went to Princeton, and as we were
growing up he joked that Princeton's motto, *Dei sub numine viget,* meant
"God went to Princeton—and you should too!" He was very proud
that his five sons attended his alma mater, spanning the years from
1950 to 1969, two becoming ministers, two lawyers, and one an educa-
tor, just as he was proud that his daughter graduated from the College
of Wooster and subsequently became an editor and college administrator.

The Princeton I knew, with its preceptorial system, its great library,
its prestigious faculty, its happy club life, its Kazmaier ("from the
single wing, a triple threat") football teams, its beautiful country set-

ting and gorgeous Gothic architecture—this Princeton was, as Woodrow Wilson once remarked during his tenure as the university's president, "the perfect place of learning."

Looking back, I realize—and appreciate—what a Princeton education meant to me. Robert Frost (whose granddaughter married my brother David) once commented, "What we do in college is to get over our little-mindedness." At Princeton, I began to see the larger picture, and I became aware that education is an ongoing experience. I was shown the value of a decent respect for the opinions of others and for the limits to our knowledge as we encounter the mystery beyond the meaning of life. Ever since I walked into the infirmary with pneumonia after the Yale game in the fall of 1950 and saw engraved on the floor there the motto "Not to be served, but to serve," I was encouraged by Princeton to lead a life of service. I was imbued with faith in the dependability of our creative resources to solve problems. My heart and mind were filled with a believable hope. Princeton freed me from the illusions of perfectionism and the delusions of cynicism and awakened me to the indeterminate possibilities inherent in life for the achievement of more love and more justice and more freedom as people come together to build themselves a new Jerusalem, a more heavenly city here on earth.

After Princeton, the three years I spent at New York's Union Theological Seminary—neo-orthodox in theology, liberal (more so than I cared for!) in politics, modernist in historical criticism, interdenominational in ecclesiology—were stimulating and enriching, good preparation for the ministry, and a validation of my decision to go to seminary rather than law school. When it came time to graduate, I declined Union's Traveling Fellowship, which would have paid my way to Europe for another year of study. I was ready to plunge into my profession, to engage myself in the life of the church where people were living and dying, hoping and hurting, growing and yearning and struggling with life's ultimate issues. So I accepted a call as assistant minister at Westminster Church in Buffalo, New York, for the grand salary of $400 a month and a small bachelor apartment on the church grounds. Commencement was just that—a new beginning.

I was following in my father's footsteps. It would not be easy, because comparisons would be inevitable. But as time went on, I would learn to be my own person. I would not try to imitate Dad's preaching style, I would develop my own. I would be myself, create my own career, utilize my own distinct talents and abilities, and let the chips of comparison fall where they might. (Later, I would have the same problem following Dick Lugar as Mayor of Indianapolis. He was a brilliant, strong, fine, hard-working person, but we had different personalities and different styles, and rather than worry about filling his shoes, I would wear my own.) As I journeyed away from home, into my profession and a little later into my own family life, I would endeavor to incorporate into my being the strengths I had come to know in my parents, I would try to avoid their mistakes and learn from their weaknesses (for we all have them), and I would go my own way with gratitude for what Mom and Dad had contributed to my start in life and continued to mean to me.

The study of history at Princeton and theology at Union obviously stood me in good stead during my years in the pastorate, but even in politics, the benefits of these studies have become very apparent to me.

My liberal arts education introduced me to the incredible creativity of the human spirit, and I believe that means that as Mayor I must be supportive of the arts and cultural endeavors in my city.

It taught me that history is the story of liberty (Benedetto Croce) and says to me that as Mayor I must work to expand the sphere of freedom in my town. I must support affirmative action and equal opportunity programs that free people from the chains of racial and sexual prejudice. I must support job training programs and economic development opportunities that free people from the curse of unemployment. I must support openness in government that frees the body politic from the dark shadows of decisions made in secret.

This education exposed me to the uses of the past as it summoned up for me the onward march of human history, and that means for me as Mayor that I must be sensitive to historic preservation issues and the potential for adaptive reuse of historic structures in my city.

My liberal arts education facilitated my ability to articulate and communicate ideas, and as Mayor, I understand not only that skill in communication, persuasive powers, the ability to put complex issues into comprehensible form, and a good command of English are essential ingredients of leadership, but also that language skills are becoming increasingly important and salable in today's interdependent world.

It reminded me that there are many different insights, philosophies, and points of view, which means for me as Mayor that I must promote tolerance and mutual respect, and I must not confuse dissent with disloyalty. Not everyone will see things the same way, but I must seek to build a community where everyone will feel at home.

My liberal arts education portrayed for me the sweep of the human drama, and as I look at its benefits now, it cautions me about jumping too quickly to a conclusion. It helps me take a longer view of things. It means that as Mayor I will plan long rather than act short for immediate political gain. I will try to raise some tough questions rather than pretend they do not exist, and I will cope with change as patiently and intelligently as I can, recognizing that there is a realm beyond human contrivance and that I cannot control everything; that, to bor-

[handwritten margin note at top: stream of time — not create, but navigate upon it ...]

row from Bismarck, I cannot create the stream of time but only navigate upon it.

This education challenged me to lead a useful life, which means that as Mayor I must promote a philosophy of government as the servant of the people. I must remember that it is people who count, people who elected me, and people I am called to serve—whether they voted for me or not.

My liberal arts education made me aware of the ambiguity and uncertainty of life, what G. K. Chesterton once called "life's wildness" which is lying in wait for us, but it also gave me resources to face that wildness with assurance, with hope, with faith that answers will come. And that means to me as Mayor that even though I do not know what tomorrow will bring, I must give people a feeling that we can cope, a belief that we can solve our problems.

[handwritten margin notes: face "life's wildness", faith that answers will come,]

"Do Thou guide him in all the ways of life, and wilt Thou use him abundantly that the Church of Jesus Christ through him may be a larger and better Church and that the world may know that Jesus is the Christ."

Grandpa had finished praying. We all returned to our seats. My father stood to deliver the "charge" to the newly ordained minister, his oldest son. He began slowly, his voice a little tremulous.

> My beloved son—and now my brother in the ministry of Christ—a wide and effectual door opens before you on this day. And your brother ministers, your family, and your friends rejoice in it with you. For you are now, you see, a part of the true apostolic succession, the fellowship of the concerned, the fellowship of Christ; and by the laying on of hands, you now share in the long line of prophets, priests, and martyrs who have not counted life dear unto themselves, but who have sought to spend it on Christ's behalf. With all my heart I welcome you to his ministry. Henceforth, you are Christ's man. . . . You have now been set apart as one whose highest vocation is to give his life away. . . . Your highest privilege is to be Christ's ambassador, to stand for him and to give your life away for love of him. You are here to magnify him, not yourself. And as you live above and beyond yourself, in the daily gift of self, you will be released from the imperious claims of self and find yourself being used in ways that you cannot now imagine. . . . And through all the days, through your labor and your leisure, through your sorrow and your laughter, through your work and your play, through your health and your sickness, through all the days, I charge you to be faithful unto him who is Head of the Church and the source of your life.

[handwritten margin note: his dad's charge to him]

Looking back, I am struck by the portent of Dad's words. "A wide and effectual door opens before you. . . . You will . . . find yourself being used in ways that you cannot now imagine."

5

Religion
and Political Campaigning

At the reception following my ordination, someone came up to me and asked, "Son, do you want to get ahead in the church?" I gave the obvious reply: "Of course I do." "Well then, there are two things you must never talk about," responded the sage. "And what might those be?" I asked. Came the answer: "Politics . . . and religion."

So much for getting ahead!

It is impossible to separate religion and politics, although their relationship is complex and tricky and always in danger of abuse or distortion. The interaction between the two is very much before the American public in the 1980s, propelled there by presidential campaign debates, the candidacies of ordained ministers, media interest, and an intense level of focus on societal issues including abortion, homosexuality, and prayer in the public schools, which are an important part of the evangelical motivation for becoming politically involved. Religion seems to be playing a more prominent role in politics and political campaigning than it has since the era of Prohibition.

Religion will always be involved in politics. There will continue to be political issues about which religious groups feel strongly and on which churches deem it important to take a stand. Religious individuals will participate in the political process in increasing numbers, ethical considerations will remain an intrinsic part of public life, and civil religion in America will endure. We cannot ignore the fact that ever since the founding of our country, religion has made an impact on political activity at point after point along the way. Certainly the issues change—from escaping the religious persecution in the Old World during the seventeenth century, to the "divine right" of a faraway king to impose taxation without representation in the eighteenth, to the slavery and abolition issues of the nineteenth—and the players change too, ranging from Cotton Mather to John Witherspoon to Henry Ward Beecher to Norman Thomas to Jerry Falwell. But it is very clear that throughout American history, religion has set the agenda and informed the dialogue of the American political process.

The surge of religion as a force in politics and political campaigning in the 1980s probably reflects what a recent Gallup poll described as the "spiritual quest of fast-growing proportions" that characterizes America today. Gallup cites a "dramatic uptrend" since 1978 in adults of all faiths and all walks of life who are becoming involved in religious education and evangelization programs, and he notes that church membership and attendance, after declining during the '60s and '70s, are "holding firm." He concludes with words that have tremendous political portent: "Not only do Americans want to see religion become stronger in our society but feel this will actually be the case."

Today, the rise of the so-called "Christian Right," also called evangelicalism or "popular ecumenicalism" (so named because it has been generated by a rank-and-file rebellion that cuts across denominational lines, against the liberal consensus of the 1960s and 1970s that prevailed among the mainstream church hierarchies), has deep roots in the American conviction that ours is a nation "under God" and that we are, in Lincoln's sublime description, "God's almost chosen people." Writing in the *Wilson Quarterly*, Paul Johnson suggests with great insight that the political engagement of the evangelicals in the 1980s flows from this conservative grass-roots reaction against the political liberalism of mainline church leadership, to which we might add that certain Supreme Court decisions on school prayer, abortion, and the like have also galvanized many religious people with firmly held beliefs into political action. Johnson believes we are experiencing the "fourth great awakening" in American life, which, like the previous three (1720–1750, 1795–1835, and 1875–1914), has palpable political outcroppings.

When I first ran for political office, as a candidate for Congress in 1972, the initial reaction of some Republicans in Marion County was, "Oh no, here comes a Presbyterian preacher. How can we get rid of him?" Their concern was triggered and focused by a controversy in which the Presbyterian Church had been engaged in the early 1970s, when it gave $10,000 to the legal defense fund for Angela Davis. Fortunately (for my political future), I had written an article and engaged in a debate on national television taking a strong stand against this donation, so I was able to mollify people who were concerned about my relationship to that particular issue. The political precinct and ward workers whose support I was seeking in the Republican primary of 1972 were in effect saying to me that they did not want any part of my candidacy if I was another "liberal" preacher who believed in supporting Communists with church dollars. "Go run on another ticket," they said to me, "if that's the way you are."

More profoundly, they were saying—and the chorus has increased tremendously in the last fifteen years—that America's moral foundations are eroding, and we must elect people who will do something to shore them up again. A key reason for the popularity of Ronald Reagan through the 1980s has been the public perception that he is a man of faith who shares this concern. People are yearning for political leaders who understand and enunciate, without sounding too pious about it, the link they believe exists between God and America, or between religion and politics.

If the Declaration of Independence could make that connection as it invoked "the Laws of Nature and Nature's God" and insisted on certain "inalienable rights" with which we are endowed by our "Creator"; if George Washington could make it in his Farewell Address in 1796 when he observed that "religion and morality are indispensable supports" of "political prosperity" and that the "mere politician" ought to "respect and cherish them"; if Abraham Lincoln could make it as he prayed that he might become "a humble instrument in the hands of the Almighty"; if Dwight Eisenhower could make it when he told the *Christian Century* magazine in 1954 that "our government makes no sense unless it is founded on a deeply felt religious faith" (that was more important, he added, than what faith it was); then, surely, political leaders today ought to be able to make that connection too (without falling, we might hope, into the traps of Messianism or idolatry), and surely we can engage in political campaigns to elect people who do so.

A tremendous number of people in our country who are concerned about specific issues and the more general problem of "moral decline" in America are turning to politics to find redress for their aggravation. This is a healthy development, because the more Americans who care about politics and become involved in political activity, the better off we are as a republic, although it can also be dangerous if it tends toward arrogance and divisiveness leading to rancorous polarization.

In discussing the relationship between religion and political campaigning, we have to recognize that there are two extremes to be avoided, which I would call separatism and absolutism.

I use the word *separatism* to define the extreme position that asserts that religion has nothing to do with politics. In this view, religion is highly individualized, privatized, and segmented; it takes place in a cloistered sanctuary separated from the real world. Morality is reduced to personal and private behavior, while the public and social dimensions are lost. It's the viewpoint many people adopt when the application of religion to current issues makes them uncomfortable—they want religion to comfort them in their troubles but not trouble them in their comforts, so they draw the conclusion that "meddling" in secular and political affairs is none of the church's business, and not properly the business of a preacher either.

When I first started in politics, and the newspapers were still putting "the Rev." in front of my name, one of the members of my congregation met me on the Circle in downtown Indianapolis, some twelve miles from 7700 North Meridian Street where Second Presbyterian Church was located, and told me in no uncertain terms, "Reverend, get your rear end back up on Meridian Street where you belong!" His view was that religion must be indifferent to what goes on in the world, and contact between the two ought to be avoided.

I know a man in Buffalo, New York, who has led a distinguished life of civic leadership. He has been involved in many worthy educational and charitable causes, and at one point in his career he wanted to run for mayor. He did not belong to a church, although he had read the Bible from cover to cover and studied comparative religion. He did not think his religious views would have any political impact. When a front-page story appeared in the Buffalo newspaper about his "agnosticism" and his disinclination to join any church, however, his candidacy in that strongly Catholic town fizzled out.

The other extreme is *absolutism.* Here an uncompromising coupling of religion and politics occurs, so that a political party or platform or candidate is viewed as the indispensable and unquestioned vehicle of a specific religious point of view and is advanced without any reservation whatsoever.

Unfortunately, this extreme usually carries a militant "us versus them" spirit with it. In theocratic New England, it led to witch hunts —and it has ever since. It's the kind of attitude that precipitated a fist fight outside a polling booth between a Bible-toting "Christian" and a supporter of a Jewish candidate for the Indiana State Senate in 1972. A vicious letter-writing campaign against the Jewish Senator had been mounted, and his candidacy was openly opposed in some pulpits and parish newsletters, both Protestant and Catholic. (He lost.)

During the Vietnam War era, absolutism translated religious convictions into foreign policy statements, draft-card-burning rituals, and lawbreaking protests. The point is not the rightness or wrongness of the stand taken, but the intolerance and fanaticism with which it is held, as in the letter I received from a liberal clergyman when I was in Congress, denouncing me for supporting President Nixon's policy on the mining of Haiphong Harbor and questioning my right to be a "Christian minister."

In 1984 I attended a fascinating symposium on the role of religion in campaigning for public office. It was held at Harvard University, jointly sponsored by the Kennedy School of Government and the Harvard Divinity School. A broad spectrum of religious opinion had been assembled, all the way from Father Drinan, president of Americans for Democratic Action, to Howard Phillips, chairperson of the Conservative Caucus, and from the editor of the *Christian Century* to the vice-president of communications for the Moral Majority. I remember how shocked I was when one attendee looked me right in the eye during an informal discussion period, shook his finger in my face, and told me in no uncertain terms, "We're out to defeat everyone in public life who does not favor the Right to Life amendment. Abortion is a more serious threat to our country than the Nazis were to Germany." What he was really telling me was that no matter what my record was in other areas, no matter where I stood on other issues, it was an either-or situation—I was either with them or against them, I either passed their test or I failed.

The danger in absolutism is the complete identification of a political position with the Divine; the danger in separatism is the complete sundering of religious and moral considerations from politics and political campaigning and the practice of government. Either way, the result would be pure power emerging as the final arbiter. Separatism errs when it suggests that religious views are irrelevant to politics; absolutism leads us astray when it implies that a politician's views on "religious issues" are the only relevant thing whatsoever. The former forgets that the core of our biblical religion is the application of the insights of ethical monotheism to life in the raw, in the here and now, and to the current events that pass by us; the latter forgets "the Protestant principle," enunciated by Paul Tillich, which, boiled down to its simplest terms, means that one can be wrong in interpreting God's Word! In contrast to separatism, we cannot say that religion does not matter in political campaigns; but in contrast to absolutism, we have to say that it cannot be the only thing that matters.

Between these two extremes, however, there lies viable middle ground where the interplay between religion and political campaigning rightfully takes place. It seems to me that it has three dimensions: intellectual, mechanical, and ethical.

In terms of the *intellectual* impact, religion prompts the formulation of issues and the direction they take.

There are issues which many people perceive as "religious"—prayer in public schools, the ERA, gay rights, pro-choice/pro-life, pornography, and several other specific items on the public agenda that "religion" (primarily the evangelical component) raises today, just as twenty years ago other religious leaders were involved in Vietnam War protests and civil rights marches. Today's interest in political activity is prompted by the evangelicals' recognition that if you really care about these issues and really want to do something about them, "the only way for change," as one of them puts it, "is to move into the arena that sets the law, and that of course is politics."

But other issues, not perceived by the general public as being "religious" or having to do with our nation's "decline in moral values," have decidedly "moral" ramifications. Theodore White has written that three basic themes are woven through American political history: war and peace, bread and butter, and black and white. All three have religious connotations. AIDS is an important issue to deal with, but so is the federal deficit; spiritual food (prayer) for schoolchildren is a legitimate concern, but so is food (to eat) for hungry people and shelter for the homeless; tax credits for parents who send their children to parochial schools is something we should consider carefully, but so is tax reform. As a matter of fact, I don't think there is a single issue that comes before those involved in government which cannot be set in an ethical and theological context.

As issues are formulated in a religious context, the dangers are twofold: first, that a single-issue mentality will develop, where a candidate's stand on one issue is used as the litmus test to evaluate his or her entire performance; and second, that biblical religion will be glibly and superficially interpreted, as it is reduced to some simplistic statements such as "Rule the world for God" (as if any human being could) or "Put God back in the classroom" (as if an omnipresent God were ever out of the classroom) or "Make ours a Christian nation" (as if Jews and Muslims and Buddhists and Shintoists and Hindus and agnostics and atheists do not belong in America). Issues are very complex, and we must always be wary of oversimplification.

Religion also can influence the direction that policies move. I do not see how it is possible to read the Bible without coming to the conclusion that God has a particular concern for those who are down and out, for those who have been oppressed by the system, and for those who do not enjoy a fair share of life's sunshine. The biblical test for assessing the health of a society has to do with how it deals with problems of wealth and poverty and oppression and freedom. The Bible pushes us in the direction of economic opportunity and racial equality. The Hebrew prophets and Jesus of Nazareth not only associated with but also stood by the poor and the oppressed, condemning the rich and the powerful who exploited them. The Bible tells us to be our brother's (and sister's) keeper, to be concerned about those who are hungry and thirsty and in prison, and it points us to a Christ who, in his first sermon, said that he was anointed to "preach good news to the poor, . . . to proclaim release to the captives and recovering of sight to the blind, to set at liberty those who are oppressed." Biblical religion should move us in the direction of love and freedom and justice, and the solutions to the grave and profound problems that affect and afflict us all will be on the right track if they promote an increase in those commodities through the formulation of public policy.

So what we are driven to, when we talk about the intellectual impact of religion on politics and political campaigning, is the recognition that the so-called wall of separation between church and state is not absolute. As a matter of fact, it is more like a combat zone. In 1976, during my first year as Mayor, when questions were raised about specifically religious decorations on public property during the holiday season, an Indianapolis newspaper commented that the issue of "the separation of church and state which was raised when the Reverend William Hudnut ran for Congress in 1972 has returned to haunt the end of his first year as Mayor of Indianapolis." But the reality is that the wall is penetrated all the time. It is much more like a membrane that is pushed first one way and then the other. There are many places where church and state come together, for, as one Catholic priest explained, "Fairness in economics and restraint in nuclear arms are moral and religious issues too."

The second dimension of religion's impact on political campaigning is *mechanical*. It can make the wheels of a political organization or campaign turn.

When I started in politics, my "power base" was Second Presbyterian Church, Indianapolis; no question about it, that congregation supplied me with my springboard. I did not use it for that purpose, but there were many powerful civic leaders in my congregation, individuals who were also involved deeply in politics (mostly Republican), and they did what they could to help me launch my second career. Churches can be very effective at mobilizing opinion and votes in a political campaign, and without any official endorsement from the church or from the pulpit of Second, there were nonetheless many members of that congregation who pitched in to help. I could not have won my first election without the dedicated assistance of numerous volunteers, including those from Second Church, who helped us with our direct mail campaigns, our phone banks, our door-to-door solicitation, and all the rest of it, not to mention the substantial number of contributors to the finance committee's effort.

It is reported that King James I of England once remarked that he would rather go into battle against a whole regiment of Scottish regulars than one Scottish Calvinist convinced he was doing the will of God. Anyone involved in politics appreciates the power of an organized and dedicated group. In the 1975 mayoralty race, when some of my opponent's supporters attempted to use Roman Catholic parishes against me, we made a considerable effort to offset that impact by organizing a "Catholics for Hudnut" group and by orchestrating the support of some prominent Roman Catholic leaders who also were Republicans.

Today, the so-called "Christian Right" is flexing considerable new political muscle. It is estimated that in 1976, born-again Christians made up 34 percent of the adult population, but at the last count, their share had increased to 40 percent—perhaps some 70 million people, based mostly in the South and Midwest. Long dormant as a political force, in the past few years they have become very active in politics and are exercising considerable influence in elections around the country. Here in Indiana, for example, in the Republican Congressional primaries of 1986, two candidates won in no small part because they received strong support from evangelicals who rolled up their sleeves and went to work with a lot of "consecrated shoe leather." The Indiana State Republican Central Committee Chairman, Gordon K. Durnil, immediately embraced those nominees, claiming that "the Indiana Republican party is very supportive of our candidates who are labeled as being with the 'religious right.' " (They lost in the fall.)

We have to be careful, however, not to give the effort to mobilize a religious constituency for political purposes more credit than it deserves. It certainly did not account for the overwhelming victories of Ronald Reagan in 1980 and 1984, although it may have been a factor. It is probably closer to the truth to say, as Seymour Lipset and Earl Raab have pointed out, that "the electoral swing toward conservatism and the emergence of a political evangelical movement were parallel developments which may have been mutually reinforcing rather than related to one another as cause and effect" in the 1980 elections. Nonetheless, as this decade has worn on, religious organizations have shown that they can produce votes. They can influence elections, particularly at the local level. They are a factor with which political professionals must contend. And right now evangelical conservatives have considerable potential to make an impact on Republican primaries.

The mechanics of a campaign involve financing as well as turning out the vote. With numerous religious lobbies registered, and with the tremendous power that large religious groups represent in terms of contributor lists that can be made available to friendly candidates, fund-raising from motivated, mobilized religious groups becomes exceedingly significant. I have never sought the financial support of religious political action committees, but there is no question that strong support from people in the Protestant, Catholic, and Jewish communities, in mainline denominations and among evangelicals, has helped my cause considerably across the years.

Sometimes, religious leaders will endorse political candidates they like. This does not often happen in the mainstream churches, but it does in the white evangelical ones as well as in many of the black churches. As a clergyman, I have had the opportunity to preach in many churches throughout central Indiana over the last fifteen years.

It was a startling experience for me when I began preaching in the black churches, because the culture was so different from that in which I had been raised as a somewhat staid, somewhat stiff Presbyterian who seemed by heritage to value structure in worship almost as much as content.

There is one black pastor in Indianapolis with whom I have had a rather interesting and somewhat up-and-down relationship. In October of 1975, on the day that I preached in his church, an article appeared in the newspaper (not by coincidence) saying that he could not support me because he did not like some of the people who were associated with me in that Republican campaign. When I preached, I did not mention the article. I went on about my campaign and eventually won the election. Then I went to work with the minority community. I appointed blacks to various boards and agencies in the City, as well as to high City Hall positions. I discussed matters of mutual concern with coalitions of black clergymen in Indianapolis on a regular basis. I tried to increase minority business with the City. I made a commitment to hire more minorities in the police and fire departments. And when my campaign for reelection in 1979 rolled around once more, I found myself preaching in the same church the Sunday before the election. Again I made no mention of politics and stuck strictly to the Bible. But at the end of the service, the pastor who had opposed me in 1975 stood up and said something like this to his congregation: "Brother Hudnut preached a fine sermon this morning. He never once mentioned that he was running for reelection as Mayor. But I want all you good people to know that he has done a fine job, I enthusiastically support him, and I hope all of you will vote for him on Tuesday."

Religion sometimes affects political advertising efforts, although putting a Christian cross on political literature, for example, is not necessarily the way to win friends and influence people. Wearing your religion on your sleeve does not assure election, but because the country is centrist, occasional religious references and expressions of belief can do little harm, and, indirectly, a message can be helpful if it has a religious connotation. For example, in 1975 our campaign, which turned out to be successful, abandoned the traditional red, white, and blue colors in favor of orange and black. And the word that we used most often in our advertising and printed materials was "trustworthy." I hope I was deserving of that adjective, but regardless, we used it to try to counteract the problems that Republicans had in 1974 when, as a result of Watergate and the breach of trust between the White House and the American people, voters deserted the Republican Party in droves. Our use of the word "trustworthy" in 1975 helped turn the situation around in Indianapolis. (President Carter did this in

1976. His pollster, Pat Caddell, sensed that the country was tired of being torn apart, and said that what people needed was "a sense of restoration, of love." Consequently, the religious angle—Jimmy Carter's sincere belief in God and his born-again commitment—was played up, and in the aftermath of Watergate, he defeated President Ford.)

In terms of the mechanics of a campaign, the question about the relevance of a candidate's personal religion is difficult to answer. I've only had people walk out of church when I was preaching (other than to sneeze or go to the bathroom) three times: once when I mentioned that we had baby-sitting service in the Sunday school part of the building (a baby was screaming in the back of the church and the mother needed encouragement to take the child out); once on the Sunday after Martin Luther King, Jr., was assassinated, when I preached a strong sermon in his behalf (the individual who walked out happened to think Dr. King was a Communist); and once the Sunday before the 1960 election, when I claimed that John F. Kennedy's Catholicism should *not* be the determining factor in whether we voted for or against him. I said he should be evaluated for who he was and where he stood on the issues. The same is true today, a quarter of a century later. Nonetheless, there's no question that the resurgence of the evangelical vote, based on a born-again conversion experience, helps candidates who share those views and can garner a lot of votes for them.

One other thought about how religion makes an impact on the organizational side of politics has to do with the involvement of women. For generations women have been very active in church work, but only recently have many churches begun to ordain women to positions of leadership, a transition that is very much to their credit. It is also a healthy sign that religious involvement of women is being accompanied by heightened political activity. This is occurring not only as women supply a large share of the volunteers in a campaign office, and not only as they assume positions of equal importance with men in the political organization itself (in Indiana, we have a very good rule and practice whereby everything is balanced between the sexes as far as party organizational positions are concerned—men and women share equally from precinct leadership all the way up to national committee representation), but also as they assume increasingly important positions in government posts and run for office themselves.

During my campaign for reelection in 1983, my opponent, John Sullivan, quite properly raised the question of the role of women in local government, criticizing me for not doing enough in this regard. Even though he lost the election, he made a valid point, and since that time we have installed women in cabinet-level appointive posts in local government—as Director of Public Works and as Press Secretary to the

Bob Irsay and I clasp hands to celebrate the Colts' arrival in front of cheering fans at the Hoosier Dome on April 2, 1984, during one of the proudest moments of my public career. Others, from left to right: Dave Frick, P. E. MacAllister, and Nick Frenzel. *Rich Miller, Indianapolis News*

As late as June 1985, Baltimore's suit for damages had me tied up in legal red tape. The suit was ultimately settled out of court. *Barnett, Indianapolis News*

Listening to "opportunities for service" with Gary Todd, host of WIBC radio's *Morning with the Mayor* program. *Greg Persell, Mayor's Office*

My successor, Dr. William G. Enright, and I discuss Second Presbyterian Church matters past and present. *George Bond, photographer*

Talking with members of the Second Presbyterian Church after the worship service. *George Bond, photographer*

As National League of Cities president, I found myself called upon by President Reagan to represent the viewpoint of our nation's cities and towns. *Associated Press*

In 1952, the Hudnuts gathered for a Christmas family portrait. Back row: David and I and Bob. Middle row: Tom on Dad's lap, Dad, Mom, Grandpa Hudnut. Seated on the floor: Holly and Stewart.

Winning smiles from Susie and the kids on election night, 1975. Left to right: Bill Rice and Laura, Ted, Susie, and Tim Hudnut. *Jim Young, Indianapolis News*

Mom, Dad, and Susie join in the 1979 post-reelection celebration at the home of long-time friends Anne and Lou Hensley. *Jerry Clark, Indianapolis Star*

On Dad's lap at age three, 1936.

In the face of federal budget cuts, we were able to finance major projects with help from the private and public sectors. *Barnett, Indianapolis News*

Senator Dick Lugar, my predecessor as Mayor, shares a victorious moment with me on election night, 1975. *Jim Young, Indianapolis News*

Susie and I rejoice upon receiving the news in 1983 that I have been elected to serve an unprecedented third term as Mayor. *Greg Griffo, Indianapolis Star*

Cooling off on a hot August day in 1983 with inner-city kids during Operation Cooldown. *Michael J. Heitz, Mayor's Office*

Demonstrating the "Hudnut hook" for
the Indianapolis Clean City Committee
in 1978. *Jerry Clark, Indianapolis Star*

Discussing policy with a few members of my senior staff. Left to right: Deputy
Mayor John Krauss, Department of Public Works Director Barbara Gole, and
Senior Deputy Mayor Joe Slash. *Greg Persell, Mayor's Office*

Mayor. In addition, women are serving as executive directors of important organizations like the Greater Indianapolis Progress Committee, the Commission for Downtown, the Indianapolis Alliance for Jobs, and the Indiana Sports Corporation. Of the twenty-nine members of our City-County Council, six are female. Nationally, the statistics are also showing a steady rise in the number of women in elective positions. A decade ago, only 8 percent of all state legislators, 3 percent of county officials, and 4 percent of officeholders in municipalities and townships were women; today, those numbers have doubled and tripled, to 14.8 percent, 8 percent, and 14 percent, respectively. The point is that we need to be sensitive to the way sexism and male chauvinism have for too long repressed women, a situation that has not only denied women access to positions of responsibility by forcing them to play a subordinate role in both religious and political activities, but one that has deprived our political and religious institutions of the benefit of more than 50 percent of our population's brainpower and creativity.

The third way in which religion affects political campaigning is in its *ethical* dimension, where it should force us to ask some pretty tough questions. To what extent do we become indebted to those who give us financial support? How much should we accept? Should we take money from political action committees, the receipt of which generally makes us beholden to them?

Once in the campaign of 1975 a leading citizen in our community handed me a plain sealed envelope, saying, "Here, this is for your campaign." It contained $1,000 in cash. We took it back to the donor immediately, thanking him for wanting to support us, but telling him we could not accept "soft" money; we preferred checks and accepted only cash that was receipted immediately and declared on financial statements.

In addition, a candidate or officeholder should never imply that a financial contribution to his or her campaign will purchase a vote or decision in the donor's favor! Individuals and political action committees tend to support candidates whose views and political philosophy they believe in, but we have to make sure there's never a *quid pro quo* between the acceptance of a financial donation and the promise of a favor.

To what extent should negative influences be permitted in a campaign? My answer would be: preferably, not at all. We must eschew mudslinging, for example, and emphasize the positive, not the negative. I've had a standing rule that when I endorse another candidate in the Republican Party, I will never say anything negative about his or her opponent in the Democratic Party. So often we seem to vote against. I think it's important to try to be *for* the best candidates, in our view, rather than *against* their opponents. I like that old Chinese prov-

Chinese proverb re mudslinging.
"You don't ... tall ... someone else's ✱ head"

erb: You don't make yourself look tall by cutting off someone else's head.

In debates held in 1974 when I was running for reelection to Congress against the man I had previously defeated, even though we never talked about it, we were both concerned about not hitting below the belt, since rumors were circulating about our private lives (we were both divorced). We tried to address the issues only. We tried to be gentlemen, and I've always appreciated the high level on which that campaign was conducted.

In contrast, I was surprised, during a TV debate while I was running for reelection as Mayor in 1983, when my Democratic opponent pulled out, to display in front of the cameras, a "Nixon-Hudnut" button that our congressional campaign had used way back in 1972. He evidently hoped to dredge up the old hatreds of Richard Nixon and tie me into them, but it did not work. People saw through his ploy immediately and scored him—not me—negatively for it.

Should we allow political advertising to play upon people's fears and prejudices? This is always unfortunate, but regrettably it is sometimes viewed as an effective tool by people who rationalize that all is fair in love and war and politics. I recall one fight where a candidate was defeated in no small part because his opponent pandered to racial fears. Phone calls were made and a whisper campaign was conducted, telling white suburbanites that if he won it would not be long before subsidized housing—that is, homes for blacks—would be built in their neighborhoods. He lost.

political advertising

In this connection, I still feel somewhat guilty about a TV advertisement we ran back in 1972, after our polling showed that busing was a key issue and something people were very upset about. The commercial showed me alongside some passing yellow school buses, saying something to the effect that I was strongly for a neighborhood school system. I regret that ad in retrospect because, in a subtle fashion, it may have fanned the fires of racial prejudice. If it did that, it was wrong, and I am sorry.

Negative advertising utilizes truth-bending, character assassination, and mudslinging, hurling electronic and printed insults at the opponent. It cheapens the dialogue in a democracy, debases the currency of political exchange, prevents substantive issues from being responsibly discussed, and, even though there seems to be an unfortunately high level of tolerance for it, turns off the voters. It is not coincidental, that the 1986 campaigns, which in the opinion of many plummeted to the nadir of negative TV commercials, drew the fewest number of voters to the polls in forty-five years. For those who take the biblical tradition seriously, with its injunctions not to "bear false witness" and to "speak the truth in love," the use of such techniques should pose

86 campaign ... in 45 yrs.
Bible + TV distortion

grave ethical questions. The survival instinct and desire to win being what they are, a natural response to negative ads in a campaign is to fight fire with fire. To be sure, self-defense is always justified and erroneous charges must be answered, without recourse to negative tactics that only prolong the vicious cycle and deepen the downward spiral. (Perhaps national legislation should be enacted to require political TV commercials to be longer than thirty seconds—how about five minutes?—or free, and equal in time allotted. That might help correct the situation.)

One other thing has to be said while we're talking about the moral dimension of advertising. It tends to highlight a candidate's surface qualities rather than his or her true character. There is nothing wrong with emphasizing a candidate's valid strengths, of course, but it's unfortunate that in our day, much political advertising on TV is so superficial. It is, however, understandable in a country where in Marshall Blonsky's words, "image is much more important than social or economic fact." There was a story going around Indianapolis about a woman who walked into a grocery store pushing a baby carriage. An acquaintance of hers approached the carriage, peered inside, and exclaimed, "What a perfectly beautiful daughter you have." To which the child's mother replied, "That's nothing. You should see her picture."

So often in politics, we are tempted to do everything possible to put a good face on things, to paint an agreeable picture of ourselves, and to enhance our own image in the voters' eyes, that sometimes we become a little phony. Fortunately, there are two good antidotes.

One is the press, a vigilant, untrusting, responsible corps of journalists who prick the balloons of political pretense and scrape away the glossy veil of puffery behind which politicians sometimes hide. I once asked a young journalist who was interviewing me why he was so cynical and why he made me feel as though I were guilty and had to prove myself innocent. He replied that in the journalism school to which he had gone, he was taught not to be too trusting of politicians because they always try to put the best face on everything and make themselves look as good as possible, even at the expense of truth.

Second, there is true religion, which points us away from plastic values toward unphony authenticity. "Be strong," says scripture, which Paul Tillich interprets to mean, "Be yourself." As Jesus asked, "What does it profit a man, to gain the whole world and forfeit his life?" He came down pretty hard on people who "tithe mint and dill and cummin" but neglect "the weightier matters of the law, justice and mercy and faith," hypocrites who "cleanse the outside of the cup and of the plate, but inside they are full of extortion and rapacity, . . . white-washed tombs, which outwardly appear beautiful, but within . . . are full of dead men's bones and all uncleanness." True religion can help us maintain our integrity in the midst of the image-conscious society in which we live.

Another question we ought to ask as we think about the ethical dimension of religion's impact on political campaigning is whether the end justifies the means. Is anything permissible if it results in winning the election? Stealing a briefing book? Breaking into a campaign headquarters? Spreading a rumor about a candidate's personal life or health? Jumping on the bandwagon of an emotional tide just to go with the flow? Our country likes fair play, and I have to hope that in the long run the voters are discriminating enough in their judgments to see through this kind of political expediency.

There's one more question to ask: Why is there so much prejudice among some religious people? Why do religiosity and intolerance seem to go hand in hand? Various studies have drawn that regrettable conclusion, and it's not a happy thought that the more people go to church, the less broad-minded and magnanimous they seem to be. Witness a study, for example, by Kathleen Beatty and Oliver Walton of "Religious Preference and Political Tolerance," published in the *Public Opinion Quarterly*, which concludes that "frequent attenders of religious services . . . exhibit lower tolerance than infrequent attenders." As a clergyman, I must confess that I am saddened by this finding, although I have no reason to quarrel with it because my own experience basically validates it. Would that everyone who goes to church could hear Reinhold Niebuhr's reminder that religiosity is no particular sign of virtue. As he suggested, "Even in religion in which man consciously seeks to submit himself to God, there is an element of sinful pretense, an effort to establish an exclusive claim upon God." And would that we could all see and hear Abraham Lincoln leaning across his table, shooting out an arm and pointing a long finger at Congressman James K. Moorhead, who was at the White House demanding retaliation against the South: "Mr. Moorhead, haven't you lived long enough to know that two men may honestly differ about a question and both be right?"

A final approach to religion and political campaigning was suggested by the first Presbyterian General Assembly. Convened in 1789, it adopted certain "preliminary principles" to guide it in the ordering of congregational life and church government. (It is interesting to note that many of these principles had been incorporated in America's Constitution when it was drafted two years earlier.) Among them are three that seem to me to set an appropriate framework for discussing the relationship of religion to politics and political campaigning. I would hope (and assume) that many others outside the Presbyterian tradition might concur.

The first principle is that *"God alone is Lord of the conscience."* In New

Testament times, Peter and some fellow apostles were officially and legally ordered not to preach publicly that Jesus the Christ had been raised from the dead. They refused to obey the order, which would have stopped them from making their Christian witness, even though this meant they were in and out of jail many times. They explained, "We must obey God rather than men."

That conviction was a cornerstone of the Reformation. Said Sir Thomas More as he went to the scaffold in England, "I am the King's good servant, but God's first." Said Martin Luther as the Roman Church prepared to excommunicate him: "My conscience is captive to the Word of God. I cannot and I will not recant anything, for to go against conscience is neither right nor safe. Here I stand, I cannot do otherwise. God help me." Notable also was the reply of John Knox to Mary, Queen of Scots, in 1560 when she chastized him for publicly criticizing her morals, asking, "What have you to do with my marriage? What are you within this commonwealth?" In the response—which historian T. H. Lindsay saw as marking the birth of modern democracy —Knox replied, "A subject born within the same, madam, and albeit I neither be earl, lord, nor baron within it, yet has God made me (how abject that ever I be in your eyes) a profitable member within the same." In insisting upon an unfettered conscience, our Presbyterian forebears rejected the theories of the divine right of kings and the infallibility of popes. They said, "The requiring of an implicit faith and an absolute and blind obedience is to destroy liberty of conscience."

As schoolchildren know, such thinking contributed to the formation of our country. The Puritans fled England's monarchical tyranny to a new world where they could worship God as they chose. The colonies rebelled against the King's dictatorial claim to tax them without representation. The Founding Fathers built into our Constitution a disestablishment of church and a guarantee of religious freedom, believing that "God alone is Lord of the conscience." Such a belief is a keystone in the arch of freedom and in the temple of democracy.

This principle means that we should ask that our thinking be directed by divine guidance, prayerfully and carefully sought. It means that we should pray hard and think hard and then speak up for what we believe, standing by our convictions and not backing down or compromising. It means that candidates and political campaigns should speak their conscience, and it means that it is permissible for candidates, right, left, and center, to refer to the religious wellsprings of their convictions. It means that when we vote, we should cast our ballots thoughtfully and according to our moral principles, making as sure as we can that we know who and what we are voting for, even while we recognize that in matters of public policy there are very few things either wholly good or wholly bad, and that we must try to discern where the preponderance of good lies and proceed in that direction.

But this first principle does not mean that we should condemn someone whose opinion is different from ours. It does not mean that we should be intolerant or judgmental. It does not mean that someone who disagrees with us is by definition wrong or less conscientious than we are. It means that people are going to see things differently, because the criterion for our opinions should be, as Lincoln put it, "the right as God gives us to see the right."

That brings us to the second principle: *"There are truths and forms with respect to which men [and women] of good characters and principles may differ."* The founding fathers of our denomination added that it is "the duty both of private Christians and societies to exercise mutual forbearance towards each other."

In the church, differences of opinion inevitably arise but, like differences within a family, they ought to be comprehended within a wider frame of loyalty and love so they do not become divisive. The same thing is true in our country. Having from the beginning practiced freedom of religion, having refused to enforce religious conformity, and having become across the last two centuries a pluralistic society composed of disparate strands, America at her best has never attempted to homogenize everyone into a uniform pattern of conduct and belief. That's probably why the Statue of Liberty is such an important symbol to Americans, and why, across the generations, refugees from political oppression, religious persecution, social bondage, and economic serfdom have consistently sought a new home in the United States rather than elsewhere. We do not have an established religion in this country. "Congress shall make no law respecting an establishment of religion, or prohibiting the free exercise thereof."

The First Amendment teaches us that it is the American way to allow people to follow God according to the dictates of their conscience. The Founding Fathers made certain that God was never to be tilted toward Presbyterians or Roman Catholics or Baptists—or Christians or Jews or Muslims or Hindus. The First Amendment deregulated the churches and privatized religion. As my pastor, Bill Enright, put it in a July 4 sermon, "Christians never try to manipulate the law their way; they live as free men, never using freedom as a pretext to shape a secular world their way. . . . You respect the State. You do not use your Christian faith to gain a political advantage . . . to gain the upper hand."

Dr. Enright went on in that sermon to tell a story about an elder in the congregation of Second Church, Dr. Steven Beering. In 1948, at fifteen years of age, the man who is now president of Purdue University entered America as an immigrant from war-torn Europe. Recently, Dr. Beering spoke of the deep emotions he felt as he stood at the railing of the ship making its way up the Hudson River and saw, for the first time, the Statue of Liberty. "America, freedom, hope, opportunity, freedom to worship God as one would," he thought. "But then," Dr. Beering continued as he was recounting this story, "thirty-eight years passed by. I did not pass that way again until a few months ago. This time my journey took me past the glorious lady in an airliner. As I strained to see her, I recalled that foggy morning long ago and felt my father's hand again in mine. As we flew by the statue, she was still shrouded in mist . . . the mist of memories and tears. Even as I rubbed my eyes, I could not make out her features. She was covered with scaffolding. If the first sight of the statue had been powerful, this one was overwhelming! For I suddenly realized that this was the real statue . . . liberty, under constant maintenance and repair."

American pluralism means that we are a nation of nations, that truth is fragmentary and no individual or group possesses it entirely, and that we must be wary of an exclusive pretension of a part of the truth to be the whole. A particular religious group may affirm its own expression of ultimate truth, but that does not give it the right to claim that others who do not see it that way are beyond the pale. Regrettably, religious groups claiming absolute truth sometimes condemn those who disagree with them as un-American, un-Christian, un-Jewish, unpatriotic, unbelieving, unenlightened, and so on and on.

Democracy respects the differences in people. In a republic where the majority rules and the rights of minorities are protected, government should be the defender of all faiths, the promoter of none. Government and its officials are the umpire, assuring fair play, not the coach, inspiring passionate play. Our system has confidence in the effectiveness of an open society. It is inclusive rather than exclusive. The key is to remember, with a measure of tolerance and modesty that sometimes escapes people with strong convictions, that two persons may sincerely hold opinions that vary radically, without either one ceasing to be a loyal American or a faithful religious believer. We should never brand dissent as treason, never equate unity with uniformity, never assume that only the orthodox are loyal. We should learn to hold to strong moral positions without being moralistic, remembering that "there are truths and forms with respect to which persons of good character and conscience may differ."

So on weighty issues of the day, in political campaigns, and in our evaluation of government officials, we must be cautious about reducing everything to a single focus and being for or against a candidate for office or a holder of office solely on the basis of his or her position on a single issue, be it abortion or prayer in the public schools or a constitutional amendment on a balanced budget, or whatever. The second principle means that no candidate carries the special blessing of the deity. There are tremendous dangers to freedom in identifying any political position with the Divine or in feeling that one political party or group has co-opted morality and truth.

Religious people involved in politics should never give the impression that someone has to see it "our way" or belong to our group in order to be a valid participant in the political process as a worker or adviser or staffer or candidate. Nor should they imply that, in pressing their viewpoints, they are speaking with the authority of scripture or church or God. As my friend Colorado Senator Bill Armstrong says, to do so would be a "horrible mistake." Reacting in the summer of 1986 to a claim by Pat Robertson that Christians "feel more strongly than others do" about "love of God, love of country, and support for the traditional family," Senator Armstrong, himself a born-again Christian, said that such remarks "feed the concern" many Americans have that evangelicals are trying to exclude non-evangelicals from politics. Asked what he might tell Robertson if he had the opportunity, Armstrong replied, "Pat, don't say that any more."

The third principle means that the proof of the pudding is in the eating. *"Truth is in order to goodness."* The test of beliefs is conduct. Faith and practice are inseparable. "By their fruits ye shall know them," said Christ. Truth leads to goodness. "Otherwise it would be of no consequence either to discover truth or to embrace it."

But what is this goodness that truth produces? I would define it in terms of freedom and justice and love.

First, whatever contributes to freedom is good, whatever deprives people of freedom is bad. I will never forget a college professor saying to us in his last lecture in a class on Colonial history, "Gentlemen, the founding of America was a great step in the freeing of mankind from the dual bondage of canon and feudal law." If truth really is contained in an idea, it will be liberating. An idea that leads to the enslavement of people has no truth in it. Political systems that produce concentration camps, one-party politics, press censorship, and so forth are false. That which liberates people from slavery—physical, spiritual, emotional, social, political, economic, psychological, intellectual bondage —is true and good.

When, two hundred years ago, John Witherspoon spearheaded the rebellion against England, I believe he had truth on his side. When, over one hundred years ago, Henry Ward Beecher spoke out from his pulpit against slavery and unjust exploitation of the Negroes, I believe he had truth on his side. When people in this century joined the civil-rights struggle of the 1960s to liberate our political process and our social system from the spiritual chains of race prejudice, I believe they had truth on their side.

Second, goodness means justice as well as freedom. In *Reformed Faith and Politics*, Professor Ronald Stone of Pittsburgh Theological Seminary has written that the biblical term for the goal of political life is "justice." Recognizing that politics is at best an ambiguous business and that sin always keeps those who embrace the kingdom of God from fully realizing it, we can nonetheless say with Stone that "the reduction of the human evil to manageable proportions is the never-ending task of anyone who, inspired by God's love, takes up the task of political responsibility." This is not to say that pure justice will ever be achieved, but rather that reasonable approximations of it can be. Justice means equal opportunity. It means each person's right to be a free human being. It means denial of oppression and liberation from the oppressor. It means a fair distribution of resources to overcome the terrible inequity of grinding poverty. And a lot more.

And third, goodness means love, for whatever increases the amount of love in the world is good and true. Whatever divides people, estranges them from each other, and makes them resentful and hostile, whatever makes people suspicious of each other and tears down confidence and mutual trust, whatever builds barriers between people or causes breakdowns of communication, whatever hurts or contributes to human misery is bad and false in politics or elsewhere.

On the other hand, those things that produce reconciliation, replace fear with understanding and contempt with respect, and promote kindliness and peace and goodwill are good. The final criterion of our believing, our doing, and our speaking is love—in politics and in everything else. In this sense, government can be an agency for spreading good. Politics can be a way of enlarging the influence of love in the world. Through the political process, it is possible to show care and concern. It is possible to bridge chasms. It is possible to build up instead of tearing down. And that is what love is all about.

When Lincoln concluded his famous Cooper Union Speech in New York City on February 27, 1860, with the words, "Let us have faith that right makes might, and in that faith, let us, to the end, dare to do our duty, as we understand it," he was not inviting us to become hopelessly relativistic about our value systems but, rather, to pierce through to fundamental bedrock morality and then let it govern our activities and relationships. That's what we come down to when we are talking about religion and its impact on politics and political campaigning—a few fundamental principles that, if adhered to, will see us through, regardless of the particular stands on the issues of the day or the different tough decisions we have to make when we are voting in the legislative branch of government or taking administrative action in the executive branch, or deciding cases in the judicial branch. It has been well said, "Believe as if everything depended on God, but act as if everything depended on you."

6

A Theology of Losing

On December 12, 1974, I gave a speech that—I'm glad to say—I've only had to deliver once in my life. It was delivered to the Congressional Prayer Group, of which I was a member, five weeks after I had lost my bid for reelection to Congress. I called it "A Theology of Losing."

Congress worked late that year, because so much of its attention had been preempted by Watergate. We were in a lame-duck session, and it was no fun (as a matter of fact, it was downright embarrassing) to walk the halls of Congress aware that I had lost the election and was on my way out. I had spoken before the group on previous occasions, so they invited me back for one last "valediction forbidding mourning."

Some of my colleagues meeting that morning would continue their service in Washington, but others—like me—would soon be heading home. We all were lucky, though, in that we could gather there as Democrats and Republicans who lived in a country where we had the freedom to run for office on different tickets—the freedom to win and the freedom to lose, the freedom to succeed and the freedom to fail.

I can remember how envious I have sometimes been across the years when I've heard about candidates running unopposed in a general election, but that is the exception rather than the rule, and America is much healthier as a result. How much better a system we have than one where there is only one party, one orthodoxy, one slate of candidates, one predictable outcome in every election. Democracy trusts the people and rests on the faith that an enlightened citizenry will elect persons of conscientious judgment and high character to represent them. In the winnowing process, some win and some lose, but we all should thank God that we live in a free system that encourages competition and believes the will of the people will prevail in the end.

Susie and I had the opportunity in 1981 to lead a delegation of public officials and private citizens to Europe, under the sponsorship of Partners for Livable Places, where we attended some meetings of the Council of Europe being held in the Reichstag in West Berlin. As long as I live, I will remember the shock and horror I felt when I saw the Berlin Wall. One afternoon we crossed through Checkpoint Charlie into East Berlin, entering (for us, the first time) a real police state where there was very little freedom. In contrast to West Berlin, where there was a profusion of political banners advertising parties from the extreme left to the extreme right, here there were no banners, no bumper stickers, no billboards, no buttons being worn by anyone advertising this or that candidate. In every direction we drove our bus, we ultimately ran into a wall and had to turn back. We were really in the middle of a well-organized prison! From the tops of the tenement houses, TV antennae were pointed west—across the barbed wire and the guns and the concrete wall to free, uncensored news from West Berlin. It was as if they symbolized a hope and yearning in the hearts of East Berliners that someday they would be free and that someday they would again be in touch with a civilization where people are not pawns on the chessboard of the state, where minorities are protected, where religion and the press are not censored, and where there is the freedom to lose an election as well as to win.

My appreciation for this freedom is very real, but so was the pain of losing my seat in Congress. I recollect now that the first thing I said to my colleagues in the Prayer Group was that losing hurts! I had worked as hard as I could—studying the issues before me and returning home nearly every weekend to discuss them with my constituents, diligently answering mail and sending out newsletters, and meeting with group after group arriving in Washington to lobby me for one cause or another. It was disillusioning and frustrating to find that my efforts had fallen victim to a tide of events beyond my control.

It is estimated that incumbents can be reelected 90 percent of the time, other things being equal. But the Watergate tragedy, coupled with President Ford's pardon of his predecessor before the 1974 elections, spelled doom for many Republicans. I had won in 1972 by about 2 percent, but that was not enough of a margin to work with—particularly when I was running against the gentleman from Indiana whom I had defeated in 1972. Andy Jacobs had universal name recognition in our district and was coming around for another try at his old seat. This time he was the one who finished with the 2 percent margin on his side. I was out. And I was down. Perhaps the defeat hurt all the more because it was the second loss I had suffered in 1974. Earlier that year, I had experienced a painful divorce and disruption in my personal life. Being separated from my children really hurt more than losing the election, and the combination of the two constituted a pretty severe blow to my morale.

Actually, my losses had placed me in a position to learn firsthand what I had been preaching about for years. As a clergyman, I had witnessed pain and suffering in many lives, and from the pulpit I had talked about how those things could be turned to useful purpose by men and women of faith. During my seminary days, I had written a long paper on Psalm 73, one of my favorites, which dealt with the whole question of theodicy (explaining God's ways), going beyond an effort to understand why good people suffer, and the wicked apparently prosper, to an affirmation of fellowship with God as being the ultimate resolution of the problem. Now I began to learn that one of life's most important lessons is that it is full of suffering and hurt and pain that can be a learning, maturing, enlarging experience for us if we approach it in the right way.

I once went with my father to see the Broadway play *The Teahouse of the August Moon,* by John Patrick. I remember being struck by one of the things the leading character said: "Pain makes man think. Thought makes man wise. Wisdom makes life endurable." This reminded me very much of Paul's advice in his letter to the Romans that we should rejoice in our troubles, "knowing that suffering produces endurance, and endurance produces character, and character produces hope, and hope does not disappoint us." Life can be difficult. In the garden of roses, there may be a crown of thorns. We don't always win. Sometimes we lose. But in losing we can win.

No matter where we find ourselves once the votes have been counted (or the promotions have been awarded or the points have been scored), it is important that we accept the outcome with grace. We should strive to be gracious winners and losers—good sports, if you please. Unfortunately, some people never learn that lesson.

Poor winners and losers are people who become spiteful in victory or defeat. A poor winner rubs it in, gloats, brags about the victory, and displays no sensitivity toward the feelings of the loser, assuming the right to punish the opposition, to exclude them, to ignore them. For example, say that I, as a Republican, win the mayoral election. If I am a poor winner, I will refuse to let Democrats serve on any boards or agencies, I will try to make sure nobody who supported my opponent gets any contracts from the city, I will see to it that promotions in City Hall go only to those who supported me, and I will take all the credit for my success.

Sore losers we all know about. They're the ones who cannot take defeat with grace. I have run into them from time to time and am always offended by them, while at the same time I find their childishness rather humorous. They refuse to shake hands after the battle is over. They would not wish you well or good luck if you paid them. They cannot bring themselves to admit that there might have been some deficiencies in their campaign or in their views on the issues. They say, "The people have spoken in their infinite wisdom, the dumb SOBs!" How well I remember a conversation with someone I once defeated (not even in a general election or a primary, but in the screening process at the beginning of an election year, when I was one of several people seeking my party's endorsement). I called up those who lost that contest to express the hope that we could work together and to say that I knew they were hurt and was there any way I could help them, only to have this fellow Republican say to me, "Well, you may have beaten me and won the Party's endorsement, but I still think I'm much better qualified than you are."

The poorest loser I've ever encountered in politics was not someone I defeated in an election, nor even a Hoosier. It was William Donald Schaefer, former Mayor of Baltimore, one of the finest mayors in the country, who led a magnificent city to fantastic renewal. When I stepped down as president of the National League of Cities in 1981, I was asked who, in my opinion, were the top ten mayors in the country, and I put Mayor Schaefer at the top of the list. Consequently, I was very disappointed by his reaction to the loss of the National Football League Colts. It was early in 1984 when Bob Irsay, dissatisfied with low attendance at Colts games and the rundown condition of Baltimore's Memorial Stadium, began examining cities in which to relocate his franchise. When he expressed an interest in possibly moving to Indianapolis, I called Mayor Schaefer and told him that I wanted to be up-front with him. I said I knew he was aware that Mr. Irsay was exploring other cities and that Indianapolis was one being looked at, that I bore him and the people of Baltimore no ill will but would obviously be an advocate for my city and try to put a deal together if, in fact, Irsay was serious. Mayor Schaefer responded graciously, remarking that he thought I was a good guy and that if Baltimore could not keep the Colts, he hoped that Indianapolis would land them. On March 2, while indicating that he and the Governor were prepared to do whatever might be necessary to keep the Colts in Baltimore, he also admitted, "[Irsay] could sign today and leave today. There's nothing in his way whatsoever. He could open up in Indianapolis next year. He hasn't done it yet. Why? I don't know."

But then, after the Colts left in late March, Mayor Schaefer instituted eminent-domain proceedings against the Colts, and nine months later he authorized a lawsuit to be filed against Dave Frick and Johnny B. Smith and me personally. All the lawsuits were finally settled out of court, but at a cost of several million dollars to the parties involved. Twice, Mayor Schaefer refused to speak to me on the telephone when I called him in early 1985 to discuss this (and other unrelated matters) with him. In March of 1985, I bumped into him at the White House, shook his hand, and made a comment to the effect that he was a pretty hard fellow to reach by phone. He retorted, "That's right," and abruptly turned on his heel and walked away. I grinned and said to some of the people around me, "There are only two people in the entire world who could corral the Mayor of Baltimore and the Mayor of Indianapolis under the same roof—the President of the United States and a federal judge." In September 1986, *City & State* magazine recognized four mayors for "managing city affairs like pros in the private sector"—Mayor Henry Cisneros of San Antonio, Mayor William Donald Schaefer of Baltimore, Mayor Ed Koch of New York City, and Mayor William Hudnut of Indianapolis. In his comment, as quoted in *USA Today* the following week, Mayor Schaefer pointedly said, "I'm very honored to be among players of the caliber of Cisneros and Koch, who are in a league unto themselves."

Why has he reacted in this manner? I don't know, but my heart is heavy with disappointment in a man I otherwise admire greatly. A first-class public official should be a better loser.

There are good winners and good losers in politics too. A good winner is somebody who is magnanimous rather than vindictive, who recognizes after the election is over that he or she has been elected to serve all the people, and who takes an inclusive rather than an exclusive approach to the job. A good loser is someone who does the right things despite the disappointment of losing—he or she does not complain, does not make excuses, does not develop a sour disposition, does not blame others, does not become childish or churlish. I was tremendously impressed when Indiana State Senator James Butcher, after losing his race for Congress in November 1986, said of his opponent, "I will honor our new Congressman and uphold him in my prayers."

Interestingly enough, the best winner and the best loser I have ever encountered in politics is the same person—Andy Jacobs. As I mentioned, I beat him after he had been in Congress for eight years, and then in 1974 he returned the compliment. In 1972, on election night, after the news was in that he had lost to me, Andy went out of his way to look me up at our victory celebration in a downtown hotel, finally reaching me by telephone to congratulate me and wish me well and pledge that he would work with me in the transition, before I assumed office in early January. And he did just that. He invited me and my staff over to his office. He made his files available to me (in contrast to some losers I have known who have purged their files and not given their successors access to them). He offered to introduce me to fellow congressmen in Washington, and he told me about problems that I would have to deal with in the district. He offered to help us set up our office in Washington, he was gracious, he smiled, he wished me well, and he stayed in touch with me during the two years I served in Congress.

Then in 1974, he beat me. I was out and he was in, but he did not gloat or smirk. We ran into each other in a TV station where we had both gone for a postmortem on election night. We shook hands, and he threw his arms around me and gave me a hug, telling me he knew how I felt. He was gentle and sensitive, and we made plans to prepare again for the transition of power from me back to him. In the years since, while I have been Mayor of the City of Indianapolis and he has been congressman, we have remained friends. He has gone out of his way on several occasions to compliment me publicly as "my mayor" and "the best mayor Indianapolis has ever had," and in all the campaigns we have been involved in during the last twelve years, we have never once allowed derogatory statements about each other to be injected by any of our campaign associates; we have always tried to be friends and gentlemen toward each other. To this day, I am grateful for the high level of the two campaigns we had against each other, and for the fact that we were able to transcend the bitter partisanship that sometimes causes permanent estrangement in human relationships.

My relationship with Andy grew from my loss—a positive grew from a negative. The Bible has a lot to say about turning failures into successes. It teaches us, paradoxically, that losing can become winning. Barren fig trees can become fruitful orchards; water can become wine; prows of boats can become pulpits; clay and mud can become people; thorns can become a crown; a cross can become a throne. In the biblical transvaluation of values, pluses are made from minuses and defeat is transformed into victory. Outcasts become disciples; prostitutes become saints; shepherds become prophets; fishermen become fishers of men; a carpenter becomes a Savior. Leaders are fashioned out of burden bearers, and the Suffering Servant is turned into the Messiah. The leaders in the Bible, as Martin Buber has pointed out, "live in failure; it is for them to fight and not to conquer." Hosea, married to a harlot, takes his heartbreaking experience and transforms it into a springboard for discussing God's "covenant love" with his people; David, an adulterer, a coward who fled from Saul and from Absalom, dancing naked before the Ark in Jerusalem, shows us that in the Bible, "the real way, from the creation to the kingdom, is trod not on the surface of success, but in the depths of failure" (Buber); Paul, a humble tentmaker with a bothersome physical disability, becomes the chief vehicle by which Christ's message is introduced into the Gentile world of the Roman Empire.

These were ordinary people, but they were used by God for extraordinary purposes. They had learned, as we all must learn, that adversity should not have the final word; if we use our losses wisely, we can find victory.

Victory is ours if we do not give up or give in. There is something much worse than losing an election or a loved one, and that is letting the defeat drag us down into defeatism. I admire Winston Churchill, youngest police chief in the history of Indianapolis, who was deposed in 1974 following allegations of corruption, for looking back later and saying, "I like to think that the real measure of a person is not how well they handle success but how well they handle disaster." On election night in 1974, with Susan McVie, my special assistant, standing on one side of me with tears in her eyes and Bruce Melchert, my administrative assistant and campaign manager, on the other, I told the crowd that had gathered, "I'll be back!" The mood in the Republican campaign headquarters was somber (the Indiana congressional delegation had flipped from seven Republicans and four Democrats to nine Democrats and two Republicans, and Mayor Richard Lugar had lost in his bid to unseat Senator Birch Bayh), but the Republican Party would recover. My hurt was acute—no reelection, no wife and children at home any more, no job—but my losses would provide an occasion for learning and a springboard for new opportunities. I would "overwhelm the overwhelming before it overwhelmed me," as a professor at the Naval Academy who was a member of the Presbyterian church in Annapolis said to me after his wife died of cancer, leaving him with three small children. Losing would not have the last word.

The loss had a galvanizing effect on me. The next year I decided to run for mayor, partially because I wanted to help the local Republican Party to bounce back from Watergate and the defeats it entailed. I didn't drop out. I do not attach any particular virtue to my decision to hang in there, but I do feel that, most of the time, true religion will keep our spirits from drooping. Its message is "never flag in zeal." Don't quit. Hang in there. With the other (better known) Winston Churchill, we say, "Never flinch. Never weary. Never despair." With scripture, we say "nevertheless." That is one of the great words of the Bible. In Psalm 73, which I have already mentioned, the psalmist, beset by doubt and suffering and bitterness, ends up with a tremendous affirmation of the abiding presence of God:

> Nevertheless I am continually with thee; . . . thou dost guide me with thy counsel, and afterward thou wilt receive me to glory. Whom have I in heaven but thee? And there is nothing upon earth that I desire besides thee. My flesh and my heart may fail, but God is the strength of my heart and my portion for ever.

God gives us the strength to come back. We can affirm the resiliency of the human spirit. People of spiritual resources redeem catastrophe by turning it into a creative moment.

We have a group of kids in Indianapolis called "The Masters of

Disaster," underprivileged kids, poor kids, "ghetto kids" some have called them. They attended one of our inner-city elementary schools. A teacher named Bob Cotter befriended them and taught them how to play chess. He taught them the values of discipline, concentration, and self-confidence, as well as the skills and techniques of the game. At first they were losing every match. But they did not give up. They persisted. And they became darn good chess players. (I had to chuckle when the *New York Times* ran an article about them showing me playing against one of the kids, identifying me as a Phi Beta Kappa graduate from Princeton University who was losing handily to the young Master of Disaster!) Eventually these sixth-graders won a national championship. They appeared on national television. They went on an exhibition tour to Japan. They were invited to the White House. And a PBS documentary was made about them. Losers? Not at all. The Masters of Disaster became champions.

Victory is ours if we use our adversity as an opportunity to grow. One of the things we were taught in seminary was that when Israel's external circumstances were in the darkest, Hebrew faith glowed most incandescently. During the Babylonian Captivity, after Jerusalem had been decimated, a Second Isaiah could appear with his infinitely beautiful poetry and his divinely inspired insight into the meaning of suffering—"Comfort ye, comfort ye my people." Difficult circumstances can become the occasion for a renewal of one's faith and hope and courage. Biblical religion does not guarantee us a smooth voyage through life, but it does guarantee us strength to ride out the storm.

During the summer of 1953, after I had finished my junior year at Princeton, I met my dad and my brother David, both of whom had just completed a year of study in England, for some travel through England and Scotland. We enjoyed poking around old cemeteries because it put us in touch with some of the exciting historic moments of the past. On the centuries-old tombstones we noticed many symbols—a cross, a star, a skull and bones, a shovel. One symbol that startled us was an anchor. We did not understand it until, after a little research, we discovered that it was a biblical metaphor derived from the book of Hebrews, which described hope as "a sure and steadfast anchor of the soul." We realized the anchor meant that, come what might, we should rest secure in the certainty that God would still be God, supporting us with everlasting arms if tomorrow brought failure, darkness, suffering, or death. Biblical hope is grounded in a steady confidence that God is faithful and that somehow, in ways beyond our ken, he rules the world and holds us all within his providential care.

When obstacles are placed in the way of accomplishing an objective, it's sometimes much easier to resign ourselves to the conclusion that our goal must be forfeited than to figure out how to make something happen. I spend a lot of time saying to people who report to me, "Don't tell me why it can't be done. Let's figure out how we can do it!" The tendency in the bureaucracy of a large organization is to become a self-protecting institutionalist, to resist change and say no to new ideas. The challenge is to manage change effectively and make positive things happen, and, if an obstacle is thrown in one's way, to figure out another way to achieve the desired result. We must have faith that takes us beyond defeat to victory.

When a lot of people tell us we cannot build a Hoosier Dome for various reasons, we keep plugging away until finally we get the job done. When a local congressman opposes our efforts to rehabilitate a derelict Union Station, we keep plugging away until we get the job done. When historic preservationists oppose our efforts to bring a phoenix out of the ashes of an old housing project called Lockefield Gardens, we keep plugging away until we get the job done. Frustration may lead us to innovation, and, quite possibly, creative thought can be stimulated by opposition that temporarily defeats what we are trying to accomplish. Like steel that is forged in the fire and hammered on the anvil, so human character becomes stronger and finer in response to pain and suffering. During some of the most discouraging moments of the Civil War, Lincoln said to Congress, "Let us renew our trust in God and go forward without fear and with manly hearts." All of us can be like the Confederate soldiers Bruce Catton described: "Men who saw night coming down about them could somehow act as if they stood at the edge of dawn."

My dad once preached a sermon called "Barnabas, Son of Encouragement." Barnabas was a traveling companion and friend of Paul's in the earliest days of the church, and, according to my dad, his name in Hebrew meant "son of encouragement." (My father never took a day of Hebrew in his life, but I'll assume he was right!) He explained how important it is for us to be sons of encouragement, people who understand that no life is without its scars, its failures, its pain, its frustrations, its sins and shortcomings. Discouragement about ourselves and about the future is far from what he called "Christ's spirit"—that spirit ought to make us adequate to meet whatever life might bring. "The Gospel of Christ," said my father, "does not produce sad, downhearted, cynical people; the true servants of Jesus are always sons of encouragement, people of hope, faith, and courage who know how to live and die in peace and joy." The same can be said of biblical religion as it is mediated to us through the Hebrew prophets. They taught us about the virtues of affliction and showed us how adverse external circumstances need not daunt the human spirit. Jeremiah, for example, was locked in the stocks and exposed to public ridicule, but he nonetheless dreamed of a new covenant between God and the house of Israel, when everyone "from the least of them to the greatest" would "know the Lord." If facing defeat can help us become sons of encouragement, if it can help us renew the wellsprings of faith and hope and courage within us, then it might not be such a bad thing after all!

As we seek to deal with the reality of losing, we gradually come to the realization that there are more important things in life than our won/lost record. After all is said and done, there are achievements that matter more—like being a good, kind, decent person, like being gentle and sensitive and compassionate, like striving and daring and reaching for our dreams, like living out our days with grace and courage and confidence. It is of greater consequence to have integrity and be devoted to excellence and to stand up for the right as we are given to see it, than to win. The important thing is to enter the arena and make the effort, perhaps to succeed, perhaps to fail, but regardless, to try. Nobody has stated the case for heroic involvement, win, lose, or draw, better than did John F. Kennedy on December 5, 1961, in his immortal words spoken about, and reflecting the philosophy of, his predecessor, Theodore Roosevelt, words from which I have frequently drawn both comfort and inspiration:

> It is not the critic who counts, nor the man who points out where the strong man stumbles, or where the doer of deeds could have done them better. On the contrary, the credit belongs to the man who is actually in the arena—whose vision is marred by the dust and sweat and blood; who strives valiantly; who errs and comes up again and again; who knows the great devotions, the great enthusiasms; who at best knows in the end the triumph of high achievement. However, if he fails, at least he fails while daring greatly so that his place shall never be with those cold and timid souls who know neither victory nor defeat.

A theology of losing takes us beyond winning and losing—to truth, to providence, to reconciliation.

It takes us beyond a narrow awareness of the pain of defeat and the joy of victory to a broader understanding of the importance of being true to one's best self. It helps us keep our priorities in order and moves us beyond expediency to integrity. Scripture enjoins us to "seek first God's kingdom and his righteousness" with the promise that other things shall be ours as well. Or, as the fourth Beatitude puts it, "Blessed are those who hunger and thirst for righteousness, for they shall be satisfied."

The biblical message is that achievement is not the only way to measure excellence. Climbing to the top of an economic or political ladder is not the only way to measure our success on the ladder of life. Sometimes, if the cause is just, the result is not as important as the engagement. I've been told there is a sign over the door in the locker room of the Dallas Cowboys that reads, "The quality of a person's life is in direct proportion to their commitment to excellence." The final outcome is never as important as whether we played to the best of our ability and performed our duties with as much excellence as possible.

If I may draw an analogy from the game of tennis, it is important to recognize that in addition to the "outer game" of tennis, which is played against an external opponent, there is an "inner game" (described by W. T. Gallwey in his book *The Inner Game of Tennis*) that takes place in the mind of the player. The "opponent" here is made up of obstacles like self-doubt, self-condemnation, nervousness, lapses in concentration, and lack of self-confidence, all of which inhibit excellence of performance. The key is to play up to and release the potential within you, to use all your talents to the best of your ability, to be what you are, to be strong. Losing is not really a disgrace unless you are just playing to beat the other guy.

Indianapolis is the home of the U.S. Clay Court Tennis Championships, and we witness this philosophy being played out on Stadium Court year after year. Once, after a particularly long and boring final which Andrea Jaeger eventually won, even though most of the Indianapolis crowd of 7,600 people had gone to sleep and a national television audience had long since switched channels (rally after rally in this moonballing match lasted more than 30 hits, some going past 50, and the longest lasting 135 hits before the point was decided), Andrea's father remarked, "I don't really care if television is pleased or the people are pleased. The philosophy that I have is one I learned from Vince Lombardi. Winning isn't everything, it's the only thing. I told Andrea a long time ago that when she comes off the tennis court, I don't want to hear how she did. All I want to know is, what is the score."

In contrast to that attitude, Arthur Ashe, who was sitting with me watching the match, commented that the great John Wooden, whom he had known at UCLA, never scouted other basketball teams. He just asked his guys to play the best they could—and, Ashe added, they were pretty successful. A great champion like Chris Evert Lloyd understands this well. Once she talked about how her husband always encouraged her to "play to my fullest potential," adding, "There's no crime in losing if you try your hardest." After a three-month layoff in 1980, Chris explained, "I just realized that I could change my priorities and not worry about winning, not worry about how Tracy Austin or Martina was playing. I could simply try to master my own game and try to reach my peak. Not once did I say to myself, 'I've got to come back.' At twenty-one, I needed it; but I'm not obsessed with it now as I was then."

As history books are written, one might conclude that only conquerors had value. Those who forced their causes through were crowned with worldly success; the weak, the humble, the unsuccessful were ignored. But in the Bible, it was precisely these people who were often chosen to be the vehicles for God's redeeming action. In the Bible, leaders are servants of others and servants of the truth, people who are led by a divine power laid upon them from outside themselves, to which they feel obligated.

In politics, this means facing tough issues and making tough choices, not being afraid to take a stand because it might mean unpopularity, not worrying so much about whether it will "play in Peoria" as whether it will play in the citadel of your own conscience. It is impossible to read John F. Kennedy's *Profiles in Courage* without learning from the lives of people like Daniel Webster, John Quincy Adams, and Sam Houston that serving the national interest rather than private or political gain is really what counts. Kennedy quotes John C. Calhoun: "I never know what South Carolina thinks of a measure. I never consult her. I act to the best of my judgment and according to my conscience. If she approves, well and good, if she does not and wishes anyone to take my place, I am ready to vacate. We are even." Most politicians would not go so far as to say they never consult their constituency, but Calhoun's commitment to do his best and let the chips fall where they may is admirable.

Of course, there are many pressures that discourage acts of political courage and force people in politics to compromise with being true to the right in an absolute sense. Politicians want to be liked. They understand that the best way to get along is to go along, and they must constantly deal in a process of give-and-take that conciliates opposite points of view and results in a balance or compromise. Officeholders usually want to win the next election, and the pressure created by an onslaught of constituents and lobbies and interest groups and organized blocs of voters may make demands on them that conflict with their own consciences. They feel a loyalty to the people and their political parties who helped them win. They want to avoid things that might cause undue hardship on their family or themselves. It's just too glib and simplistic to say, "Do what's right." It's too easy an answer and one that can only be offered by people who have never had to bear the responsibility of public life.

Another thing that a theology of losing helps us discover on the other side of winning and losing is God's providence, a subject that brings to mind my grandfather and his favorite hymn. He used to talk about it at our summer hymn sings and often asked that we all sing it together, to the tune of "Finlandia," because it meant so much to him as an expression of the way biblical faith can carry us beyond suffering and pain.

> Be still, my soul: the Lord is on thy side;
>   Bear patiently the cross of grief or pain;
> Leave to thy God to order and provide;
>   In every change he faithful will remain. . . .
>
> Be still, my soul: thy God doth undertake
>   To guide the future as he has the past.
> Thy hope, thy confidence let nothing shake;
>   All now mysterious shall be bright at last.

The pain of losing, with its accompanying feelings of remorse, self-doubt, rejection, and alienation, could leave us discouraged, defeated, crushed in spirit. The experience of losing could tempt us to doubt ourselves, our friends, our future, even God himself. But it could also prompt us to faith; we could let *our* "cross of grief or pain" introduce us to a faithful God who undertakes "to guide the future as he has the past." That was my discovery. It was my experience that "the everlasting arms" were with me as much in defeat as in victory—even more. God surprised me in the valley of my shadow. He came to me through the consolation tendered me by friends and family. He visited me in the midnight of my soul and held my hand. It was like the time when, climbing a mountain in the Adirondacks, we misjudged our time and had to finish in the inky darkness. We held one another's hands, Dad leading, inching our way along the trail, feeling it with our feet, until finally we emerged from the forest, safely home once again.

It is important that we "let go, let God." I love the parable in Mark 4:26–29, about the seed growing secretly. The farmer plants his seed and goes to bed; while he is sleeping, the seed sprouts and grows, in some unknown way. Which is to say, in the midst of events that impede growth, God is still at work bringing forth his harvest. Even in our time of repose, his purposes are being worked out. "While I drink my little glass of Wittenberg beer," Martin Luther once dryly observed, "the gospel runs its course." That has to be the best thing ever said about drinking beer!

When you lose, you should not get too uptight. You should "let go, let God." That is, you should let things happen, believing that God's providence is at work. This does not mean passiveness. It means deep confidence, an almost childlike trust in the Father's ability to make things work out. It means acceptance of the fundamental process, the grace and mystery and sensibleness of life. It means faith in the order and goodness of life, both human and natural. Letting go after a loss means allowing joy to come into your life, rather than contriving to have a good time or pretending to turn yourself into a winner. It means learning to appreciate the love and beauty already happening around you, rather than trying to manufacture something that you think is not there. It means letting your problem be solved unconsciously as well as by conscious effort, and it means giving no thought for the morrow, unwinding, relaxing, trusting. On the last night of his life on earth, Jesus said to his disciples gathered in the upper room, when they all knew something awful was about to happen and a sense of foreboding hung over their gathering like a dark cloud, "These things I have spoken to you, that my joy may be in you, and that your joy may be full."

It is also important to discover that "God moves in mysterious ways, his wonders to perform." In his providential care for his children, he opens another door for you when one is slammed in your face. We don't always recognize it right away, but looking back, we see it. As the old saying has it, our extremity is God's opportunity. "Leave to thy God to order and provide."

Finally, a theology of losing can take us beyond prudential calculations of victory and defeat, based on who received more votes, to an understanding of the importance of mercy in life. Call it love, compassion, magnanimity, forgiveness, grace, or reconciliation. It is a quality that can redeem us from self-pity if we lose, from self-congratulation if we win. It can lift us above bitterness in defeat, above vindictiveness in victory. It's the quality all true religion possesses, be it Jewish, Christian, or something else.

This is the quality that Micah possessed when he reminded the Hebrew people that the Lord required them to "do justly, love mercy, and walk humbly" instead of worrying about who was righteous and who was not and becoming obsessed about rewards due one group and punishments due the other. It's the quality Paul yearned for in the young church of his day, so sundered by bickering and jealousy and in-fighting, exhorting them to "put on love, which binds everything together in perfect harmony," instead of taking sides and telling some that they were out, others that they were in. It's the quality Jesus displayed on the cross—he, the so-called loser by the standards of those who had put him on trial and convicted him, praying, "Father, forgive them," on behalf of those who had him crucified, instead of bitterly denouncing them and condemning them to be outcasts for eternity far from the reach of the love of God.

Pain or loss that we endure can evoke the quality of mercy in us. Suffering can gentle us, and losing can release love within us. Individuals who have endured some form of pain often become more sensitive men and women, for they are lifted to a higher level of insight and maturity. The quality of mercy represents a new plateau beyond the peak of winning and the valley of losing.

Two examples in American political history came readily to mind: President Ford's willingness to pardon Richard Nixon, and President Lincoln's willingness to pardon the South.

Gerald Ford's pardon of his predecessor in the fall of 1974 struck me at the time as being exceedingly infelicitous—not because I thought Mr. Nixon should be brought to trial, but because I resented the way it made campaigning for reelection much more difficult for beleaguered Republicans like me who already had their hands full with the Watergate tragedy. It gave our opponents one more issue. It brought Nixon-haters out of the woodwork all over again. Congressman Jacobs used it against me all fall in debate after debate, appearance after appearance. I was invariably asked about the pardon, and usually my response was something to the effect that the President did it in order to save the country the embarrassment and indignity of a trial in federal court of a former Chief Executive; to which Congressman Jacobs would invariably reply that it was a greater embarrassment to the country that President Ford got Mr. Nixon off, as if everyone is equal and no one is better than anyone else in our democracy, except the President, who apparently is above the law. I kept asking myself, Why couldn't President Ford have waited just a few weeks until the November elections were behind us?

In retrospect, however, it seems to me to have been the right thing to do, and I'm not going to quibble about the timing. Jerry Ford lanced the boil. He took America beyond the point where "winners" were calling for a trial to make sure that justice was served and Mr. Nixon was punished, and where "losers" were complaining about the press and defending the Republican record, to the point where a Presidential expression of forgiveness authorized by the Constitution was understood to be an essential precondition to the restoration of national unity. He lifted us all to a higher level of reconciliation than would have been possible had Mr. Nixon been put on trial. Along with others, I lost the ensuing election, but now I have to ask, "So what?" The Presidential pardon put Watergate behind us once and for all. The healing process began. The country started to mend. Losing an election was worth it. Ford did the right thing, the brave thing, the wise thing, the compassionate thing.

The most sublime expression in American political history of the ability to transcend winning and losing is undoubtedly the magnanimity of Abraham Lincoln. Lincoln's humility before a sovereign God who stood above and beyond both sides of the tragic conflict, and his willingness to forgive his critics and enemies, as well as the South, expressed that kind of love in action which alone can carry us beyond power politics and self-interest, beyond "brutal victory and cruel defeat," beyond judgment and self-righteousness. In Lincoln's goodness, in his kindness and magnanimous spirit, American political thought ascended—as John P. Diggins concluded in his brilliant study *The Lost Soul of American Politics*—"and ascending, reached spiritual ecstasy."

Lincoln understood the partiality of all human perspectives. He fathomed the truth that all virtue does not necessarily inhere in the winner, nor all vice in the loser. Although he practiced the spoils system, Lincoln's spirit ran counter to its philosophy, and when Cabinet members protested his appointment of a Democrat, they received the reply, "Oh, I can't afford to punish every person who has seen fit to oppose my election. We want a competent man in this office." He recognized the taint of self-interest and sinfulness in the North as well as in the South. He acknowledged "the judgments of the Lord" on both sides. And in doing all this, he pointed the country beyond victory and defeat to a national reconciliation, a reformation, a rebirth, based on mutual compassion and forgiveness, where the wounds of all would be healed and the ones who had borne the battle, as well as their widows and orphans, would be cared for. As he wrote to a correspondent, "I shall do nothing in malice. What I deal with is too vast for malicious dealing." And thus he lifted us to a higher plane of community that would restore a feeling of national unity and well-being.

Whenever we lose, our natural human tendency is to justify ourselves and make excuses; whenever we win, our natural human tendency is to feel victorious and to gloat about our triumph. But we must learn that there are values beyond winning and losing, values that we must try to incorporate in our approach to victory and defeat. I suppose many Christians value Jesus Christ because he can provide us with strength and success in this life, even though worldly success runs counter to his whole character and mission. His sacrificial and crucified spirit should instruct us in how to handle victory and defeat, and perhaps illumine for us the way in which anguish and suffering become the vehicles for higher meaning in politics, and certainly higher meaning in life. Lincoln implies in his Gettysburg Address that the death of good, young, innocent, brave men on both sides had to do with much more than achieving a victory for their own side; it had to do with redeeming America from the sins of the past, making some kind of atonement, and ushering in a "new birth." Just so, for us; we have to recognize that spiritual ordeals through which we pass can lead to renewal. Our pain, our suffering, our losing need not prompt us to despair, or become defiant, or endure stoically; they can free us from forces that enslave the spirit and can make us better human beings.

"I shall do nothing in malice."

Just because our biblical faith embraces the pain that life's defeats bring us and helps us to understand how loss can become gain, this does not mean that ours is a religion of losers; quite the contrary. Biblical religion enables us to rise above power politics, where all that counts is winning and losing, to a level of understanding of ourselves and life and destiny that is more enlightened and constructive.

A theology of losing, then, is really what life and scripture encourage us to develop as we travel our pilgrim way. For we all lose. All God's children hurt. We all have problems, but we need not be overcome by them. We need not give in. We need not become poor losers. We can be surprised by God when we lose, and we can learn that there are more important things in life than winning and losing. We can be true to truth. We can discover the comfort of God's presence and the guiding hand of his providence. We can grow in the measure of mercy that we possess. And we can go forward into our tomorrows as better persons, praying with Sir George MacLeod of the Iona Community off the coast of Scotland, "O God, wield well Thy tools in the workshop of the world, that we who come rough-hewn to Thy bench may be fashioned to a greater beauty and purpose by Thy hand. Amen."

7

Decisions, Decisions, Decisions

Early in December each year, when the Indiana Society of Chicago meets in (where else?) Chicago, my wife and I visit Winnetka Presbyterian Church, where my brother Bob is the pastor. We enjoy his preaching and sharing in the warmth and joy and openness of an unusually close-knit congregation. He always asks me to speak at the adult forum hour on some subject related to religion and politics, and in December 1985 he suggested the topic "How a Christian Makes Decisions in Public Life."

"Part of his background is that Bill is a good Republican," Bob told the congregation, "which is to some a contradiction in terms and to others redundant. Another part of Bill's background is that he was a four-letter man in high school. All his life he has wanted to appear on the front page of a sports section, and finally he got his wish—in Baltimore!—where the four-letter man became a four-letter word. We're delighted Bill could take time out from the suit that Baltimore has lodged against him as a conspirator. We have two brothers who are lawyers, neither of whom has volunteered to pick up his defense, which suggests that maybe the defense is not as viable as Bill would hope, although of course they are not criminal lawyers either. Bill has been a trial to many of us for years."

Bob's large dose of raspberries continued, including a reference to a statement of mine that had recently been included on the quotation page of *U.S. News & World Report.* "The magazine reports that Bill has asked the question, 'Are we ready to peel the hot potatoes?' regarding the federal budget—an observation whose sagacity was exceeded only by the remarkably culinary metaphor, in view of the fact that Bill, to my knowledge, has never peeled a potato, hot or cold, in his life." Eventually, Bob ran out of stories to tell on his older brother, presented me as the Old Gray Mayor, and let me proceed with my thoughts on making decisions in a biblical context.

To begin with, the question of whether or not one's faith—one's biblically based view of life, one's Christianity—helps one make decisions in the public arena, or in any other for that matter, has no easy answer. The obvious response is, "Yes, it does, and here's how." That's the answer the question begs. That's the answer we want to give. But while on the one hand I say, "Yes, it does," first I must say, "No, it does not. Not necessarily." We cannot just glibly assume that Christian faith makes a difference in our decision-making process.

Why do I say, "not necessarily"? For one thing, people coming at a problem from different points of view can all reach the same conclusion. The result may be the same regardless of the frame of reference from which the decision-makers move into that position. For example, I sit down on Monday mornings with my senior staff, and with the President and the Majority Leader of the City-County Council. Assume one is Christian, one is Jewish, one is agnostic; one goes to church regularly, another never darkens the door. We talk over problems, we share ideas, we decide. We are different people with different backgrounds and beliefs, but we agree on the course of action to be followed. The decisions are pragmatic—they do not involve our theological and biblical perspectives, or lack of them—so why do our beliefs matter? What difference does it make that I am a confessing Christian?

In the second place, before we too quickly assume religion can make a difference in our decision-making, we must remember that conscientious believers often disagree on what course of action should be followed. There are Christians on both sides of practically every issue. Is there a right biblical answer in every situation? I doubt it. The Bible is not a book of pat answers. During the Civil War, there were good church people who supported the North and equally good people who supported the South. The pro-life/pro-choice controversy finds devout Christians on both sides of the issue, equally sincere, equally passionate. Sincere religious people belong to all political parties and espouse different solutions to problems our country faces. So what difference does it make, what we believe, if our beliefs lead us in exactly opposite directions?

And then, third, there are even times when Christianity—or certain versions of it—can be quite irrelevant in the decision-making process. Reinhold Niebuhr used to talk about the irrelevance of righteousness. As an example, he explained that while there is a place for pacifism in the total picture, in terms of international relations if we were all pacifists, the people with the guns would run over the people with the butter. When Nazi storm troopers were marching across Europe a generation or two ago, pacifism seemed irrelevant. (Now, half a century later, however, nuclear pacifism may be terribly timely and helpful.)

On a more local level, those of us in city government sometimes deal with people who tend to think solely in terms of "moral" issues—like substance abuse, massage parlors, adult bookstores, that sort of thing. While these activities merit attention, they do not constitute the whole story. There is more to urban America than this, and it disappoints me that some "good Christians" do not seem to have many helpful suggestions when it comes to the really tough issues of our day—jobs, housing, quality education, crime, protection of the environment, and the like. I remember visiting with a group of ministers about a couple of these "moral" concerns. During the course of our conversation I asked them if each would help by hiring an economically disadvantaged youth in the summertime to mow grass or wash windows—just to give the young people jobs and some sense of self-worth and to keep them off the streets. No response. No helping hand. All they gave me was criticism of government job-training programs. I left the meeting very disillusioned, somewhat angry, and convinced that Niebuhr was right: there are some forms of righteousness that are extraordinarily irrelevant.

Now, with all these disclaimers behind me, let me say that "Yes, of course, biblical faith really should and often does make a difference in my decision-making process—for the better, I hope." I'd like to think that it establishes the *context* in which I try to make my decisions, it refers me to the proper *source* of those decisions, it points those decisions in a certain *direction,* and it informs the *style* in which the decisions are made. Let's look at each in turn.

I believe my life is wrapped up in God's providence. That is the *context* for my decision-making. God's love supplies purpose beyond the pain of life; his truth supplies meaning beyond the perplexity. The purpose of my existence is to let God's purpose flow through me, as ink flows through a fountain pen, so I can better express his love. I am here to help out—to be a burden bearer, a servant, an agent of reconciliation—and I believe God wants to branch out into life through me.

Within this context, it is possible for me to sit somewhat loose in the historical saddle. I need not fret too much or be too anxious about my decisions. I can let go of them because God is there, because "there's a divinity that shapes our ends, rough-hew them how we will." I know that things can very well work out in spite of me as well as because of me. In the constant friction and restlessness and nervousness of the decision-making process in which I am unremittingly involved, I can be somewhat nonchalant, because I know I am justified by faith—by grace received in faith—not by works, not by my own merit, not by whether my decisions are right or wrong. As is written in both the Old and New Testaments, "The just shall live by faith." Jesus said that the hairs of our head are numbered. He also said that not a sparrow falls to the ground "forgotten before God," adding, "Fear not; you are of more value than many sparrows." Jesus was reminding us that our lives are comprehended within the providence of a loving heavenly Father and that we can live out our days with the confidence that nothing can separate us from that love. This confidence provides us with a steady point on our compass amid the swirl of history. In the midst of change and decay, the One who changes not "abides with me."

Abraham Lincoln exemplified serenity in the midst of chaos as well as anyone in American public life. Although subjected to the vilest criticism, facing antagonists on both sides who would have happily dissolved the union to see their views on slavery prevail, and horrified by the waste of life and property occasioned by the Civil War, Lincoln did not capitulate to cynicism or nihilism. He maintained his poise. He stayed in touch with the Infinite. He had a profoundly biblical understanding of God's providence, and a sincere desire to align himself with God's purpose, praying, "not that God be on our side, but that we be on His." He was able to transcend the push and pull of events around him and serve as a balance wheel for the nation. His strong biblical understanding of the providence of God supplied him with a context in which to make his decisions. In his famous interview with the distinguished Quaker Mrs. Eliza Gurney, Lincoln spoke of God's "wise purpose" and said, "We cannot but believe, that He who made the world still governs it."

In this interview, Lincoln also spoke of having been placed in a "very responsible position" as "a humble instrument in the hands of our Heavenly Father . . . to work out His great purposes." He said that he desired "that all my works and acts may be according to His will." God's will thus becomes the *source* of the decisions we make. The politician who is operating from a grounding in biblical faith should seek God's will and try to do what is right in the light of his or her understanding of that will.

One historian, James G. Randall, says that "there is ample reason to believe that Lincoln [in reaching his historic decision to issue the Emancipation Proclamation] had not only endured anxious hours, but had undergone a significant inner experience from which he emerged with quiet serenity." Lincoln rooted his major decisions in his solid knowledge of the Bible and his deep immersion in a life of prayer. He once referred to the Bible as "the best gift God has given to man." And his friend, newspaperman Noah Brooks, recalled, "He said that after he went to the White House, he kept up the habit of daily prayer."

Lincoln sets us a good example. Important decisions that we make must be grounded in an effort to discern God's will. Bible reading, quiet meditation, prayer, participation in public worship, conversation with close friends and loved ones, counseling—all these can help. They are vehicles for God to break through to us and communicate his will to us. They can be very helpful and must be used if we really want to align our will with God's and follow his lead in our decision-making. "Whatever you ask in prayer, you will receive, if you have faith."

Before making an important decision, our task is to seek God's will and the rest will flow from that. "Seek first his kingdom and his righteousness, and all these things shall be yours as well." In his famous essay on Tolstoy's philosophy of history, Isaiah Berlin divides the world's great thinkers into "hedgehogs" (those who "know one big thing," who have a unitary vision of life and truth and reduce everything to a coherent system) and "foxes" (those who observe the variety of the world, who know "many things" and pursue "many ends," who do not insist on relating everything to a single central vision, but instead lead lives, perform acts, and entertain ideas that are "centrifugal rather than centripetal"). Brilliant though this analysis is, it probably oversimplifies. Won't the biblically oriented person be both a hedgehog and a fox? On the one hand, he or she will relate everything to God's will, to "his kingdom and his righteousness," but on the other hand, God's will is going to play itself out in a host of ways in life and take us down many different centrifugal paths. To mix the metaphor, it's like the falconer and the gyre of the falcon—the bird flies out and around in many different directions but always comes back to its master in dead center. We seek to discern the will of God, then we act. We cultivate fellowship with him, then we move responsibly into history. The pendulum swings between disengagement and involvement, between withdrawal and penetration, and we live out our days balanced between the two.

When we are faced with a major decision, one that takes time and thought to work through, it is clear that we should prayerfully and carefully seek God's will. But what about the little choices, the countless day-to-day decisions a Christian in public life must make? We may not consciously stop and ask what is God's will in each particular instance, but I think we can try to do that in a general sort of way.

I was quite touched not long ago in church to hear our pastor, Bill Enright, describe how a prominent member of Second Church tries to let his religion influence his decisions. He said this individual confesses that he tries to ask himself maybe half a dozen times a day when he is making decisions, "What would Jesus have me do?" In discussing his statement, my mother reminded me that she was raised with the same philosophy, sincerely trying to "live in Christ's light and walk in his way" each day, as we used to say in our family prayer around the dinner table. It is crucially important to make one's decisions on the basis of "firmness in the right, as God gives us to see the right," and not on the basis of self-interest or expediency. The source of my decision-making process should be God's will, not mine. "God be in my head and in my understanding." That's the controlling principle.

It is instructive to note that Lincoln did not let serenity paralyze him. His faith moved him in the *direction* of engaging in life's struggle. His belief, deeply rooted in his quiet hours and significant inner experiences, that God's will was being worked out in the "fiery trial" through which the nation was passing, did not bog him down in uncertainty or irresolution. He acted decisively. He engaged history. He proceeded with "executive confidence." He said, "We—even we here —hold the power and bear the responsibility." Lincoln conscientiously sought to know the will of God in fulfilling his day-to-day responsibilities, living in a balance between his belief that "the will of God prevails" and his determination to "do the very best I know how, the very best I can." He combined moral resoluteness with a faith in the providence of God that gave him a vantage point over the struggle in which he was involved. His biblical faith propelled him into the fray, not away from it.

My father used to tell us as we were growing up that there were three important decisions we would have to make in life: where we would work, whom we would marry, and what we would believe. He encouraged us in each instance to try to discover God's will for our life, but he also advised us to lay the decision out on a yellow pad, listing the pros and cons on each side of a penciled line. He taught us that God's will has to be figured out, and that it must be related to the critical decisions we make as we travel through life.

Biblical religion will help direct our decision-making process, not only because it thrusts us into life as responsible actors in the drama of history but also because it moves us in the direction of love and justice and freedom. God's will is to enlarge those values in our world. The principle, mentioned in chapter 5, "Truth is in order to goodness" applies here. It means that our decisions are true and right if they lead to an increase in the amount of love and justice and freedom in the world.

We have to ask ourselves if our decisions help people, whether they bring healing where there is hurt and reconciliation where there is polarization. I love the sentence, so profoundly biblical, from Alan Paton's introduction to *Cry, the Beloved Country:* "I look forward to the day when we shall realize that the only lasting and worthwhile solution to our grave and profound problems lies not in the love of power, but in the power of love, without which life would be an intolerable bondage, condemning us all to an existence of violence, misery, and fear." Our decision-making process should be characterized by active compassion and sensitivity to human hurt and distress. It should move us in the direction of wanting to release more of the "power of love" in life. "Make love your aim."

justice too

Make justice your aim too, God commands us. He wants our decisions to move in that direction also. "Let justice roll down like waters," thundered the prophet Amos, "and righteousness like an ever-flowing stream." Perfect justice cannot be achieved in our finite world, but we can work toward it, we can approximate it. The biblical goal for human society is a just ordering of relationships—wholeness, fairness, health, peace—and biblical religion forces me to ask of my decisions if they move things in this direction.

freedom too

And also, I must ask if they move things in the direction of more freedom. The Bible is a story about oppressed people going free. Moses led the Israelites out of captivity into the Promised Land. Jesus came to free people from sin. If my decisions can free people from poor housing or hunger or racial prejudice or sexism or poverty or illiteracy or any other kind of chains, my decisions are proceeding in the right direction. "Stand fast in liberty."

Love and justice and freedom are constructive, not negative, forces in life. So another way of putting all this is that biblical faith will propel our decision-making in a positive direction. With Isaiah, our Hebraic-Christian faith believes that "every valley shall be lifted up, and every mountain and hill be made low; the uneven ground shall become level, and the rough places a plain." Biblical faith believes that "the way of the Lord" can be prepared even in the wilderness, and that even in the desert "a highway for our God" can appear. Biblical faith centers on the transforming possibilities in life. It takes gigantic negatives like sin and death and turns them into plus signs, so that with Paul we can exult, "Thanks be to God, who gives us the victory through our Lord Jesus Christ."

So much of our decision-making is negative. We see problems instead of solutions. We think in terms of the downside rather than the upside. We fail to see the positive possibilities in a situation and concentrate on the negative potential.

In government, the tendency of "bureaucrats" is to tell you why something cannot be done, why it won't work. In fact, what we need are positive thinkers who can achieve breakthroughs. I grow terribly tired of people in government who never want to stick their necks out. They never want to risk anything. They pass the buck to someone else. They lay the blame elsewhere. They hunker down and only speak when spoken to. They protect their turf. They never think creatively or bravely. They're negative, that's all there is to it.

Government needs positive thinkers to help make positive decisions. That's what we try to do in Senior Staff meetings. We try to see the big picture and to analyze all the factors involved. We evaluate the pros and cons of different options, we sift through everything, decide which course of action seems the best, and then go ahead. We want to accomplish positive results. We do not have a caretaker philosophy of government. If we did, the Hoosier Dome would never have been built and many other things that have had a positive effect on the revitalization of our city would never have occurred.

In addition to pointing decisions in certain directions and establishing the context of those decisions and introducing us to their proper source, biblical faith also determines the *style* in which our decisions are made. It shapes decisions in four distinct ways.

First, it prompts me to make decisions modestly. We do not possess all knowledge; we can be wrong. "Now we see through a glass, darkly." In addition, we cannot always know what is going to happen—maybe God has other plans. After working with the State of Indiana to land a Chrysler minivan production line in an empty plant in Indianapolis, we were near to closing the deal when, in the spring of 1985, President Reagan announced he was lifting the voluntary restraints on import quotas, and Lee Iacocca immediately canceled Chrysler's plans. I tell people one of the reasons why I like my job is that it is full of surprises. No two days are alike. Every day when I drive downtown I wonder what's going to pop up or break open that I have not anticipated, and usually there is something! So a little modesty in making one's decisions seems to be in order, when one realizes how they can often be changed by things beyond one's control, and that there is a realm beyond human contrivance.

And a little modesty is also in order when one realizes how credit should be spread around. Much more can be accomplished if we do not worry about who receives the credit for a positive accomplishment. Politicians usually want it all for themselves. They like to announce the grants. They enjoy turning the good news to their own advantage. And in the process, they quite often forget others who had a hand in bringing the good projects to fruition or making the good news happen. But if it is true that we are all like the rooster who thinks his crowing makes the sun rise every morning, then it follows that we should be cautious about taking more credit than we deserve. I am grateful for the compliments I receive about the revitalization of Indianapolis and the progress of our city, but I do not deserve all the credit by a long shot. Many people have had a hand in it. A little modesty is always in order. As the Bible enjoins us, we should not think of ourselves "more highly" than we ought to think.

Second, biblical faith leads me to make my decisions as openly as possible. It makes me want to be up-front with people. "Speak the truth in love." I cannot dissimulate or prevaricate. Being candid, admitting when you've made a mistake, not answering "No comment," not stonewalling or giving the impression you have something to hide, helps to build a trusting relationship with others, especially, I think, the press. I loved it when one of my department heads recently admitted publicly, "We screwed up!" James Madison, principal designer of the First Amendment and an important advocate of the public's right to know, was absolutely on target when he wrote, "A popular government, without popular information, or the means of acquiring it, is but a prologue to a farce or a tragedy, or perhaps both."

Jesus talked things over with his disciples. He was straight-up with the money changers in the Temple. He was wide open with the people on Palm Sunday. The health of our democracy depends upon the openness and forthrightness of our public officials. We learned that during Watergate. In the summer of 1974, while I was a member of Congress, we were practicing for the traditional Republican-Democrat baseball game. I happened to be standing on first base with Senator Lowell Weicker. It was just a week or so before President Nixon resigned, and he remarked, "If only the President had been open about what had occurred, none of this tragedy would have happened." Candor would have served our nation well.

In a speech he gave in 1985, Neal Peirce offered rules for those of us who constantly deal with the media. He credits them to Eileen Shanahan, a veteran journalist. She said, "Never prevaricate. If you lie and the press catches you, you'll be pilloried. And they won't believe you in the future either. Move very fast to get information out when you're in trouble. Unlike wine, troublesome information does not improve with age. Getting it all out there on the first day can save one the Chinese water torture of a little more leaking out daily." All this advice centered around the importance of forthrightness in the decision-making process. "Having done all . . . stand fast."

Third, biblical faith supplies us with resolve. It gives us the staying power to hang in there with our decisions and to stand firm. This does not mean that faith makes us rigid or inflexible, but that it provides us with the spiritual strength to maintain a commitment, to be firm in our course of action as God gives us to see it. We had to make a very tough decision a few years ago to close a fire station because of shifting demographics in Indianapolis. The people in that neighborhood were furious. They brought in the ashes from a recent fire in the area and dumped them on my receptionist's desk and yelled and screamed and said we didn't care about them. But we had thought the situation through. We were confident the closing was the best solution, so we stuck to our guns and eventually things worked out all right.

Finally, biblical faith helps us to understand how things are interrelated. Individuals cannot exist in isolation; members of the body cannot function alone. Where one part hurts, everything hurts. Biblical religion helps us overcome the dichotomy between individuals and community. It teaches us that life's meaning has to do not merely with the autonomous self, but with society and history as well. "Seek the welfare of the city . . . , for in its welfare (shalom) you will find your welfare" (Jeremiah 29:7). We must think in terms of what is good for *us* as well as for *me.* We must consider how our decisions will affect others.

With this as background, what about the decisions I have made? I believe they could be placed in one of the following five categories.

1. Sometimes I decide not to decide! It can be a mistake to jump into a battle prematurely—to do so can lead to a lot of stress over an issue one does not have to be involved in. Let me cite two examples.

In the debate that rages in our country over abortion, people from both sides of the issue come to me and ask for my view. They want to know where I stand. I explain that my job in the executive branch of government is to enforce the laws, that decisions about abortion are made at the federal and state level, and that I must keep the peace for everyone involved in these disputes. My personal views are not relevant to the fulfillment of my executive responsibilities, and therefore it is not necessary that I take a public stand on this issue.

Back in the days of Watergate, I did not jump on the impeachment bandwagon, even though it might have been to my political benefit to do so. President Nixon had befriended me as a freshman congressman. I had gone to Congress on his coattails, for he won my district by fifteen percentage points and I carried it by two. A cardinal political maxim is that you do not forsake old friends to make new ones. So . . . I was not going to forsake Mr. Nixon prematurely, and decided not to decide until right at the bitter end, when everyone realized that the "smoking gun" had been found.

2. Sometimes I decide expediently. I cannot say that high moral principle *always* informs my decision-making process in the political arena! ("Some things are too important to leave to principle" is a standard joke among politicians.) Often there is just no point in having a big brouhaha over a decision of little significance.

When I was first elected Mayor, I chose as police chief a man who lived outside the county. I felt strongly, however, that the police chief should be a resident of the area he serves, so I told him I would appoint him only if he would promise to relocate. He said he would within six months, as soon as his daughter finished high school. But he never did. He broke his promise and told me that if I didn't like it, I could find myself a new chief. The police department during those initial years of my administration had had some rough going, and we needed the stability and good management the new chief had brought to his department. My decision not to force the issue was an expedient one, but probably the right one as well.

It was also expediency that prompted me to go before the State Legislature in 1985 and support seatbelt legislation. I hoped it would send a strong signal of good faith to the different automobile companies we were working with in Indianapolis and might even lay good groundwork for future economic development opportunities with the manufacturers who wanted the legislation to pass. Many people objected to the bill as an infringement on their personal freedom, but it was not a big deal to me one way or the other. I supported the legislation, which was the expedient choice to make.

3. Sometimes I make the wrong decision. It would be absolutely foolish of me to say that all my decisions have been proper. I am a frail, finite, fragile child of God like everyone else, and I certainly make mistakes. The key, I suppose, when I make an erroneous decision, is to admit it and not to stay bound to the wrong course of action.

admit it, shift course

Sometimes my decisions are wrong from the beginning, and these are quite often the result of anger or frustration. For example, when a very important bond issue that would have made possible $45 million worth of redevelopment projects in the heart of our city and throughout the neighborhoods was defeated in the spring of 1985, I was very upset and disappointed, and in a news conference I made some comments about the motives of the people who had led the remonstrance that I should not have made. I made the wrong decision, and subsequently apologized for it.

In other situations my decisions are wrong because of their consequences. During the winter of 1984–85 we decided to have a public discussion about the possibility of a new landfill in our community— some 2,000 tons of trash accumulate on a daily basis in Indianapolis and we have to put it somewhere! When we realized what fierce and antagonistic reactions people had, and when we saw how they berated our Director of Public Works at the meetings we scheduled, we knew our decision had been an error. Citizens stormed the City-County Building, they participated in phone-in and write-in campaigns to my office, and they passed "rat patrol" buttons all over town.

But God's providence is an amazing thing. Our adversity must have been his opportunity, and the door that slammed in our faces resulted in another's opening somewhere else. Because we backed off the idea of more landfill, we came up with the solution of burning our garbage and trash instead of burying it. We are now in the process of instituting a plan that makes a great deal of economic and environmental sense whereby, in a joint venture with the private sector, we are going to build a resource-recovery mass burn facility that will take our trash, burn it up, turn it into steam, and leave a very modest residue of sterile ash that can be recycled or buried in existing landfill space. The steam will be sold to private companies—"trash to ash to cash," we call it!

4. Sometimes I decide easily. Amazingly enough, some of the most significant decisions are made without difficulty because the correct choice seems very clear.

It did not take long to decide whether or not to enter into conversations with Bob Irsay when it became known to us that he was considering a relocation of his Baltimore Colts franchise. The upside of being in the NFL with all the resulting positive consequences for our city far outweighed the downside risks.

The decision to resist the Justice Department's lawsuit against Indianapolis, seeking to dismantle our affirmative action program, also was an easy one to make because I firmly believed, as explained in the next chapter, that the Justice Department was wrong legally, morally, and politically.

Our city, like a dozen others, has been interested in the possibility of securing a major league baseball franchise. We have made a presentation to the expansion committee, but we have no idea when and if a franchise might be awarded to Indianapolis. Consequently, it would be imprudent of us to proceed with the construction of a new $30- to $40-million open-air, grass-turf, 40,000-seat stadium built to Major League specifications, and we have decided not to do it until we are sure we would have a franchise. In the case of the Hoosier Dome, we expanded the Convention Center and were able to justify the decision irrespective of whether or not an NFL team played in it. But in this case, a free-standing facility would have no other use than baseball. Some of our most avid baseball fans want us to build it anyway and provide a new home for the Indianapolis Indians, our triple A team. But we have decided not to proceed. The risk would be too great. The decision was relatively easy.

5. Most of the time, I decide with difficulty. In a job like being the mayor of a large city, there are many tough decisions that have to be made in an atmosphere of almost constant publicity and unremitting criticism.

Back in 1977, I deliberated carefully on a decision to appoint a black as Deputy Mayor. This had never been done in our city, but I felt the time was right. I learned of a capable young accountant who was identified with the black Republicans in Indianapolis, so I began laying the groundwork. I talked to a number of different political types, made sure the City-County Council would not reject my nomination when confirmation time came, and sounded out the movers and shakers in our community. I knew there would be some raised eyebrows and possibly some open criticism, and I did everything I could to make things go smoothly, announcing the appointment on Martin Luther

King, Jr.,'s birthday. Joe Slash has turned out to be a first-rate public servant, and I have never had any occasion to regret my decision to appoint him. Fortunately, a decade later, we can look back at this decision with some surprise that it caused such concern, but at the time it involved sticking out my neck pretty far. It was the right decision, but a tough one.

Mention difficult decisions and I cannot help picturing police cars and hearing sirens wailing! One of the toughest decisions I've ever had to make was to support the Public Safety Director and Police Chief when they came to me in 1977 and recommended terminating the take-home car program we had for our police officers. I was concerned about how the rank-and-file officers would react if we made this decision, but that concern was counterbalanced by the realization that the program was no longer practical. When it had been instituted by my predecessor, Richard Lugar, the cars cost the city about $1,500 apiece. By the mid-1970s, however, they were up to $5,500, with no signs that the trend would ever reverse. We just could not afford to continue the expense, so we terminated the program and computed into the salaries and wage and benefit scales of the police department a figure to make up for the loss of that privilege. We did our best to compensate the officers who lost the cars, but nonetheless the disgruntlement was enormous. Everything came to a head one hot August afternoon when the officers circled the City-County Building (where my office just happens to be), turned on their lights and sirens, locked the car doors, and threw the keys into a basket. A difficult decision had been made and the consequences were distressing, but amazingly enough we unscrambled the mess and lived to tell about it!

A lot of decisions are tough because they fall into the category of "no win." They are lose-lose. We decide to override our Department of Transportation about a street plan because the neighbors object, and the paper says we caved in to neighborhood pressure; we decide to uphold DOT and we are depicted as insensitive to neighborhood needs. We build a mass burn facility to convert our trash into steam, and the community is told that we are gambling that we won't contaminate the air with dioxins; we don't build it and continue to dump the trash into a landfill, and the community is informed that we are polluting the groundwater with dioxins and other awful stuff! We provide a business with tax abatement and other incentives, and we are accused of unwarranted government subsidy of the private enterprise system; we don't provide those benefits, and the business collapses and it's our fault. I once received some bad press because my code enforcement people filed a lawsuit against a little church, so I issued a policy stating that we would not sue any churches or not-for-profits until I personally talked to the pastor or head of the organization to explain the problem and its consequences. You know what happened then. I was accused of favoritism and having a double standard and not treating everyone equally! Lose-lose!

Nonetheless, difficult issues ought to be faced—preferably before a crisis arises and the course of events leaves you no choice. When we did an actuarial study in 1984 and discovered that ten years out we would be facing a very substantial unfunded liability problem in the police and fire department pension funds, we decided to take corrective action immediately, rather than follow the advice of some people who said, "It's not our problem. Let people solve it later." But that would not have been responsible.

Our city has all the typical big-city problems, which must be faced and dealt with, not ignored or put off—pollution, the need for clean air and water, trash disposal; high unemployment among young minorities, and dislocation caused by the transition from the Industrial to the Information Age; the need for funding city services and maintaining our capital infrastructure; housing, transportation, police-community relations, education; and so on. Leaving them for someone else to solve would possibly avoid some controversy, but in the long run it would constitute a disservice to the people. Those who have been elected to govern ought to be willing to make difficult decisions and accept the consequences. Political leaders at their finest have the "guts" to take on the really hard issues and to be true to what they know is right and best.

At the federal level, it is crucially important to face the problem of the federal deficit, a much more serious problem, in my opinion, than tax reform. Unless taxes are going to be increased, the solution lies in slowing down spending by the federal government all across the board, reining it in to a sustainable rate of growth and looking elsewhere than to the so-called "controllable" urban social programs for savings. Gramm-Rudman is a step in this direction, although a side step for Congress, since responsibility for budgetary restraint is shifted to an automatic trigger mechanism. When we are facing severe shortfalls in funding and a frightening scarcity of resources, it is imperative that all areas of government spending share in the sacrifices. No cow should be sacred, no program sacrosanct.

This will require the "weaning of America"—a process in which the people of this nation reduce their expectations of government at all levels, stop looking to government for solutions to all their problems, and begin to take some of the responsibility for those problems on themselves. Ever since the New Deal, the trend has been to boost government assistance programs. But those days are over. The train

needs to be slowed down. We must stop going to Washington with a
tin cup in our hands, always wanting more. Government at all levels
must learn to practice creative frugality.

The cities have taken their fair share of the cuts since 1980. Two
thirds of the first round of cuts—$35 billion—came from 14 percent
of the budget. And not a dime has been gained on the federal deficit.
Entitlement programs and the defense budget need to be given the
same kind of microscopic scrutiny that urban programs have received,
for these lie at the heart of the fiscal crisis in Washington today and
ought not be put off until tomorrow. Tomorrow is today.

It's a political problem, and it requires political will to solve it. We
need statesmen on both sides who will rise above demagoguery and
talk about the national interest. The deficit will not be reduced until
liberals start talking about capping the entitlement programs and conservatives start talking about capping defense. It's easy for liberals to
support social service programs and criticize the military-industrial
establishment, and for conservatives to do the opposite. Not until
conservatives honestly recognize that the Pentagon should be run on
a more businesslike basis and that waste and mismanagement there
should be curbed, not until liberals honestly recognize that ever-
escalating entitlement programs will require outlays that the American
economy will not be able to sustain, and not until these two groups
engage in responsible dialogue and forge an effective bipartisan coalition, will we be able to disenthrall our country from the debilitating
effects of political rhetoric and focus on finding a solution to the grave
fiscal problem of restraining growth of government spending that
vexes us all. Liberal claims that the President and conservatives are
mean-spirited and insensitive to the problems of the poor, the disadvantaged, and the elderly are unfair; so are conservative allegations
that any liberal who questions spending or demands accountability at
the Pentagon is unpatriotic or "soft" on the Soviet Union.

The only questions are: Will political leaders have enough wisdom
and courage to act? And will they have enough feelings of partnership
to cooperate for the good of the country? Will the American people
have enough patience and tolerance to let them try? It may mean
shaving some points off one's margin of victory, or maybe even losing
an election, but would that be so bad if in the process our country's
dialogue could be focused on this overriding issue and a solution could
be found?

The difficult decisions, like those just described, require discern-
ment, because there are no easy answers. People feel very strongly on
both sides of an issue, and there are weighty arguments in favor of each
side. You simply have to make up your mind and do the best you can,
knowing that we live in a realm of indeterminate grays rather than a

grays, not black + white

realm where there are absolute blacks and whites. Nobody has put it any better than Lincoln did when he said, "The true rule in determining to embrace or reject anything is not whether it has any evil in it, but whether it has more of evil than of good. There are few things wholly evil or wholly good. Almost everything, especially of government policy, is an inseparable compound of the two; so that our best judgement of the preponderance between them is continually demanded."

The final thing to be said about decision-making and biblical faith is that once we have put our hand to the plow, we must not look back. If we do, we are not "fit for the kingdom." After bringing our best thinking to bear on a decision, and after making that decision, we proceed to other things. We do not agonize any more or let ourselves be paralyzed by worrying whether it was right and whether things are going to work out. Knowing we are justified by faith, not by works, we relax. At the end of the decision-making process, we find ourselves back where we started—in the context of God's love, under the umbrella of his providence. If a mistake has been made, we admit it and then look for a way to correct our error. But we do not fret constantly. "Do not be anxious!" The grief may be there, but so is the grace. At the end of the day, we let go of our decision and move on to another.

8

"An Empire of Laws"—
For All

"I am embarrassed to be associated with the same denomination and Presbytery that you are associated with."

"You are proposing to turn Indianapolis into a cultural wasteland."

"What you permitted was an exact enactment of the crucifixion 2,000 years ago."

"I hope you get assassinated."

These comments stem from four controversies I was embroiled in during my years as Mayor. They were made by (1) a fellow Presbyterian minister who was aggravated by a City zoning decision; (2) the head of the Indiana Civil Liberties Union discussing an anti-pornography ordinance I was supporting in the Indianapolis City-County Council; (3) a local clergyman who was upset about the removal of the Nativity scene from Christmas decorations in an Indianapolis city park; and (4) an anonymous letter writer who did not like my views on affirmative action.

Remarks like these can be discomforting, but sometimes they must be endured. You can't cop out on your responsibility just because you want everyone to like you—or because you can't decide which side of the fence to sit on.

Ministers tend to be thin-skinned. They want to be liked. They prefer smoothing over to ruffling feathers. So when one of them, like me, is thrown into the hurly-burly of political life, it can get a little rough. Being subjected to criticism that is not only stinging but often unfair—a category into which I think the above expressions of opinion fall—can hurt.

Ministers quite properly try to see both sides of an argument. In marriage counseling, for example, they learn there are very definitely two sides to most questions; the issues are rarely clear-cut. Nearly every time as Mayor that I have had to deal with a police–community relations problem, the same thing has been true—there has been something to be said by and for the police; something to be said by and for the aggrieved citizen. Just so, in these four controversies, there was right and wrong on both sides. All that could be done was to determine where the preponderance of right lay, and then to act. To do nothing would be irresponsible. As Lincoln said, "We cannot escape history." Just because life gives us few absolutely clear choices between good and evil, just because all our decisions must be made in the fog of ambiguity, just because we ought never presume to equate God's will with our limited perspective or our finite actions, all this does not mean we should not engage in responsible decision-making and decisive action. The religious person who engages in the political process has a frame of reference that transcends the finitude and ambiguity of that process, but nonetheless engages in it with humble resolve. He or she exercises the biblical ethic of responsibility.

When controversies arise, you don't back away from them. If you can't stand the heat, get out of the kitchen; Harry Truman was right. If you stay in the kitchen, you take the heat. And take it you can, if you think you are right and have confidence that your cause is honorable and just. According to my father, Dr. Fosdick used to advise his students to pick their battles carefully, and never to fight a major battle on a minor front. To all of us there come opportunities to join the fray, to stand up and be counted. To back away from them is cowardice; to choose them carefully is wisdom; to rise to them is courage of a high order. I like Reinhold Niebuhr's prayer: "God grant me the courage to change what can be changed, the serenity to accept what cannot be changed, and the wisdom to know one from the other."

The following are four controversies I have been engaged in since becoming Mayor which I consider significant, although others might have chosen differently. Each of them involved high-running emotions and bitter words and hyperbolic accusations, yet in every instance there were significant lessons to be learned.

We obviously learn about handling the heat, but beyond that we learn some important things about our country. We realize that ours is "an empire of laws and not of men" (a distinction I discovered in Politics I at Princeton when we read Harrington's *Oceana,* dating back to the seventeenth century), and if we are going to realize our dream, to which we pledge our allegiance, of "liberty and justice *for all,*" we must do our best to be sure that in terms of public policy and private practice everyone is treated equally.

There is biblical basis for the idea that we should not take the law into our own hands but rather, as Paul suggests in Romans 13, be "subject to the governing authorities." Granted, the Bible amply supports the other truth too, which is that when our conscience dictates that we should oppose existing authority, under God we have the right to do it. That having been said, however, we must recognize that anarchy and chaos are the alternatives to having an orderly community based on laws duly passed and willingly obeyed. And I think that is what Paul was driving at when he went on to talk about paying taxes to whom taxes are due, revenue to whom revenue is due, respect to whom respect is due, and honor to whom honor is due; even though I would not go so far as to equate all earthly authority as coming from God, nor after fifteen years in politics would I be tempted to identify all governmental authorities as "ministers of God"!

Paul also said in his letter to the Romans that "all Israel will be saved." I like his emphasis on the word *all.* Christ prayed that all might be one. Proverbs reminds us that "the rich and the poor meet together; the Lord is the maker of them all," and we are told in Acts that "God has made of one blood all nations of men to dwell on the face of the earth." In short, a careful reading of scripture seems to propel us toward an inclusive rather than an exclusive approach not only to religion but also to the practice of democracy. The thrust is toward universality, not parochialism; the image is more properly that of mother than virgin; the spirit, one of compassion and tolerance; the commitment, to equality for all.

The first two cases had to do with abiding by the law, observing due process, doing things "decently and in order," as we Presbyterians would put it. Classical political philosophers like Harrington, Locke, and Montesquieu, building on Plato and Aristotle and influencing the thought of the founders of our country, warned against taking the law into our own hands. They believed that just as personal liberty depends upon the empire of our reason, the absence of which would betray us to the bondage of our passions, so in the state, the government through law enthrones reason, subdues passion, and secures liberty. They disagreed with Machiavelli and Thomas Hobbes, who believed laws are nothing but "words and paper" without "the hands and swords of men" to enforce them. They bequeathed to us the notion that the spiritual force of a government resting on law constitutes "the soul of a nation or city" (Harrington).

Lincoln picked up these themes early in his career. In his 1838 Lyceum Address in Springfield, worried by the violence and lawlessness that led a howling mob to lynch the abolitionist editor Elijah P. Lovejoy at Alton, Illinois, just three months before, Lincoln observed that even though emotions played a role in the revolutionary founding of our Republic, to sustain our system of government requires "reason, cold, calculating, unimpassioned reason." He pleaded, "Let reverence for the laws . . . become the political religion of the nation; and let the old and the young, the rich and the poor, the grave and the gay, of all sexes and tongues, and colors and conditions, sacrifice unceasingly on its altars." Naturally, in the exigencies of this or that historic moment, the pendulum swings one way or the other between freedom and order, but throughout the framework of both is supplied by law. Our government is "an empire of laws and not of men."

The zoning controversy had to do with the efforts of the Villages, Inc., a wonderful nonprofit organization founded in Topeka, Kansas, in 1964 by Dr. Karl Menninger to provide "family homes" for abused, abandoned, and neglected children, aged six and above. What can be more worthwhile than that? Many, many children growing up without viable families benefit tremendously from the twenty homes operated by the Villages in our country. It's a beautiful expression of compassionate action motivated by a very pure love.

Unfortunately, when the Villages decided to establish themselves in Indianapolis, they did not follow the advice that other City officials and I gave them when they came in to visit with us. We recommended that they work with the appropriate zoning authorities in our Department of Metropolitan Development to make sure that everything was proper for zoning their group home in a well-established, high-income neighborhood on the north side of our city. They did not feel, however, that the single-family dwelling they had purchased could be rightfully defined as a "group home," since in their interpretation one family would reside there, regardless of the fact that the houseparents would have ten unrelated children living with them. Feeling no obligation to go through the rezoning procedures for this home, they embarked on the project on their own.

Inevitably, trouble soon arose. The zoning authorities took issue with the independent action of the Villages and hauled them into court. In the opinion of our Administrator, the home did not qualify as a "one-family dwelling," as permitted in that neighborhood, and rezoning for "foster family care" or a "boarding home" or a "group home" or a "child caring institution," depending on the number of youngsters involved, would have to be obtained.

The Marion County Municipal Court ruled in favor of the Villages; then, upon appeal by the City, the Indiana Court of Appeals reversed the local court's decision. Still the matter was not settled. The local court prepared an order to terminate the Villages' use of the property, but when the parties could not agree on a proper effective date, a petition was filed with the appellate court requesting instructions.

After oral arguments were heard and the date agreed upon, the Villages' attorneys, who still contended they were immune from zoning requirements, appealed the issue all the way to the Supreme Court.

In the meantime, the neighborhood rose up in arms. We received several inquiries asking why the City was permitting "institutional use" in an area zoned for single families. There were a couple of neighborhood meetings, attended by some 150 people, most of whom were opposed to the facility. The situation became emotional and stories began to circulate about the neighborhood escapades—accusations of peeping Toms and break-ins and that sort of thing—of some of the children in the home, which had been opened without a permit.

Naturally, the supporters of the Villages rallied to try to mount a counterpressure campaign on City Hall. I received many angry letters charging that the City was being unfair. One stated there was "no excuse for the meanness exhibited by the City" and went on to assert that "rejection by a city which claims to be a great place for families and by an administration headed by a prominent Christian minister" constituted a kind of final humiliation for children who "have been sexually and physically abused, abandoned and left at bus depots, spent years living out of the back of cars, separated from siblings, had adoptions terminated, and the list goes on." The first criticism referred to at the beginning of this chapter came from a letter written by the pastor of a local Presbyterian church who had on his staff the wife of the Director of the Villages here in Indiana, so naturally he was directly and emotionally involved in the debate. He wrote that "along with many other citizens with whom I have spoken, I object to you and your administration's efforts (through a local City Council member) and your lack of sensitivity toward today's youth, in what is your apparent concern for only votes in the next election. To play politics with the lives of children—I thought that an ordained minister would be above that ploy." He sent copies of this letter (some of the choicer parts of which I have chosen not to quote) to State Senators, local Presbytery officials, neighborhood associations, and even U.S. Senator Bob Dole, a member of the Board of the Villages.

My response to these angry people was that while I was supportive of the cause of the Villages, I was also concerned that they came into our City and refused to follow due process, not filing for a zoning variance in order to establish their institution properly. I talked with Dr. Menninger about the situation, explained to officials of the organization that we wanted to help resolve the issues, and told them we would try to secure the proper zoning for them if they would come in and work with us. But I reminded everyone involved that we are a government of laws and not of men and that we could not cavalierly disregard due process in the community.

I suggested that if they did not like the law, they should work to change it. Which they did. Once again, I found myself caught in the middle as people lined up to support or oppose Senate Bill 487, introduced in the State Legislature to allow children's boarding homes and childcare institutions in areas zoned for residences and dwellings if certain standards were met. Neighborhood leaders wrote, urging me "to fight with . . . vigor the attempt to achieve . . . neighborhood destruction through the proposed legislation," while I also had letters from the Episcopalian Bishop of Indianapolis and other clergy, as well as many laypeople, supporting the effort to secure passage in the 1985 meeting of the General Assembly. The legislation, however, did not pass.

Nor did the final effort to secure a favorable decision from a local zoning board at the end of the litigation process. The zoning variance was heard after the Supreme Court declined to accept the case, but when the argumentation was held and all the neighbors appeared, in spite of our staff's positive recommendation, the zoning board voted not to grant the variance. The matter was ended—happily for those who opposed the Villages; sadly for those who supported their efforts.

In this instance, we appeared caught between love and justice, and we failed to achieve a synthesis. But elsewhere we did, for there is another Villages project in our community. This home too was established without proper zoning, but the neighborhood did not become aroused, and with city staff support, a variance was applied for and received—demonstrating, I hope, that contrary to the emotional accusations hurled at us, Indianapolis does indeed "have a heart."

In an issue involving pornography and the First Amendment, the City lost and was on the receiving end of decisions that reaffirmed the supremacy of the law over what we—believing our cause to be just and believing it to be grounded in love of neighbor and concern for moral values—wanted to accomplish.

Going into the fray, I knew that City government already had certain weapons in its arsenal to use in its efforts to control pornography—licensing powers, zoning regulations, law enforcement through the vice squad, and so forth—to say nothing of the people's right to set up economic boycotts and to picket establishments purveying materials they found offensive. However, I was aware that a substantial segment of opinion in our community felt that government should be doing more to curb the spread of pornography, adult bookstores, X-rated movie houses, massage parlors, and all the rest of it. I also knew that over the years, the Supreme Court had indicated that some aspects of speech were beyond the bounds of First Amendment protection, including libel, child pornography, obscenity, and shouting "fire"

in a crowded building. Finally, I was aware that there was a correlation
—perhaps not precise or scientific, but one that nonetheless existed—
between the presence of these kinds of establishments in a neighborhood and decreasing property values, on the one hand, and increasing
crime rates, on the other. Our Department of Metropolitan Development ran a study in a neighborhood where a go-go place with its
attendant activities had burned to the ground, and they discovered that
over the course of the next eighteen months property values began to
increase and crime statistics started trending downward. A subsequent
DMD report stated, "The best professional judgment available indi-
cates overwhelmingly that adult entertainment businesses—even a
relatively passive use such as an adult bookstore—have a serious negative effect on their immediate environs," and if that were not enough,
Herbert Case, Detroit's prominent police chief, has stated, "There has
not been a sex murder in the history of our department in which the
killer was not an avid reader of lewd magazines."

It had come to my attention that my colleague, Mayor Don Fraser
of Minneapolis, whom I had known when we were in Congress together, had vetoed an ordinance that attempted to link the anti-pornography battle with civil rights. He felt it was unconstitutional (and
he was right), but the idea of trying to tie the fight against a blighting
influence in our community with a fight for the civil rights of women
appealed to me. At a National League of Cities meeting in early 1984,
I asked Charlee Hoyt, a member of the City Council in Minneapolis,
if she would secure a copy of the proposed legislation for me, and I
introduced her to Beulah Coughenour, a member of our City-County
Council who was interested in sponsoring such an ordinance in Indianapolis.

Beulah and I looked at the Minneapolis statute; then she began
working to refine it with the help of Professor Catharine MacKinnon
of the University of Minnesota, and Indianapolis attorneys working in
City Legal and the Prosecutor's Office. Subsequently, Beulah introduced it to the City-County Council. Our City Attorney, John Ryan,
had grave reservations about the constitutionality of such an initiative,
but we decided to pursue it anyway. We assumed that this was untrod-
den terrain and it might at least engender some national dialogue that
would lead to a breakthrough in efforts being made throughout the
country at the local level of government to rid communities of what
many people regarded as "sleaze and trash" that had a deleterious
effect on morality and precipitated a great deal of neighborhood violence and crime to boot.

The Indianapolis Anti-pornography Ordinance found pornography
to be a form of sex discrimination and a violation of women's civil
rights, based on sociological and psychological studies introduced at

the City-County Council hearings as exhibits, which showed that violent pornography heightens male aggression toward women and reinforces the notion that women are subordinate to men and enjoy that inferior status. The finding was also based on testimony from several victims of pornography, including individuals who had been sexually abused either in the making of pornography or in the use of it during sex crimes. It read:

> Pornography is a discriminatory practice based on sex because its effect is to deny women equal opportunities in society. Pornography is central in creating and maintaining sex as a basis for discrimination. Pornography is a systematic practice of exploitation and subordination based on sex which differentially harms women. The bigotry and contempt it promotes, with the acts of aggression it fosters, harm women's opportunities for equality of rights in employment, education, access to and use of public accommodations, and acquisition of real property, and contribute significantly to restricting women in particular from full exercise of citizenship and participation in public life.

pornography + women's rights

The ordinance was rather specific in its definition of pornography as "the graphic sexually explicit subordination of women, whether in pictures or in words," which included one of five specifically described scenarios of women being sexually abused.

The ordinance allowed a woman to file a discrimination complaint against makers, sellers, distributors, and exhibitors of pornographic materials in the local Office of Equal Opportunity, which would then investigate and hold a hearing. If the OEO Board found that the materials were indeed pornographic, it could not enforce its decision without first seeking a judicial determination. If a court found materials to be pornographic, only then could the Board issue a cease-and-desist order that could prohibit the production, sale, distribution, and exhibition of the material. (Men, children, and transsexuals were also given the power to file discrimination complaints if they could prove they were harmed in the same way.)

This Indianapolis ordinance differed from the Minneapolis one in three respects: a narrower definition of pornography, the requirement of automatic court review, and the prohibition against women filing action directly in court. The support represented an interesting coalition. It included religiously oriented conservatives like Mrs. Coughenour who were concerned about cleaning up the city and who realized there was a lot of support for regulation of adult bookstore activities, plus liberal feminists who believed, with Professor MacKinnon, that "pornography plays a major part in establishing and maintaining male supremacy in our society," plus those who were concerned about pornography as a public safety issue.

On May 1, 1984, I signed into law the ordinance, which had passed the City-County Council by a vote of 24–5, but knowing that we were going to be sued immediately, I declared that the ordinance would not be enforced until—and unless—its constitutionality was upheld in the courts. Within two hours, a lawsuit was filed challenging the ordinance by a coalition of trade associations representing booksellers, publishers, and libraries, as well as certain businesses such as video outlets. The American Civil Liberties Union was *amicus* in the case, and U.S. District Court Judge Sarah Evans Barker, a very capable and respected attorney who had recently been appointed by President Reagan to fill a vacancy on the court, preliminarily enjoined enforcement of the ordinance pending the lawsuit. Briefs were filed and oral arguments were heard on the plaintiffs' and the defendants' cross motions for summary judgment; then Judge Barker found the ordinance unconstitutional on November 19, 1984, stating that it violated First Amendment free speech rights and was unconstitutionally vague.

Her decision was not unexpected, but I was rather startled by the shrill hyperbole of the opposition. Articles appearing around the country had jumped on us for promoting censorship without respect for the First Amendment. Sheila Seuss Kennedy, a former City Attorney who worked with the plaintiffs in this case, called the ordinance "an outrageous attack on freedom of thought and expression," and Michael Gradison, Director of the Indiana Civil Liberties Union, said, "Whether they call it by any other name, it's still censorship. . . . It would turn Indianapolis into a cultural wasteland." The *New York Times* editorialized that "censorship is no one's civil right," a local TV station told its listeners the whole thing was "foolishness," and the *Village Voice* suggested that if our ordinance went into effect, "Vladimir Nabokov, *The Godfather*, William Faulkner, the Bible, Alfred Hitchcock, *Lady Chatterley's Lover*, Lina Wertmüller—all [would be] forbidden in the new America."

Judge Barker ruled that the ordinance regulated speech protected by the First Amendment and was therefore unconstitutional. She ruled that the City-County Council's definition of "pornography" and its characterization of such as sex discrimination "has sought to regulate expression, that is, to suppress speech," and as such violated the First Amendment. She concluded, "Although the State has a recognized interest in prohibiting sex discrimination, that interest does not outweigh the Constitutionally protected interest of free speech. For these reasons the ordinance does not withstand this Constitutional challenge."

The City appealed to the U.S. Court of Appeals, 7th Circuit, in Chicago, where nine *amicus* briefs, six of which supported the ordinance, were filed by various interest groups. After hearing oral arguments, the court found in August 1985 that the ordinance violated the First Amendment. The City filed a petition for a rehearing in the Court of Appeals, which was denied, and prepared an appeal to the U.S. Supreme Court, which the highest court declined to hear by a 6–3 vote.

And so the matter ended. Looking back, in spite of the ridicule that was heaped upon us in some quarters and the final disposition of the case in the courts, I feel it was a battle worth fighting. Perhaps new ground was broken. Perhaps a tighter law can subsequently be written. Somehow, I cannot believe that the First Amendment was ever intended to protect speech or conduct that inflicts injury on people or contributes to illegal behavior; and since, in my opinion, pornography does that, there must be some way to tie the fight against it into the fight for equal opportunity and civil rights for women. As Tottie Ellis succinctly commented after the Attorney General's Pornography Commission issued its report in the summer of 1986, "The issue is more than freedom of the press or liberty. It is protection against poison."

Time alone will tell how the country resolves this difficult issue. But one thing is clear: it must be resolved within the framework of the law. We have a Constitution and a Bill of Rights that must be upheld. We are "an empire of laws and not of men."

Two other cases illustrate the importance of applying the law and administering justice equally. That's a lot easier said than done, because all too often a comfortable majority has no desire or feeling of moral obligation to give up its privileges for the sake of achieving a higher degree of justice for an uncomfortable minority. (Look at the trouble, for example, that has arisen in the last two or three decades over opening up, to minorities and women, the membership of organizations and quasi-public institutions that had previously been dominated by an exclusive white male membership.)

A debate erupted during the holiday season in 1976 when the customary Nativity scene was not erected in University Park in downtown Indianapolis after the practice was called into question by the Indiana Civil Liberties Union (ICLU) and the Jewish Community Relations Council (JCRC). The City's Department of Parks and Recreation, responsible for maintaining that park, made the decision, but a similar display was included in the decorations on Monument Circle, a state owned and operated facility.

The JCRC felt that using a Nativity scene on public property violated Constitutional prohibitions against mixing religious and government functions, and the Executive Director of the ICLU said that the decorations, owned and installed by the City's Parks Department, meant that a government agency was taking action favoring one religion (Christianity) over another. So the usual display was scaled way down, and the decorations that year featured only an innocuous flashing electric star, an evergreen tree, and a sign saying "Season's Greetings." The Parks Department even decided not to decorate light poles to resemble candy canes or to include the customary Santa Claus!

Immediately, the protests began to come in. I appealed to the public to stay calm during the holiday season and said that after the first of the year, we would try to establish guidelines for the future. In a statement to the press, I said, "I am sorry about the unfortunate furor that has arisen over the matter of Nativity displays on public property. The angry feelings it has engendered, particularly the anti-Semitic hostility, are not in keeping with the spirit of brotherhood, goodwill, and freedom that ought to characterize our observance of both Christmas and Hanukkah." Catholic, Jewish, and Protestant leaders issued a joint statement at the same time appealing to "interfaith harmony and fellowship" and deploring "any actions or statements which are designed to arouse hostility toward one another or incite one community against another." Nonetheless, one local pastor accused church and state, "both of them, together" of "putting Christ out," and another clergyman said the removal of the Nativity scene was, as already mentioned, "an exact enactment of the crucifixion 2,000 years ago."

After the holiday season, I met with representatives of the Indianapolis Christmas Committee as well as various religious leaders and officials of the ICLU and JCRC. My effort was to try to hammer out a policy that would be jointly agreeable to all parties concerned, steering a middle course between the prohibited government establishment of religion on the one hand, and a complete secularization of the holiday traditions on the other.

My conclusions, made public in February 1977 in an open letter to the community, were that in our pluralistic society with a Bill of Rights that guarantees freedom of religion (not freedom *from* religion), many different expressions of religious faith are tolerated and government should be neutral. Public funds should not be used to give support to one form or symbol of religion over another. However, I indicated that in a nation that quite often and quite consciously does breach the so-called wall of separation between church and state—from earliest times we have not institutionalized atheism in our country and have acknowledged our dependence on Almighty God, putting "In God We Trust" on our coins, providing public support for chapels and chaplains at all levels of government and in every branch of the armed forces, pledging "this nation under God," and holding religious services from time to time on public properties—it would seem appropriate that temporary privately funded displays, some secular and some religious, on public property at appropriate times like Christmas and

Hanukkah be permitted, provided that fair and equal access was guaranteed.

The issue never went any further, because no lawsuits were filed questioning this resolution of policy. Although some civil libertarians claimed the City should have taken the position that public property would be open to *no* religions rather than to all, they were pleased by the privatization of the funding for the holiday decorations (no public funds would be used in preparing the displays) as well as the City's statement of neutrality with respect to all faiths. The Director of the Jewish Community Relations Council also supported our efforts, saying, "There is no longer a clear Constitutional violation involved and the JCRC appreciates the Constitutional sensitivity demonstrated by the Mayor's office." I was pleased with the opinion printed later on the editorial page of the *Indianapolis News* and signed by Teryl Zarnow, who wrote:

> In his statement last winter Mayor Hudnut deplored the religious prejudice that surfaced during the debate as an affront to the American ideal of mutual respect. Part of that prejudice came from a misunderstanding of the issue involved. As the Mayor emphasized, the question raised was not religious but basically Constitutional. The way in which the issue was resolved demonstrates that this was so. The agreement was reached with care and understanding—the public should perceive it in the same spirit.

To my mind, our privatization of the funding and operation of the religiously oriented displays represents a better solution than the one promulgated by the Supreme Court in 1984 when, in a 5–4 decision, it gave permission in the Pawtucket, Rhode Island, case for the erection of a publicly funded crèche as part of its Christmas display on the grounds that it did not violate the Constitutional separation of church and state.

But the main point here is that public policy should be "fair for one, fair for all." The Christian majority should not impose its religious beliefs, practices, and symbols upon a non-Christian minority through laws that "establish" or favor one form of religion over another.

Last, we come to the Justice Department's lawsuit against the City of Indianapolis, seeking to force us to modify our affirmative action commitments in the police and fire departments, an action that made me so irate at one point that I referred to the instigators as the "Injustice" Department. I was utterly flabbergasted, dismayed, and angered when, on April 29, 1985, the U.S. Department of Justice filed a motion in U.S. District Court in Indianapolis to require us to eliminate the hiring goals for minorities and females that had been set forth in the

Consent Decrees signed with that same Justice Department back in 1978 and 1979.

In the early 1970s, a few minority officers had alleged discrimination in the hiring and promoting practices of the Indianapolis Police Department, a lawsuit was filed, and our fire and police departments were in conversation with the Justice Department when I was elected Mayor in late 1975. In January of 1976 I issued a directive to all departments to implement a voluntary affirmative action program so that the demographics of City employees would more closely represent the community they serve, with the specific suggestion that all fire and police recruit classes include 25 percent minority recruits. Our goal—and hope—was to narrow the gap between the percentage of minorities in our community's work force and the percentage of minorities in these two departments. Working with the Justice Department, we agreed that our voluntary guidelines already in force would become binding by law until such time as our long-term goals (approximately 17 percent) of community representation were reached. In 1979, a similar Consent Decree was approved that established a 20 percent short-term goal for women in police department recruit classes. Thereafter, a short-term goal was set for the fire department providing that the percentage of women hired should match the percentage of women applying to the department. Additionally, promotion goals were established in both departments in order to have each rank reflect the percentage of minorities in the rank from which the promotions were occurring. As more minorities were hired at entry-level positions, the percentage of minorities in the upper ranks would start to increase.

This system was working well and some progress was made. At the end of 1975, our fire department had 7.9 percent minorities and no females, and the police department had 9.8 percent minorities and 6.8 percent females, but by the end of 1985, the fire department's percentages had increased to 13.3 percent minorities and 1.4 percent females, and the police department's had increased to 14 percent minorities and 11.1 percent females. Moreover, things were going pretty smoothly; nobody was actively complaining about our commitment to affirmative action and equal opportunity, and no lawsuits were being filed, even though now and then a disgruntled white male would make some negative comments about reverse discrimination when he was passed over for promotion.

Consequently, we were surprised when we received a letter from the U.S. Department of Justice, dated January 8, 1985, indicating that in their opinion, the Supreme Court's decision in *Firefighters Local Union #1784* v. *Stotts* 467 US 561 (1984)—a case arising originally in Memphis, Tennessee, required us to modify our Consent Decrees. We responded with a long letter on February 20 indicating that we did not believe that *Stotts* could "clearly and without equivocation be read as broadly as the Justice Department claims," that we thought our interim hiring and promoting goals were "within the four corners of our Consent Decrees," and that we consequently would not "voluntarily join in a motion to modify the current Consent Decrees."

The ensuing two months were the quiet before the storm, because on April 29, 1985, the Justice Department filed its motion in the U.S. District Court to require Indianapolis to modify its Consent Decrees to eliminate the hiring goals. Their motion directed that a modified approach "substitute for the hiring goals an enhanced recruitment program, coupled with procedures that ensure nondiscriminatory selection." I held a news conference that day in which I said that we would "fight it as hard as we can" because we had come "too far along the road of minority involvement to turn back now." I indicated that in my opinion we had experienced too much success with our affirmative action program simply to give up as the Justice Department was suggesting, and added, "If we want a higher standard of hiring than the Justice Department requires, I do not understand why they feel they cannot permit us to do that."

I was angry and astounded for a couple of reasons. First, Indianapolis was the largest Republican city in the country, and I was surprised that a Republican administration in Washington would go after us first, since over fifty other jurisdictions and agencies were involved in this particular issue. I was also mystified that the routine courtesy of notifying either of our Senators, any of our Congressional delegation, our Republican State Chairman, or myself that this action was coming had not been observed. But secondly, and more substantively, I felt that the Justice Department was absolutely wrong in initiating this action. In the various debates that ensued on national TV and in the newspapers, I elaborated on this belief, indicating that in my opinion, they were wrong legally, morally, and politically.

First of all, we thought that the Justice Department's reading of *Stotts* was unreasonable. We felt that decision concerned a very narrow set of facts dealing with layoffs and the seniority system and that a broader reading of *Stotts* to call into question all hiring and promotion goals and affirmative action programs in government jurisdictions around the country was unwarranted.

Nor could I fathom any justification of the Justice Department's motion upon the basis of a proper reading of the Declaration of Independence and the U.S. Constitution. Not that I am an expert in these matters, but I happen to agree with Abraham Lincoln when he said, "Most governments have been based on the denial of equal rights of men; ours began by affirming those rights." (In those days, nobody was troubled by the use of the generic word "man," and I am sure that if

he had lived a hundred years later, Lincoln would have been sensitive
to the problem of equal rights of women as well as minorities.)

I thought the Justice Department was also morally wrong. I could
not square what they were doing with my understanding of the biblical
injunction to be our brother's (and sister's) keeper and to bear one
another's burdens "in love." Our country has not come as far as it
should have in its march toward the realization of the dream when
everyone might sit down at the table of brotherhood and sisterhood
together. Nonetheless, in the preceding quarter of a century or so,
considerable progress had been made in the struggle for equal opportunity and equal treatment and the affirmation of civil rights for all
Americans regardless of race, sex, creed, color, or national origin. Why
turn the clock back? Why, allegedly in the name of justice, say that
affirmative action was discriminatory and unconstitutional when, for so
long, minorities and women had been excluded from the mainstream
of American life? In a society where the average black family made
$8,000 less than the average white family, and where the average
woman received about 65 percent of what the average male received
for comparable work, why not take remedial steps to correct such an
unjust situation? Cutting through the arguments about reverse discrimination, why not say that the speedy and full integration of minorities and women into American life is a reasonable and urgent national
priority and that a strong commitment to affirmative action and equal
opportunity through a rather systematic approach using goals and
guidelines is a legitimate means to attaining that overriding national
goal? It could be said that affirmative action has some unfortunate
effects and some obvious defects; but where sizable groups of people
have been prevented from enjoying a full and equal share of the pie
of American opportunity for so long, we have to ask if correcting the
so-called evil side effect of reverse discrimination is any more morally
compelling than redressing the historic injustice done to those groups.
(Charles Krauthammer made this point in the September 16–23, 1985,
issue of the *New Republic,* and I agree with him.)

And third, I thought the Republican administration in Washington
through the Justice Department was making a political mistake—small
"p" and capital "P."

It was a political mistake (small "p") because it made it harder to
govern at the local level of government. I suggested in a letter to the
White House staff on May 7, 1985, that we did not need the grief of
this lawsuit. In the words of some old Hoosier philosopher, "If it ain't
broke, don't fix it." As a result of the Justice Department's action,
things got pretty stirred up in Indianapolis for a while. There was
increased tension between the blacks and whites in the Police Department, the Fraternal Order of Police decided to take the side of the

Justice Department, then Assistant Chief Joseph Shelton, the highest ranking black in the department, said he was going to resign from the FOP, then all the blacks in the department started talking about resigning as a bloc, then the FOP reversed itself, and so on. None of this destabilization would have occurred if the Justice Department people, who have never had to administer the affairs of a large city and seemed to be proceeding purely on ideological grounds, had left well enough alone.

The Justice Department's action fanned the fires of racism in our community, stirred up emotions, and threatened our unity and tranquillity. It brought a lot of latent resentment to the surface and gave bigots an excuse to attack (hence, the hope for my assassination mentioned at the beginning of this chapter). If a mayor's job is to hold things together and prevent a community from flying apart—as I think it is—the Justice Department wasn't helping us very much!

It was also a mistake politically (small "p") because it ran counter to the announced Reagan philosophy of decentralization of government. President Reagan came to power riding the wave of resentment against the heavy hand of centralized government and advocating the right of states and local government to make their own decisions and to have a greater share of the power and resources allocated to them through a devolution of authority back from Washington to state capitols and cities. Now, here was the national Administration's Justice Department suggesting that we did not know how to run our own affairs at the local level and that they were going to tell us what was best for us and make us change our ways—"forcing us to be free" as it were. And on top of this, there was the preposterous contradiction of the current Justice Department headed by Attorney General Meese reversing actions that President Carter's Justice Department had taken just eight years previously. The destabilizing influence of putting local government on this kind of yo-yo was considerable.

It was also a Political mistake (capital "P"). I felt that the Justice Department's action would stir up increasing antagonism toward the Republican Party on the part of many elements who were already pretty well disaffected and felt shut out of its embrace. The message sent out by the Justice Department implied that we as a Republican Party did not care about the historic problems of minorities and women in achieving their rightful place in American society, that we were a party of people who had "made it," and that in the name of color blindness we ought to throw it open so that everybody could compete on an equal footing—which really meant reverting to a discredited system where white males were awarded most of the jobs and received an incredibly disproportionate share of the pie. As one white police lieutenant remarked to me, "Had the Justice Department won and our city lost, we would have been driven back into the old caste system of segregation, and we don't need that."

In my opinion, the Republican Party would be better advised to reach out toward the dispossessed, the minorities, the elderly, the women, the poor, the outcast, the ones who have not had an equal chance and would not have without some kind of government help, rather than narrowing its base inward. Under Ronald Reagan's leadership (and I disassociate him from Attorney General Meese's actions in this instance, even though the President at news conferences has responded somewhat ambiguously to questions about affirmative action), the base of the Republican Party had been considerably broadened to include many groups that had hitherto been regarded as traditionally part of the Democratic Party coalition. But the message here was exclusive, not inclusive, and I thought that was a mistake. The genius of American politics is tied up with the ability of both major parties to occupy the viable middle between the extremes. If either party is captured by ideologically oriented people who want to force their own particular social agenda on the country, that party will become a minority party. Possibly that is particularly true of the Republican Party, which must work hard to be inclusive or be resigned forever to the oblivion of minority status. (I was pleased in this regard that the Indiana Republican State Chairman, Gordon Durnil, not only supported the effort of the Republican National Committee to establish a minority subcommittee, but also sprang to my defense when I was attacked by Clarence Pendleton, the Chairman of the U.S. Civil Rights Commission. Our City-County Council, composed of 23 Republicans and 6 Democrats, unanimously endorsed my position on affirmative action, and while few churches indicated any support for our stand, I was grateful when the Presbyterian General Assembly, meeting in Indianapolis in June 1985, voted to commend us for doing battle on behalf of equal opportunity.)

I tried to take our case privately to Washington. In September of 1985, a meeting had been arranged with Attorney General Edwin Meese in connection with a meeting of the Advisory Commission on Intergovernmental Relations, of which we were both members; but he left the meeting early, before I arrived. Later in the day, when I went over to the Justice Department, I was told that he could not see me and was referred to William Bradford Reynolds, the Assistant Attorney General heading up the civil rights division of the Justice Department. Mr. Reynolds and his lawyers spent the better part of forty-five minutes with me, and it was obvious that the conversation was headed down a nonproductive path. Mr. Reynolds kept telling me that the overwhelming majority of blacks, according to polls he had taken, disagreed with affirmative action and that our city was guilty of unconstitutional discriminatory hiring practices based on a rigid quota system. I responded that what we were really trying to accomplish, in addition to holding the community together and running local government as smoothly as possible (with which endeavor he was interfering), was to increase the number of job opportunities in our fire and police departments for women and minorities on the basis of race- and sex-conscious policies applied to a pool of equally well qualified applicants. I told him that we did not have a rigid quota system but, rather, goals toward which we were moving, and I thought we were within our Constitutional prerogatives in doing this. I tried to explain that rather than envisioning our hiring and promoting policies as a vertical list where better qualified white males were passed over to get to less qualified females and minorities, we should think in terms of a circle, everyone inside that circle being equally qualified and nobody being "passed over" in the selection process.

But Mr. Reynolds did not buy my reasoning. He was convinced that he had the Constitution on his side and said he was going to proceed with the litigation against us. Knowing that our motion to dismiss the Justice Department's complaint against our city had been filed and was lodging in the federal court system, knowing that it represented one facet of a very complex problem that had many ramifications with different cases working their way to the Supreme Court, and knowing that I was not going to make any progress with Mr. Reynolds on my request to the Justice Department to reconsider its stance, I stood up and shook hands with him and said, "I'll see you in court."

At the same time as I visited with Mr. Reynolds, I wrote Mr. Meese a letter outlining our city's position and asking him to reconsider, but he never answered the letter. I also wrote the President in January 1986, reiterating my request that the Justice Department abandon its efforts to push this matter further and asking him to stand strong in support of the Executive Order on Affirmative Action (11246) as it was originally promulgated in 1965 by President Johnson and subsequently amended in 1971 by President Nixon to include "goals and timetables." I asked President Reagan not to yield to the pressure on him from the Attorney General and others to modify or terminate that Executive Order. I told him that in Martin Luther King, Jr., birthday celebrations the day before it was dramatically presented to me how strongly many Americans feel about the need for a commitment at all levels of government to affirmative action, and I hoped he would not yield to the pressure to "turn the clock far back on civil rights advances over the last twenty-five years." My letter was never answered.

Even though we resolved to maintain a strong voluntary recruitment and promotion program for minorities and women regardless of what happened in the courts, we went into the federal courts asking that the

Justice Department be caused to withdraw its action against us. In the summer of 1986, three cases, two involving the cities of Cleveland, Ohio, and Jackson, Michigan, and the other involving the Sheet Metal Workers Union, were decided by the Supreme Court. These decisions handed a clear victory to the proponents of affirmative action and a decisive defeat to Messrs. Meese and Reynolds and Pendleton. Cutting through all the legalese, the decisions boiled down to this: The Supreme Court carefully considered and rejected the arguments against race-conscious relief—including the use of goals and timetables in hiring and promoting—which benefit persons not identified as individual victims of past discriminations. I responded not only on behalf of myself and the City of Indianapolis, but also for the U.S. Conference of Mayors, as chairman of its subcommittee on civil rights, when I said, "I have felt in my heart all along that our position was correct." The Justice Department subsequently ended its fight (without comment) to throw out the Indianapolis Affirmative Action Plan contained in the Consent Decrees. Assured that our hard-fought battle in the area of equal opportunity would survive, I can say I'm glad we won this one and am grateful for the checks and balances that keep the American system of government working for *all* its citizens.

These four controversies have taught me several lessons, beginning with the way in which people sometimes react to controversy. In each case, I was appalled at the amount of downright meanness demonstrated by some individuals and was disheartened, not because the opposition made me think I was wrong in the stands I was taking but because it laid bare the emotional irrationality lurking just beneath the surface in so many people's hearts. Where were "the better angels of our nature" that Lincoln talked about? I saw the "beast in the jungle" spring many times. I was saddened by the vicious personal attacks, the accusatory epithets hurled at me, the anonymous letters full of hate and spite and threats on my life, the abusive phone calls, and the unfair and untrue things said about me and my family. Everyone in public life is subjected to this kind of abuse from time to time, but it is never easy to take. I must confess that one of the most disillusioning aspects of being in political office is the irresponsible and emotional way in which people erupt when their vested interests are threatened—not always, of course, but more frequently than I care to admit in a country founded on the hope that people will think and act and react responsibly and reasonably.

In each of these four cases, as well as many other situations, I have been made acutely aware of racial, religious, and sexual prejudice as well as the fear, hatred, mendacity, pettiness, and vindictiveness in

unredeemed human nature. I have tried to deal with this negativeness
in one of three ways.

First, *ignore the negativeness* and rise above it with the hope that reason
and decency will ultimately carry the day, that the generous fairness
in the American spirit will not be extinguished, and that people of
goodwill and large heart and sound mind will prevail over those who
live in the shadows of life. Some remarks are better left undignified by
an answer. You don't have to react every time the editor prints a critical
letter about what you're doing, or every time you receive unfavorable
publicity, or every time you hear about an unflattering rumor being
circulated about you. As the Good Book says, sometimes you have to
"shake off the dust from your feet" and go on to the next town. I
remember when Barbara Walters implied on national television on
election night in November of 1974 that I had lost the election because
I was having an affair with a doctor's wife in Indianapolis, I was out-
raged at the gross distortion of truth (which was that I was single at
the time, and dating a woman whose ex-husband was a physician); but
after talking with lawyers about it, and being told that unless I could
prove malicious intent there would be no point in pursuing it, I decided to let it pass.

Second, *rebut it* with the truth. If factual inaccuracy or misstatement
of a situation is involved, sometimes it pays to respond with the facts
of the matter. We have to live with the hope that truth will prevail, and,
occasionally, it seems to be prudent to try to correct the misimpres-
sion, to state the facts as you see them and not to take an unfair
accusation lying down. "Speak the truth in love," admonishes scripture. Once I received a very angry letter from a constituent who did
not think I was being fair to President Nixon in some of my remarks.
I waited awhile before answering his letter, wrote him a gentle reply
in which I tried to state my case as honestly as I could, and, when I
returned to Indianapolis, he and I had dinner together. He acknowledged that he had been wrong and I was right—and our friendship
endured!

Third, *transmute it.* Redeem it. Turn it around. Make a positive out
of the negative if you can. "Love your enemies and pray for those who
persecute you." Maybe you can convert your accuser. During the Villages controversy, I had a relatively irate and negative letter from a
couple who were members of the church where the aforementioned
minister was pastor. Rather than writing them back, I telephoned the
couple, talked with them about the situation, and told them what some
of the other side of the story involved. In the course of conversation,
I found out that the husband and I had gone to the same college and
that we both enjoyed tennis. We made arrangements to play, and to

make a long story short, in the time since then we have won two tournaments together in men's doubles!

Having said all this about some aspects of the opposition I have received across the years, let me add that my heart has also been gladdened by expressions of support "at home and abroad" on some of these matters. When members of my family call me from around the country to say they applaud my stand on affirmative action which they have seen on TV, when people write me from far and wide to thank me for what I am doing, when the leaders of the NAACP and the Urban League and U.S. Senators and fellow mayors from around the country say, "Keep it up. Don't back off. You're right," it certainly encourages me and gives me strength to continue. When rabbis and leaders of the National Conference of Christians and Jews and of B'nai B'rith express appreciation for my sensitivity to their concerns, I am gratified and fortified. In short, the positive, supportive comments keep me going. Thank God for people with good hearts and tolerant spirits who provide us with a positive support system to endure the trials we face in public life! And the same should go for the church, which should always reinforce you in doing what you think under God is right and provide you with a measure of solace and comfort—not judgment— when you enter its fellowship.

But even more significant than this whole business of learning how to handle abuse and controversy, I think these four different issues helped me to learn some pretty fundamental things about our country. In the Villages case and the one dealing with our anti-pornography ordinance, I have learned the importance of respect for the law. Three centuries ago, Harrington was right, and he still is right: "The liberty of a commonwealth consists in the empire of her laws." If the law is bad or unjust, it should be changed. Even if we suppose, along with Mr. Bumble, one of Charles Dickens' characters, that "the law is a ass, a idiot," we do not have the recourse of flouting it but the obligation to work to change it. We do not have the option of shooting people with whom we disagree, bombing churches, stealing files out of people's desks, breaking into offices, preventing people from entering doctors' offices, and all the rest of it. Peaceful civil disobedience is another honorable way of dealing with a law we do not like, providing we are willing to bear the consequences of our actions. But however we choose to express our feelings, respect for due process is required, regardless of the intrinsic merits of a cause. Because the alternative is anarchy—or dictatorship.

In the Christmas decorations case and the one on affirmative action, I learned the importance of respect for differences of opinion, and for the majority being sensitive to the problems of a minority. We must be sure the rights of everyone to equal opportunity and free expression are preserved. Government must not take the side of one against the other; government must work to assure that *all* are fairly included, and none are unfairly excluded.

The American republic lives out its days hanging in delicate balance between liberty and security, individualism and collectivism, justice and injustice, majority rule and minority rights. Ours is a society based on civil liberties and human rights, where dissent is tolerated and individual expression encouraged; yet, so that society does not degenerate into the chaos of an anthill or the tyranny of despotism, the security of a lawful ordering of life is required as well as a balancing of different powers and interests. These polarities exist in dialectical relationship with each other, and the health of the state lies in the dynamic equilibration of their competing claims.

The American dream is that the ideals of "liberty, equality, and fraternity" might be shared by all, not just the privileged few. It belongs to Catholics and Jews and other believers, and to nonbelievers, as well as to Protestants; to ethnics of many different heritages as well as to WASPs; to minorities and women as well as to white males; to the downcast and dispossessed as well as to the fortunate and well-off. Government has a particular responsibility to help everyone achieve that dream, especially those who live, to borrow Hubert Humphrey's phrase, in "the dawn, the shadows, and the twilight of life." It has been said that good managers do things right, but good leaders do the right things, and to those of us in positions of governmental leadership, there often come opportunities to do the right thing. With firmness we should seize them so that each of us, in his or her own way and time, can help make the dream of liberty and justice for all, under law, come true.

9

Building the City

The Bible takes what is happening in the city very seriously. The prophets did most of their preaching there. Jesus was born there, spent a goodly portion of his ministry there, and was crucified and resurrected there. Paul boasted of being "a citizen of no mean city." In the large concordance for the Revised Standard Version of the Bible, there are more than 1,200 references related to cities and citizenship.

The city is where God's children are—where they live and work and worship and play, where they succeed and fail, hope and surrender, die and come to new life. The city is where the action is and where the church must be if it is to discover and proclaim and manifest God at work in the world. I do not mean to slight the farmlands or the beaches or the mountaintops and the religious inspiration available there. But let's face it! Seventy percent of America's people live in cities, and there are over fifty population centers across the country with more than a quarter of a million people living in them. Our lives, our business and professional and social and educational and religious worlds, are grounded in the city. The city is the hub of communication and transportation networks, the cockpit where crucial commercial and political decisions are made, the arena where conflicting communities of interest are battling it out.

The city is fulfillment and frustration, justice and injustice, poverty and affluence, sophistication and ignorance, organization and chaos. It is dynamic, explosive, and vital; it is dull, static, and decaying. It is ambiguous—it releases the best in people and the worst in them. It prompts some to dream, others to despair. And it is where most of us live and move and have our being. Biblically oriented people believe that God meets us in many places, and certainly today that must include the city. It is the Palm Sunday message all over again—Christ is riding into the city today, meeting us, challenging us, judging us, calling us. Just as the Hebrew prophets came to city dwellers in days of old, just as Jesus did in his day, so we have to recognize that God is coming to us amid the urban crises of our time, confronting us where the problems are, and the suffering, and the opportunities, and the challenges—in the midst of decay and abandonment and rebirth and change. The church's job is to discern where this is happening and to help the "new creation" take shape.

Scripture presents us with at least three views of the city; first, the real city, the city that is, the city where there are tons of problems; second, the ideal city, the city that could be, the envisioned city where there aren't any problems; and third, the potential city, the city that is coming into being, the city where solutions to problems are being found.

First, the Bible recognizes that *real* cities gave God a very hard time! He destroyed Sodom and Gomorrah with fire and brimstone because they were so bad. ("The smoke of the land went up like the smoke of a furnace.") Jeremiah gave a rather biting commentary on the Babylon of his day: "Her cities have become a horror, a land of drought and desert." And in the New Testament, we read that there wasn't even any room for Christ and his family in the city where he was born—he was shunted off to a stable. When he was preaching, he was not always received well. ("All the city came out to meet Jesus; and when they saw him, they begged him to leave their neighborhood.") Jesus wept over Jerusalem when he saw what was going on there, and he was finally put to death there.

All of which suggests that cities are where goodness is trampled, where justice is undercut, where the powers of darkness are at work to drag humanity down to defeat, and where the forces of poverty, pollution, hunger, crime, and depersonalization cast long shadows across the pathway of life.

A mayor sees this every day. I remember the first time a murder occurred in our city after I had been elected. I felt tremendous feelings of sadness and remorse and heartache, because I did not want my city to be a place where people hurt or killed each other. As we travel the city streets, our wheels occasionally hit potholes, but I want our roads to be smooth all the way. Some people in our community live in very inadequate housing, but I want them all to live in nice places. Many are out of work, but I want everyone to have a job. (Once in a political campaign I misspoke, and instead of saying, "I want our city to be a place where everyone who wants a job has one," I said, "I want ours to be a city where everyone who has a job wants one." I couldn't understand why people were laughing at me in the middle of a serious campaign address!) For me, in short, it was a rather rude awakening to be elected Mayor and then to realize that Indianapolis would not be transformed overnight as a result of my election, that sin and death as well as taxes would continue to be in residence.

Nonetheless, the Bible dreams of "a new Jerusalem" and so should we. The real city is the stage on which God is playing out his drama of redemption, and holy religion holds before our minds and hearts the vision of an *ideal* city where all problems have been solved. Like Abraham we keep journeying toward "the city which has foundations, whose builder and maker is God." And like the prophet John we continue to dream of "the holy city, new Jerusalem, coming down out of heaven from God, prepared as a bride adorned for her husband; and I heard a loud voice from the throne saying, 'Behold, the dwelling of God is with men. He will dwell with them, and they shall be his people, and God himself will be with them; he will wipe away every tear from their eyes, and death shall be no more, neither shall there be mourning nor crying nor pain any more, for the former things have passed away.' "

Translated for today, biblical idealism means that one's faith for his or her city involves the belief that its capacity for good can be developed, its tendency toward evil harnessed. Those who stand in the Judeo-Christian heritage believe and hope that in stark contrast to the reality of a Babylon corrupted, impoverished, and dessicated, upon which God's stern judgment fell, the city can become the vehicle for God's new creation, to be born and come alive.

It is impossible to blueprint the city as God's new creation, for it is an ideal toward which we strive rather than a reality which we experience. Not that we have already attained . . . but we press on toward the goal for the prize. Our biblical hope for the city is that it will become the place where our humanity and true community are fulfilled under God. We ought not dismiss as irrelevant the vision that the famous old preacher Cotton Mather had back in 1710, when in his essay "On the Golden Street of the Holy City" he issued a summons to his fellow countrymen and women:

> Come hither, and I will show you an admirable spectacle! 'Tis a heavenly city . . . a city to be inhabited by an innumerable company of angels, and by the spirits of just men. . . . Put on thy beautiful garments, O America, the holy city.

Our hope for the city is that it will become a holy place, a place where neighbors will work and dwell together in peace, where the differences that divide people will be transcended by common purpose, and where a new community will be achieved beyond the chaos of conflicts between social classes, races, nationalities, and economic pursuits. Here justice will supersede injustice, reconciliation will bridge chasms of alienation, love will cast out fear, and compassion will redeem indifference. And here, as my father liked to say, the human race will be transformed into the human family.

This is what the city under God can become, and our hope is that with hard work and by God's grace the gap between the ideal and the real in the city will gradually be closed.

Applying the general biblical theme to the situation in which I find myself, I have a dream about my city. I want Indianapolis to be known as a community that aspires to excellence and grows toward greatness, where the public, the for-profit, and the not-for-profit private sectors work together as partners for progress. I dream of a city where quality growth is encouraged, where the delivery of basic services is uninterrupted by work stoppages or cash-flow problems, and where race relations are characterized by mutual respect and appreciation. I want ours to be a sound city, whose management is progressive but prudent and whose financial condition is sound—triple-A rated all the way. I want it to be a place where the arts flourish; where every child receives a quality education and every needy person a warm meal, shelter, and a job; where moral values will be upheld and spiritual ideals will be exalted and the blighting influences of pornography will be kept in check. It is my dream that Indianapolis will become a city where people care about people, where the human spirit can be released, where the heart can celebrate, where relationships are humane and we treat each other with dignity and sensitivity.

I hope Indianapolis can prove the validity of the American dream that people can unite across all the lines of race and creed and culture and heritage and economic station and social class that tend to divide them, living together in peace and mutual respect and governing themselves on the principle of justice tempered with mercy.

And so, in the third place, scripture points us to the *potential* city, the city that is becoming what it should be, making a transition from the real to the ideal, where problems are being solved and successes are being experienced. "Thus says the Lord: I will return to Zion, and will dwell in the midst of Jerusalem, and Jerusalem shall be called the faithful city, and the mountain of the Lord of hosts, the holy mountain." Jesus taught us to pray, "Thy kingdom come, thy will be done, on earth [and in the city] as it is in heaven." The process of what Christian theology calls sanctification is working itself out not only in individuals but in the corporate structures of the urban community. The church has the responsibility and the opportunity to be the servant and healer in our urban areas, and the bottom line for the Christian is to join the battle in the city and to help it become what under God it ought to be.

The Bible is not a book of ideas, it is a collection of stories about God acting through people. It is a book of verbs, not nouns and pronouns, and its mode is active, not passive. We read about plowing and planting and sowing and reaping; about living and believing and hoping and loving; about sailing and working and building and serving. It challenges us to build a better city.

"Come, let us build ourselves a city." I discovered that phrase from Genesis one day while looking for a suitable text to talk about motivating people to become involved in the effort to make a positive difference in Indianapolis. Actually, I have never preached a sermon on the story of the Tower of Babel. Its vestiges of polytheism are difficult to explain, and I always had a difficult time trying to understand why God would scatter people over the face of the earth and cause them to become confused and to speak in different languages if they were once united. I know it is intended to serve as a rebuke for our pride, but it is still a tough story for an expository sermon, and I avoided it! Nonetheless I love the phrase, "Come, let us build ourselves a city," taken from that story. It's probably more of a pretext than a text, but it makes the point pretty well—as does the tragic epitaph at the end of the story, "And they left off building the city."

As I walk around Indianapolis and watch the construction activity taking place, old buildings coming down and new ones going up, cranes and boom lines swinging out across the city streets, mile after mile of pavement being torn up to put in new utility lines, I am often reminded of an anonymous poem that puts the challenge to be the builder of a better city rather well.

> I watched them tearing a building down,
> A gang of men in a busy town;
> With a ho-heave-ho and a lusty yell
> They swung a beam and the side wall fell.
>
> I asked the foreman, "Are these men skilled,
> And the men you'd hire if you had to build?"
>
> He gave a laugh and said "No, indeed!
> Just common labor is all I need.
> I can easily wreck in a day or two
> What builders have taken a year to do."
>
> And I thought to myself as I went my way,
> Which of these roles have I tried to play?
>
> Am I a builder who works with care,
> Measuring life by the rule and square?
> Am I shaping my deeds to a well-made plan,
> Patiently doing the best I can?
> Or am I a wrecker, who walks the town
> Content with the labor of tearing down?

good — for wrecker or builder of the city?

The challenge is to be a builder, not a wrecker, and this says something to me about the role of mayor in a rather specific way.

A mayor should be a consensus builder, trying to bring people together around commonly perceived goals to follow a commonly agreed upon strategy to reach them. While it is true, as Samuel Johnson once dryly observed, that "nothing will ever be attempted if all possible objections must first be removed," it is also true that more can be accomplished if the various leadership entities within a city share a common vision and a common sense of direction. Cooperation makes more sense than confrontation, and in most cases partners can achieve much more together than they can separately—just as on the hearth one ember will soon fade and die, whereas many embers lumped together will generate heat and light for a long time.

Those communities are fortunate who have a commonly shared view of their priorities and their ways to achieve them. One of the best examples in America for a consensus-building organization at the local level is the Goals for Dallas program in Dallas, Texas. It is an important mechanism for sharing information and building awareness at the grass roots. It brings together top community leaders, public and private, with a sense of team spirit to tackle the city's problems. It involves hundreds if not thousands of people in shaping goals and formulating plans for that city. In Indianapolis we have several organizations—among them the Greater Indianapolis Progress Committee, the Corporate Community Council, the Commission for Downtown, the Indianapolis Chamber of Commerce—which share the goal of progress for our city. Our citizens have discovered that there is no conflict between private profit and public responsibility and that quality of life and working together to enhance business opportunity go hand in hand. Creative civic thinking can turn the exercise of social responsibility into money-making and job-producing ventures that increase private gain, while also benefiting the city as a whole.

Second, the mayor should be a cheerleader, to pursue the basketball metaphor so popular in Indiana. Of course, the mayor also acts as the coach, sitting on the sidelines to strategize, and as a player, out there on the court hustling and staying involved with one project after another. But there is no substitute for enthusiasm and a can-do spirit to galvanize the forces of progress, and as a cheerleader the mayor helps people to focus on hope and optimism and to see their city as a good place to live and work and invest and raise a family. The beautiful thing about the mayor's job—probably one of the most rewarding in all of government—is the opportunity to communicate a believable hope to people about what their city can become.

The mayor can also play the role of facilitator, bringing together different groups and interests around the table to talk, to discuss, to thrash out, and to find common ground upon which all can stand. While this function may not be in the job description, most mayors have opportunities to facilitate dialogue all the time—all it takes is the interest in doing so and the ability to perceive where those opportunities lie.

In Indianapolis, we have a housing project, built in the 1930s and one of the oldest in the nation, named Lockefield Gardens. Located in the downtown where many of our current minority leaders had their roots, Lockefield Gardens fell on hard times in the late '60s and early '70s. The project was abandoned and enclosed with barbed-wire fences. Weeds grew rampant, windows were smashed, and rats moved in. It was a festering sore in the heart of our city, adjacent to Indiana Avenue and the Indiana University School of Medicine. Something had to be done. The problem was obvious to all, but no one could agree on a solution.

For years we struggled with this vexatious issue. Some people wanted the structures demolished so the city could begin again; some argued that all 748 units should be preserved and restored; some supported the idea of giving the whole area to Indiana University and allowing that institution to determine what should be done. In 1977 a confrontation occurred when opposing groups made an appearance before the Advisory Council on Historic Preservation in Washington, D.C.

City representatives speaking for the official power structure of the community were there to ask for permission to raze Lockefield. Another group, representing neighborhood leaders and supported by Senator Birch Bayh, appeared on behalf of saving the project. We were there in adversarial roles, each seeking to further our ends as we perceived them. But we were all citizens of Indianapolis, and we all wanted what was best for our city. It seemed ludicrous that the decision should be left to officials in Washington, individuals who had no real feeling for the character of our community. I stood up and asked that we all return home and make a commitment to beginning an open-minded dialogue to see if we could reach a compromise.

State Representative William A. Crawford described the results at a groundbreaking speech along Indiana Avenue. "We agreed, and came home and began to talk *to* each other and not *at* each other." A task force was formed by the Greater Indianapolis Progress Committee, consisting of representatives from neighborhood associations, business and professional leadership in the midtown area, Indiana University, the Health and Hospital Corporation, the city's Department of Metropolitan Development, and the U.S. Department of Housing and Urban Development. The process in which we engaged was essential to achieving the result we desired.

We agreed to compromise. We were able to reconcile opposing

viewpoints and find viable middle ground after months of discussion and work. As a result, part of the original project was demolished, making way for 300 units of new housing, and 200 units were saved and are now in the process of being restored. Some of the land was deeded to Indiana University for its medical school campus, and a new street is being constructed through the middle of the complex. The blight is gone; the bloom is on. Disintegrating tendencies were successfully overcome by constructive thought and action.

I appreciate what Representative Crawford said at the groundbreaking: "As a youngster who grew up in Lockefield Gardens and for eight years walked by this very site daily on my way to St. Bridget's Grade School, I can remember what this area once was. I see it as it is now, and because of the leadership of Mayor Hudnut, I am confident that it will be an area we will all be proud of in the future. Because of his leadership, we can see what can happen when we talk to each other and not at each other. Thanks to him, we have, in the historic 1980 Memorandum of Understanding, a vehicle that can become a model plan for neighborhood development because it emphasizes cooperation and dialogue over competition and divisive debate."

Everyone who worked on the project deserves credit for what happened. My role as facilitator was deemed successful because of the reconciling spirit fostered by the many men and women on the Task Force which made positive accomplishment possible.

And, fourth, the mayor is *a packager,* who helps to bring the different pieces of a puzzle together. The mayor and City Hall staff can arrange for land assemblage and financing so that economic development plans can come to fruition. Local government can provide tax incentives and inducements such as property tax abatements, tax-exempt development bonds, and tax-increment financing and can also leverage other public monies to stimulate private sector investment.

One of the unfortunate aspects of the so-called Reagan Revolution is that while it has quite properly focused on bringing the federal budget under control, some very good programs have fallen into disrepute. Things like General Revenue Sharing, Urban Development Action Grants, and Community Development Block Grants have been lampooned by officials in Washington who have given the American people the mistaken impression that they are extravagant frills, a waste of taxpayers' dollars. There is, however, a vital connection between these government grants and economic development, between the use of public money and the investment of private funds that can result in new and restored properties for our cities.

My brother Bob distinguishes between the major vocation that we all have, the means by which we earn a living and where our primary sphere of service lies, and the secondary forms of service that come to us, extra things that we do to serve the needs of others and help build the city. It's probably the job of the pulpit to ask questions that point the laity in the direction of the extra things they can do to help. Many cannot, do not, will not do anything, but the city desperately needs capable, talented, caring people who are willing to go the second and third miles. The pulpit must ask if we are willing to do that. Are we shouldering any extra burdens to help build a better city? What are we doing to break out of our comfortable private cocoons to help the disadvantaged and the unfortunate? What are we doing as corporate managers to exercise leadership in helping to solve the tough problems of our times and to fight the battles that must be fought—against poverty, unemployment, racism, sexism, pollution, urban blight, crime, delinquency, drug addiction, neighborhood deterioration, and all the rest? What are we doing as individually concerned people to build the kingdom of brotherhood and justice and love and peace here where we live, in a city that is becoming a new creation? What are we doing to make life more humane and tolerable where we touch it? What are we doing to live responsibly in our time? The pulpit can only ask the questions and point the rest of us in the direction of understanding that biblically oriented people's ministry in the city takes many forms, and it is on the wings of such ministries that the new creation will be ushered in and God's kingdom will come a little closer to realization.

There are several ways in which each of us can help.

First, we can **create and participate in dialogue.** In an open society, in a democracy, it is important to talk, to share, to listen to one another and learn from one another, and to discuss who we are and where we are going. The dialogue is more important than the specific issues being discussed. This is extremely important in the city, because people become angry if they feel no one is listening. When they have no voice in the decision-making process, they can explode. Certainly we learned that from the riots in Miami a few years ago, when it became clear from the postmortems that leaders of the minority communities, both black and Hispanic, were frustrated by the feeling they were outsiders looking in. If people are included in the conversation, they feel they can make a contribution; if they are excluded, they may see confrontation as their only alternative.

A few years ago, tensions escalated between the black and Jewish communities in Indianapolis owing to several anti-Semitic remarks made by Minister Louis Farrakhan, a guest speaker at Indiana Black Expo. (Black Expo is an annual celebration of the minority community's contributions to the cultural, religious, educational, civic, and business life of our country, drawing many nationally prominent figures to its programs.) In response, a few women leaders from each of those communities came together to form a discussion group, which they named Dialogue Today. Its original purpose was to facilitate interaction among people after Farrakhan's irresponsible rhetoric inflamed certain elements of the community, with the hope that greater understanding would develop between the two groups and potential polarization would be averted. In the time since it was founded, Dialogue Today has grown into a broad-based, ongoing forum consisting of a good cross section of women who are opinion leaders in the black and Jewish communities. The group has made a meaningful contribution to increasing the amount of harmony and mutual forbearance and enlightenment in our community. Chances are, people who have dialogues with one another will not fight with one another.

There are many opportunities for citizens of a community to express their opinions and to participate in the dialogue rather than to employ the cop-out that one person cannot make a difference. And there are opportunities to listen, to consider what we hear, not only in government but throughout the city in our workplaces, our schools, our churches and temples, our social organizations, our neighborhoods. Even though Isaiah was talking about a conversation between God and his people, the advice "Come now, let us reason together" has a lot to recommend it.

Which leads to a second way we can all help build community, and that is to serve as "agents of reconciliation." Paul tells us in his Second Letter to the Corinthians that God has entrusted the message of reconciliation to us. Part of our job is to overcome the salient cleavages in modern urban life—between black and white and brown, or between center city and the suburbs, for example. We must combat the forces that tend to pull a community apart with those that reinforce the center.

Each of us needs to ask whether we contribute to polarization or reconciliation in our city. Every time we laugh at an off-color ethnic joke, every time we reinforce patterns of sexism or racism, every time we brush off somebody else's concern and say we don't care, every time we criticize without offering a constructive alternative, every time we drive through town without seeing the pain and hurt around us, we contribute to polarization. But every time we stop to listen, every time we shoulder a burden, every time we recognize that the chains that bind a brother and sister bind us, every time we display a caring, compassionate attitude, we help to build the city by promoting reconciliation.

In the city we need to respect each other and be sensitive to each other. In his book *The Art of Loving,* Erich Fromm says that respect "denotes the ability to see a person as he is, to be aware of his unique individuality. Respect means the concern that the other person should grow and unfold as he is. Respect thus implies the absence of exploitation." That is the path to reconciliation. Our tendency as sinful human beings is to like only our own kind, but we must show respect for one another in the city. We must exercise a due regard for the uniqueness and individuality of the other person, and we must be willing to guarantee him or her the right to be different and the right to an integrity of their own. Sensitivity goes even farther than respect. It implies concern, compassion, and empathy. It does not allow us to belittle or ridicule or demean people just because their point of view—or their clothes, income, life-style, religion, skin color, residence, or political party—is different from our own. All of us are children of God. All of us are human beings. And all of us want others to be sensitive to our hurts and our dreams.

Following from this, a third way we can build a better city is to **foster a larger sense of community,** which may mean transcending the narrow limits of self-interest in favor of the common good. When the Bible tells us that we are "our brother's keeper," it means we must see how we are wrapped up in each other's destiny. Sometimes this is very difficult to understand.

For example, in one of the major plants in our city where we manufacture a very important product line, management and labor cannot agree on a new way of doing things, a new contract. So that business goes elsewhere. And for a while, all is well and good. But maybe the word goes out that there was a failure to work together in Indianapolis, maybe the parent corporation decides it would be easier to do business elsewhere. Maybe five or ten years out, jobs disappear because of the inability to make something work in the here and now.

In church we sing, "In Christ there is no east or west." The Hebrew scriptures enjoin us "to dwell together in unity" (not uniformity). By the same token, America dreams of a new unity where Protestant, Catholic, and Jew, Irish, Pole, and German, native American, Japanese-American, and Hispanic, upper, middle, and lower class, black and white and brown and red, Republicans and Democrats and Independents, can all live together and get along together and work together. Contrary to a country like Japan, where nearly all of the people are Japanese through and through for generations, urban America is a heterogeneous society. The key to holding it all together is the necessity for regarding each other as brothers and sisters, not strangers; as neighbors, not enemies. And also, the key is to understand that what affects somebody else really affects me. Cancer in one part affects the whole body.

A fourth thing we can do to help build a better city is to **protect the environment.** At the individual level this means obeying the laws regarding trash burning and littering and disposal of hazardous wastes. It means volunteering to participate in clean city campaigns. It means understanding the connection between jobs and clean air and clean water. A city can have a more successful economic development enterprise if it makes a strong commitment to environmental protection, but fighting pollution is not necessarily a politically popular thing to do. There is no political will, for example, in many state legislatures to force a vehicle emissions testing program on car owners, even though cars are one of the major pollutants of the air. We are fortunate that in our city many of our citizens do participate in a voluntary inspection program being carried out by local government in cooperation with some of the city's larger employers.

Gradually, it seems to me, an awareness is growing in our community, as well as throughout America, of the importance of promoting those kinds of projects and programs that combat environmental degradation and the pollution of our air and water. Progress is being made, although we have a long way to go before we can feel satisfied that we are good stewards of the precious treasure of God's earth that he has given us.

As we talk about preserving the environment, it is easy to see that another thing we must do to help build better cities is to implement an ethic of urban conservation. We must be good stewards of all our resources. We must recycle, we must preserve, we must not waste. The historic preservation movement is a controversial thing, because sometimes it is perceived as standing in the way of progress and holding out for old buildings for no other reason than that they are old, regardless of whether they are suitable for adaptive reuse. Yet sometimes the historic preservationists tell us something that is very important, which is that we must learn to conserve the resources of our community and avoid the kind of bulldozer mentality that ramrods a project through a neighborhood.

I like the parable about the barren fig tree in the Gospel according to Luke. Don't uproot it right away. Work with it awhile. Fertilize it. See if you can get it to bear fruit. It is important that we treat our cities with the same kind of care, with the same sense of responsibility for protection and preservation.

Another thing we must do if we are to help build the city is to forge strong neighborhoods. In early 1986, our local government conducted a series of nine neighborhood forums, one in each of the townships in Marion County, to give people a chance to come in and talk with me and other city officials about what was on their minds. About 3,000 individuals took part in the meetings, resulting in well over 1,000 "opportunities for service." Many of these people were concerned about drainage problems, others had questions about public safety, about transportation, about city parks. We collated all the concerns, put them into the system, and tried to solve some of the problems through routine office procedures. We funded some solutions with property tax dollars set aside in cumulative building funds and undertook some of the larger projects through bond issues. Those who attended showed concern for their neighborhoods and took advantage of the opportunity to suggest improvements. Along with their neighbors, they established a feeling of identity and voice for their communities.

Government cannot always oblige people. Sometimes they ask the impossible. Sometimes you do not have the resources to do what people want or you simply cannot help them because to do so would hurt many others. But it is important for concerned citizens and members of congregations to be involved in their neighborhood associations. So often it seems that people separate religion from what is going on in the world around them. They forget that churches and synagogues can exist "outside the walls," that strong religious institutions can help develop strong neighborhoods as they feed talent, resources, and commitment into community-based organizations and neighborhood associations. Protestant, Catholic, and Jewish congregations can and do play a significant role in organizing and catalyzing neighborhood development. It is interesting to note that three of the strongest neighborhood associations in Indianapolis—Butler-Tarkington, Meridian-Kessler, and Irvington—hold many of their meetings in churches. Another neighborhood association meets in the Jewish Community Center. There is important symbolism there.

And wouldn't it be wonderful if neighborhood parks and schools could be adopted by religious congregations or civic groups like the Kiwanis Club or the Chamber of Commerce businesses? The Indianapolis Hebrew Congregation has a Loaves Program in which thirty to forty volunteers purchase, cook, and serve dinner one night a week in a community center located in a less fortunate part of town, to anyone who needs a hot, nutritious meal. Our Chamber sponsors a program called Partners in Education (PIE), which achieves excellent results. Member companies work with schools not only to develop what you might call citizen skills, but also to build new housing in older neighborhoods. We have four houses in one block in the Old Northside neighborhood, built by students from Tech High School with the help of local contractors and unions who have pitched in to help these young people develop various mechanical skills. The result is new housing in the city as well as a higher level of self-esteem on the part of the kids involved in the program. Churches could do the same thing.

What we are really talking about is releasing positive potential. In a city, builders will work hard at doing that on many fronts, and certainly it is important to develop the potential of youth in this endeavor.

Job-training programs can be a very effective tool in providing young people both specific skills and positive work-related attitudes that will serve them and their cities well in the future. Gene Glick, one of our city's finest public-spirited businessmen, whose large operation has built apartments all over America, has made a real contribution in this area through his Pro One Hundred program. With the assistance of Job Training Partnership Act funds, Pro One Hundred puts 100 disadvantaged youth to work on the city's golf courses each summer. They mow the fairways and greens, they pull weeds, they rake, and they build new tees and cart paths and clubhouses. In addition to the physical contribution they make, the participants learn marketable skills as well as important work habits that will make them more disciplined and responsible young people.

Many others in our community contribute by participating in Partners 2000, a joint effort of the Chamber of Commerce, the Greater Indianapolis Progress Committee, and local government. The original goal was to place 2,000 young people in summer jobs, but we have now exceeded 3,000. Private sector employees donate literally hundreds of hours to match applicants with job slots offered by local businesses, schools, and government, and while minority youth unemployment remains high in our city, the fact that 3,000 youngsters find a constructive and meaningful work opportunity during the summer is a plus, not a minus. The many employers who offer jobs and volunteers who administer these programs are builders, not wreckers.

In the development of a city that people can enjoy, it is very important to promote cultural and artistic activities. We must realize that we do not "live by bread alone" and that we can all help to develop a well-rounded quality of life in our city for everyone to enjoy if we support these kinds of projects and programs. A woman once stopped me as I wandered around Monument Circle during one of several summer festivals held in the center of Indianapolis, to offer a compliment about the way in which the city had been made so much more festive and enjoyable during the time I had been Mayor. I appreciated her comments but was quick not to take the credit for the events sponsored by many organizations, whose members work hard all year to promote programs and projects that celebrate urban life.

The support we give to the arts is essential, not only because of their intrinsic entertainment and edification value but also because they contribute greatly to a city's potential for economic development. Concerned citizens in Indianapolis saved the historic Indiana Theater from the wrecking ball, restored it, and created a lot of jobs and vitality in the heart of a blighted city block, and within a few years we had a new office building on one side of the theater and a new hotel on the other. The arts are beleaguered today. Too often, hard-pressed public officials find it easy to give low priority to—and cut spending for—artistic and cultural organizations that ask them for support. Some opinion leaders think that government has no role to play in this area whatsoever, which does not make it any easier to plug money into public budgets for the arts. The federal government spends more on military bands than on arts and humanities grants.

But all this having been said, opportunities constantly arise to enrich the cultural life in every community. Maybe we can help just by attending, by taking a picnic and going to hear the symphony play in a city park, for example. Maybe we can send a financial contribution or help by raising money. Perhaps we can participate in the work of a voluntary board that runs a museum or a theater or a ballet. And who knows? Our contribution might even be made by singing or acting or dancing or playing! Pericles, in his famous Funeral Oration in 430 B.C., recommended to the Athenian citizens, "Honor the Gods, adorn the city, serve your fellowman." In the cities of today where God's people live, we must help to "adorn" them by supporting those creative, artistic, and cultural expressions that give wings to the human spirit and voice to the frustrations and aspirations, the agony and the ecstasy, the comedy and the tragedy, in the human situation.

Another thing I consider to be very important is to **encourage political involvement.** The right to vote is precious but so often taken for granted, so often neglected. It's a tragedy that more people who are eligible don't vote, particularly in the off years when there is no campaign for President. People offer so many excuses—I forgot to register, voting is too complicated a process, I didn't feel well, the weather was bad, I couldn't find my precinct polling place, I was out of town, nobody was worth voting for, there's not a dime's difference between the parties—but the fact of the matter is that our free way of life depends on enlightened participation by the citizenry in the political process.

And of course, at its best, that participation includes much more than voting. It may also involve activities on behalf of a candidate, working in a campaign headquarters, raising money, being a precinct committee person or a ward leader in the party of one's choice or attending rallies and conventions. Or maybe you might even run for office. Citizens can serve on governmental boards or agencies in an appointive capacity, share in forums and debates, become informed on the issues and the candidates. I'm always appalled at the number of people who have no idea who is running for what office and in what year their terms begin and end, or who represents them in the City-County Council, or in the State Legislature, or even in Congress.

I remember a teacher of mine back in the ninth grade in Monroe High School in Rochester, New York, who was quite disgusted with us because we did not seem much interested in learning about *Macbeth*. She said to us, "Tell me you hate Shakespeare, tell me you love Shakespeare, but don't tell me you don't care about Shakespeare, because he's one of the greatest figures in all of human literature!" I use that line often when I am talking with students about the importance of political involvement. "Tell me you like this or that candidate or this or that party, tell me you don't like this or that candidate or this or that party, but don't tell me you don't care!" Apathy is the enemy of freedom. Our country was founded on the supposition that people would engage in responsible political activity. Edmund Burke was right when he said, "The best way to assure the triumph of an evil cause is for good people to do nothing."

Everyone can do something! Everyone can contribute to his or her city in some way. Everyone can find some way to help build a better city. Everyone can volunteer. People are a city's most valuable asset. Volunteers contribute immeasurably to the upbeat spirit of a city. A Walker Research poll with 200 Indianapolis-area residents during February and March 1986 tells us that 91 percent of the people interviewed indicate they are proud to say "I am from Indianapolis," 90 percent feel that business and government leaders work together, 82 percent agree that people volunteer for community projects, and 53 percent rate our future as very optimistic. Edward Leary, the historian who wrote a book on our city for its 150th anniversary in 1971, spoke of the civic pride and the "roll up your sleeves and get with it spirit" of the people here. There can be no doubt that the enthusiastic spirit of voluntarism in our community is one of the keys to understanding the growth and progress we are experiencing.

There are many reasons why people volunteer. Sometimes they are personally touched by tragedy or illness that makes them want to become involved with agencies like the American Red Cross or the Mental Health Association or with causes like the resettlement of Soviet Jews or refugees from Cuba or Southeast Asia. Sometimes they volunteer out of a sense of gratitude for all the blessings they've received. Sometimes they join up because they feel civic pride or a religious obligation to do their part. They answer, "Yes, I am my brother's keeper." And sister's! Many people volunteer for the sheer fun of it and the joy of belonging to a worthwhile cause. I love John Wesley's prayer, "Lord, let me not live to be useless"; it's good for two reasons: first, it says something important, and second, it's short! Putting others ahead of self, having a sacrificial spirit, not insisting on "me first," wanting to give and share and serve and volunteer—all this is crucially important in building the city. "If any man would come after me, let him deny himself and take up his cross daily and follow me. For whoever would save his life will lose it."

Every city offers a broad range of volunteer opportunities to its citizens, and in Indianapolis we are blessed with thousands of individuals who understand that the hours they contribute help to make their city a better place to live. In 1947, John Gunther, in his book *Inside USA,* called Indianapolis "the dirtiest city" in the United States; three decades later, Keep America Beautiful gave us an award for being the cleanest city in the country over 500,000 in population. This progress was largely due to a joint effort between concerned citizens and local government officials to launch a clean city program and an anti-litter campaign (complete with a TV commercial showing the Mayor giving the "Hudnut hook" to some trash), and to establish the first municipal environmental court in the nation. Scores of volunteers over the years have helped to make Indianapolis the home of the U.S. Clay Court Tennis Championships. Each year, hundreds of volunteers help raise money for our PBS TV station, only 11 percent of whose budget comes from tax dollars. For more than a quarter century, the volunteers who make up the 500 Festival Associates fill the month of May with gala events leading up to the 500 Mile Race. More than 6,000 volunteers made the National Sports Festival held in our city in 1982 the first to end up in the black, and some 20,000 volunteers will welcome 6,000 athletes to our city in 1987 for the Pan American Games. Other citizens volunteer in completely different areas, such as the Mayor's Concerned Neighbors CrimeWatch program, started in 1976 with the help of our police department and the *Indianapolis News.* Today thousands of people are involved in more than 1,000 block clubs in our community, each volunteering to look out for his or her neighbors and each contributing to the city in the process. The list goes on and on and on.

President Kennedy was right; we should not ask what our country can do for us but, rather, what we can do for our country—and our city. "The fields are already white for harvest." There are more opportunities out there waiting to be seized by people who care than there are caring people to seize them. Anyone who says there's nothing for him or her to do must be wearing blinders and ear muffs. Elizabeth Barrett Browning said it eloquently in *Aurora Leigh:*

> Earth's crammed with heaven,
> And every common bush afire with God;
> But only he who sees takes off his shoes,
> The rest sit round it and pluck blackberries.

In October 1982 I was invited to attend a conference in Zurich, Switzerland, sponsored by the Swiss National Committee. The theme of the meetings was "Say Yes to the City," and I was asked to speak

Europeans love their cities more than we...

about partnership in Indianapolis and how it has contributed to the progress we have enjoyed. In my remarks I noted that, at least in my opinion, Europeans love their cities much more than their American counterparts. They caress them. They nurture them. They plan them. They embrace them. They preserve them. They rejoice in them.

I went on to say that in America, some people want to say *no* to the cities. They leave the city to live and work in the suburbs. They believe the cities are places where only old people, poor people, minority people, and criminal people live. They believe the cities are plagued by problems and should be abandoned for a better life elsewhere.

many hate the city, say "no" to it

But I say *yes* to the city, and many others share a positive attitude about their city's future. Cities can be livable and lovable. They are manageable, they are renewable, they are our greatest resource. They can be fun, and they can work. They can be the place where our true humanity and the creativity of the human spirit are realized, where our destiny to live together in viable community can be fulfilled, where the new creation can be ushered in.

the "yes"

Each of us has the opportunity to help our cities realize their potential for good; each of us can contribute by saying yes to the city.

"Come, let us build ourselves a city."

Epilogue

In the little hamlet of Johnsburg, New York, nestled into the gentle wooded slopes of the Adirondack Mountains near Windover, there is a tiny white clapboard Methodist church, complete with creaking floor, a bell in the steeple, uncomfortable pews, and a pump organ. For four generations, our family has worshiped there in the summertime, joining the lumberjacks, carpenters, farmers, highway workers, and store owners in its sparse but devoted and warm congregation. When we attend, Hudnuts often outnumber all the others. For years, members of our clan sang in the choir while Dad played the organ. Occasionally, those of us who are ordained ministers would preach the sermon and conduct the service.

The pastors changed about every three years. One of them, who served the church when we were quite young (and Mom had to feed us raisins to keep us still during the sermon), was Reverend Anton Beza. When he left, he bequeathed to the church a beautiful gift—a mural that he painted on the front wall behind the pulpit and the communion railing. It depicts the mountains nearby, the recognizable hills and vales painted in hues of green and blue and crowned by a clear azure sky tufted with white clouds. On one side of the mural, robed in white, is the figure of Jesus, approaching us, beckoning us, calling us to follow him. The painting, seen first when we were young, has been engraved on the tablets of our minds ever since, a reminder of our roots, our family, our calling.

"Jesus calls us," as we used to sing at family hymn sings, to follow him. If we were Jewish, it might be God or one of the prophets calling us. If we were Hindu or Muslim or Buddhist, it might be the founder of that religion calling us. But whether we know him as "the God of Abraham, Isaac, and Jacob, of Sarah, Rebecca, and Esther" or "the God and Father of our Lord Jesus Christ," or something else, he comes to us from the hilltops and the valleys, by night and by day, along wooded paths and asphalt streets, where the seas are rough and where the waters are calm, in the country and the city, saying, "Follow me." Live usefully. Deny yourself. Work hard. Wear the yoke of service. Help out. Do your best—and leave the rest.

Very few of us will ever stride across the pages of history and leave large footprints. But each of us, no matter what he or she does, can plant a good seed and hope for a fruitful harvest. We can expand the sphere of God's kingdom by answering the call to lead a life of service.

> For not with swords' loud clashing,
>   Nor roll of stirring drums,
> But deeds of love and mercy
>   The heavenly kingdom comes.

Each of us can make an effort to help others and the community where we live to achieve a better life.

It has been said that lighting a candle makes more sense than cursing the darkness. Credit belongs to the person who engages in the fray, not to the one who sits on the sidelines. Whether we fail or succeed is not as important as whether we make the effort. We live life more significantly by doing the good immediately in front of us than by thinking that life is vain and fruitless if we do not make a huge mark. Herbert Butterfield, in his book *Christianity and History,* makes the point that if we allow ourselves to be used by God to accomplish his purposes, we will be more effective than if we try to control things in a sovereign manner as though we were princes of earth. It is far better to work for the little good in our own corner of the world, in each chapter of our lives, with the hope that like leaven in bread or salt in meat, our small efforts will improve the quality of life where we touch it, than to be forever thinking that we will accomplish nothing unless we become famous, receive much attention, pile up lots of money, or wield political power.

Sometimes we will stumble, sometimes we will succeed. So we must be steadfast in our effort and humble in our attitude. We must let God's strength perfect itself in our weakness. We must live out our days with joy and confidence. Like the Pilgrims, we must believe that "more light is let to break forth from God's holy Word," that each new day brings new opportunities to serve and to build, and that life is full of exciting new surprises from God. And as we travel, we can borrow my father's favorite prayer:

> O God, light of the minds that know thee, strength of the wills that serve thee, and life of the souls that love thee, from whom to be turned is to fall, to whom to be turned is to rise, and in whom to abide is to stand fast forever—grant us thy forgiveness and thy blessing, and though we are unworthy, do thou lift us up to thee. Amen.

Index
of Names